AMC'S BEST DAY HIKES IN THE
BERKSHIRES

FOUR-SEASON GUIDE TO 50 OF THE BEST TRAILS IN WESTERN MASSACHUSETTS

RENÉ LAUBACH

SECOND EDITION

Appalachian Mountain Club Books
Boston, Massachusetts

AMC is a nonprofit organization, and sales of AMC Books fund our mission of protecting the
Northeast outdoors. If you appreciate our efforts and would like to become a member or make
a donation to AMC, visit outdoors.org, call 800-372-1758, or contact us at Appalachian Mountain
Club, 5 Joy Street, Boston, MA 02108.

outdoors.org/publications/books

Distributed by National Book Network.

Front cover photograph © René Laubach
Back cover photographs © René Laubach; © 2/Caroline Woodham/Ocean/Corbis
Interior photographs by © René Laubach, unless otherwise noted.
Maps by Ken Dumas © Appalachian Mountain Club
Cover design by Gia Giasullo/Studio eg
Interior design by Eric Edstam

Library of Congress Cataloging-in-Publication Data
Laubach, Rene.
  AMC's best day hikes in the Berkshires : four-season guide to 50 of the best trails in western
Massachusetts / Rene Laubach. — Second edition.
     pages   cm
  Includes bibliographical references and index.
  ISBN 978-1-62842-012-8 (pbk. : alk. paper) -- ISBN 1-62842-012-X (pbk. : alk. paper) 1. Hiking—
Massachusetts—Berkshire Hills—Guidebooks. 2. Walking—Massachusetts—Berkshire Hills—
Guidebooks. 3. Berkshire Hills (Mass.)—Guidebooks. I. Appalachian Mountain Club. II. Title.
  GV199.42.M42B474 2015
  796.5109744'1—dc23

                                                                                    2015011034

The paper used in this publication meets the minimum requirements of the American National
Standard for Information Sciences-Permanence of Paper for Printed Library Materials, ANSI
Z39.48-1984. ∞

Outdoor recreation activities by their very nature are potentially hazardous. This book is not
a substitute for good personal judgment and training in outdoor skills. Due to changes in
conditions, use of the information in this book is at the sole risk of the user. The author and the
Appalachian Mountain Club assume no liability for accidents happening to, or injuries
sustained by, readers who engage in the activities described in this book.

Interior pages contain 30% post-consumer recycled fiber.
Cover contains 10% post-consumer recycled fiber.
Printed in the United States of America,
using vegetable-based inks.

10 9 8 7 6 5 4 3 2 1   15 16 17 18 19 20

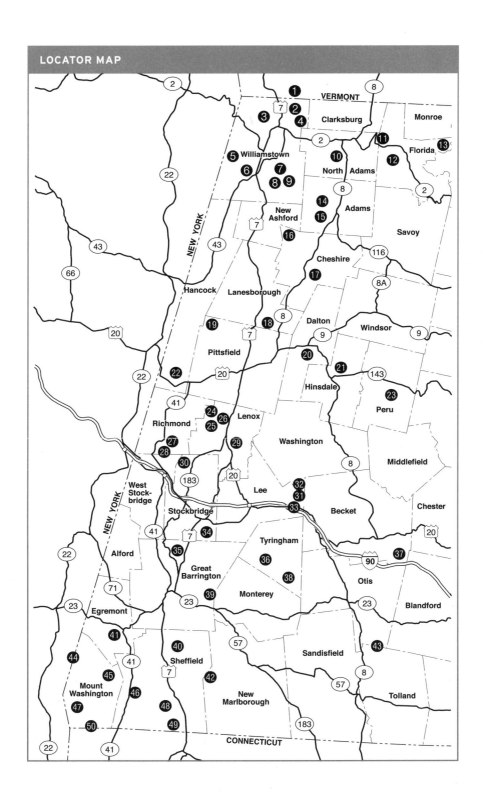

*This book is dedicated to my late, good friend
Don Reid, who loved the outdoors.*

CONTENTS

SECTION 2: CENTRAL BERKSHIRES

SECTION 3: SOUTHERN BERKSHIRES

NATURE ESSAYS

AT-A-GLANCE
TRIP PLANNER

#	Trip	Pg.	Location (Town)	Rating	Round-Trip Distance & Elevation Gain	Estimated Time
	NORTHERN BERKSHIRES					
1	The Dome	2	Pownal, VT	Moderate	5.2 mi, 1,715 ft	3.5 hours
2	Mountain Meadow Preserve	7	Williamstown, MA; Pownal, VT	Moderate	4.0 mi, 430 ft	2.0-2.5 hours
3	Hopkins Memorial Forest and Taconic Crest Trail	12	Williamstown, MA; Petersburg, NY; Pownal, VT	Strenuous	10.4 mi, 1,650 ft	5.5 hours
4	Pine Cobble and East Mountain	18	Williamstown, Clarksburg, MA	Moderate	4.8 mi, 1,340 ft	3.0 hours
5	Berlin Mountain	24	Williamstown, MA; Berlin, NY	Strenuous	4.7 mi, 1,545 ft	2.75-3.25 hours
6	Field Farm Reservation	30	Williamstown, MA	Easy	2.9 mi, 120 ft	1.5-2.0 hours
7	Greylock Range Traverse	35	Williamstown, Adams, North Adams, MA	Strenuous	12.7 mi, 2,390 ft	6.5-8.0 hours
8	Hopper Trail to Greylock Summit	41	Williamstown, Adams, MA	Strenuous	9.0 mi, 2,390 ft	5.0-6.0 hours
9	Stony Ledge via Haley Farm Trail	48	Williamstown, MA	Moderate-Strenuous	5.6 mi, 1,460 ft	2.5-3.0 hours
10	Mount Greylock and Ragged Mountain via Bellows Pipe Trail	52	North Adams, Adams, MA	Strenuous	8.8 mi, 2,140 ft	5.0 hours
11	Hoosac Range Trail to Spruce Hill	58	North Adams, MA	Moderate	5.4 mi, 540 ft	2.5-3.5 hours
12	Spruce Hill via Busby Trail	63	Florida, North Adams, MA	Moderate	2.6 mi, 670 ft	1.5-2.0 hours
13	Dunbar Brook	68	Florida, Monroe, MA	Moderate-Strenuous	6.25 mi, 1,010 ft	4.0 hours

Fee	Good for Kids	Dogs Allowed	X-C Skiing	Snow-shoeing	Trip Highlights
		✓		✓	scenic summit, boggy wetlands
	✓	✓		✓	wildflower meadow and panoramic views
		✓		✓	Taconic ridgeline vistas, Snow Hole
		✓		✓	stunning views
		✓		✓	views from summit
	✓	✓	✓	✓	meadows with bucolic mountain vistas
		✓		✓	four summits, the best vista in MA
		✓		✓	boreal forest and Greylock summit
		✓		✓	most outstanding vista in MA
		✓		✓	magnificent view of Greylock's east face
		✓		✓	stunning vistas
		✓		✓	fabulous views, migrating hawks in fall
		✓		✓	old-growth trees and roaring brook

#	Trip	Pg.	Location (Town)	Rating	Round-trip Distance & Elevation Gain	Estimated Time
14	Saddle Ball Mountain	74	Adams, Cheshire, New Ashford, Williamstown, MA	Strenuous	10.4 mi, 1,675 ft	6.0-7.0 hours
15	Mount Greylock State Reservation–Cheshire Harbor Trail	80	Adams, MA	Moderate-Strenuous	6.6 mi, 1,930 ft	4.0-4.5 hours
16	Mount Greylock State Reservation–Jones Nose and Rounds Rock	86	Cheshire, New Ashford, MA	Easy-Moderate	2.6 mi, 235 ft	1.5-2.0 hours
17	Cheshire Cobbles and Gore Pond	92	Cheshire, Dalton, MA	Moderate	7.6 mi, 1,250 ft	3.5 hours

CENTRAL BERKSHIRES

#	Trip	Pg.	Location (Town)	Rating	Round-trip Distance & Elevation Gain	Estimated Time
18	Ashuwillticook Rail Trail–Lanesborough to Cheshire	98	Lanesborough, Cheshire, MA	Easy-Moderate	7.4 mi, 20 ft	3.0 hours
19	Pittsfield State Forest–Lulu Cascade, Berry Pond, and Tilden Swamp	103	Pittsfield, Lanesborough, Hancock, MA	Moderate	5.0 mi, 1,000 ft	3.0-3.5 hours
20	Warner Hill	109	Dalton, Hinsdale, MA	Moderate	6.3 mi, 430 ft	3.0-3.5 hours
21	Old Mill Trail	115	Hinsdale, Dalton, MA	Easy	3.0 mi, 155 ft	1.5-2.0 hours
22	Shaker Mountain	120	Hancock, MA	Moderate	6.5 mi, 790 ft	3.0-4.0 hours
23	Dorothy Frances Rice Sanctuary for Wildlife	125	Peru, MA	Easy-Moderate	3.8 mi, 570 ft	2.5 hours
24	Pleasant Valley Wildlife Sanctuary–Fire Tower Loop	130	Lenox, MA	Strenuous	3.0 mi, 825 ft	2.0 hours
25	Pleasant Valley Wildlife Sanctuary–Beaver Ponds Loop	136	Lenox, MA	Easy	1.5 mi, 115 ft	1.0 hour
26	John Drummond Kennedy Park	141	Lenox, MA	Easy-Moderate	4.8 mi, 355 ft	2.5-3.0 hours
27	Lenox Mountain–Burbank Trail	148	Richmond, Lenox, MA	Easy-Moderate	3.2 mi, 540 ft	1.5-2.0 hours
28	West Stockbridge Mountain–Charcoal, Walsh, and Ridge Trails	153	Stockbridge, West Stockbridge, Richmond, MA	Moderate	2.2 mi, 530 ft	1.0-1.5 hours
29	Schermerhorn Gorge Trail	157	Lenox, Lee, Washington, MA	Moderate-Strenuous	3.7 mi, 620 ft	2.0-2.5 hours
30	Stevens Glen	162	West Stockbridge, Richmond, MA	Easy-Moderate	1.4 mi, 320 ft	1.0-1.5 hours
31	October Mountain State Forest–Finerty Pond	166	Becket, Washington, MA	Moderate	6.0 mi, 870 ft	3.5 hours

Fee	Good for Kids	Dogs Allowed	X-C Skiing	Snow-shoeing	Trip Highlights
		✓		✓	flower-filled meadow with wonderful views, boggy wetlands
		✓		✓	state's highest summit
	✓	✓		✓	great vistas, prolific blueberries in season
		✓		✓	fantastic vista point, scenic pond
	✓	✓	✓	✓	wildlife-rich wetlands
$		✓		✓	trifecta of water attractions
	✓	✓			attractive northern hardwoods, evergreen stands, Greylock view
	✓	✓	✓	✓	industrial history
				✓	sojourn back in time
	✓	✓	✓	✓	wild woodlands
$				✓	fine summit views
$	✓			✓	active and easily observed beaver colony
	✓	✓	✓	✓	interesting local history, views
	✓	✓		✓	attractive woodland, pleasing lookout
		✓		✓	mature woodland, pleasing vistas
		✓		✓	cascading brook and massive trees
	✓	✓		✓	towering trees, cascading brook
		✓		✓	serene pond ringed by mountain laurel

#	Trip	Pg.	Location (Town)	Rating	Round-trip Distance & Elevation Gain	Estimated Time
32	Basin Pond	171	Lee, MA	Easy	3.1 mi, 290 ft	1.5-2.0 hours
33	Upper Goose Pond	175	Becket, Lee, Tyringham, MA	Moderate	3.7 mi, 385 ft	2.5 hour.
	SOUTHERN BERKSHIRES					
34	Ice Glen and Laura's Tower	180	Stockbridge, MA	Moderate	1.9 mi, 580 ft	1.5 hours
35	Monument Mountain Reservation	185	Great Barrington, MA	Moderate	2.7 mi, 765 ft	2.0 hours
36	Tyringham Cobble Reservation	191	Tyringham, MA	Easy-Moderate	2.0 mi, 380 ft	1.5 hours
37	Becket Land Trust Historic Quarry and Forest	196	Becket, MA	Easy-Moderate	3.0 mi, 400 ft	1.5-2.0 hours
38	McLennan Reservation	202	Tyringham, Otis, MA	Easy-Moderate	2.5 mi, 448 ft	1.5-2.0 hours
39	Benedict Pond Loop and Ledges	207	Great Barrington, Monterey, MA	Easy-Moderate	3.0 mi, 240 ft	1.5-2.0 hours
40	East Mountain and Ice Gulch	212	Sheffield, Great Barrington, MA	Moderate	7.2 mi, 680 ft	4.0-4.5 hours
41	Jug End State Reservation and WMA	217	Egremont, MA	Easy	2.9 mi, 365 ft	1.5 hours
42	Questing Reservation	222	New Marlborough, MA	Easy	2.3 mi, 300 ft	1.5 hours
43	Tolland State Forest—Gilmore Trail	226	Otis, Tolland, MA	Easy	3.5 miles 75 ft	2.0-2.5 hours
44	Bash Bish Falls	231	Mount Washington, MA; Copake Falls, NY	Easy-Strenuous	2.0-2.6 mi, 470-900 ft	1.5 or 2.5 hours
45	Upper Race Brook Falls and Mount Race	237	Sheffield, Mount Washington, MA	Strenuous	6.2 mi, 1,625 ft	4.0 hours
46	Guilder Pond and Mount Everett	243	Mount Washington, MA	Moderate	4.2 mi, 825 ft	2.5-3.0 hours
47	Alander Mountain Trail	248	Mount Washington, MA	Moderate	5.0 mi, 790 ft	3.0-4.0 hours
48	Lime Kiln Farm Wildlife Sanctuary	254	Sheffield, MA	Easy	1.75 mi, 135 ft	1.5 hours
49	Bartholomew's Cobble Reservation	259	Sheffield, MA	Moderate	3.2 mi, 310 ft	2.0-2.5 hours
50	Sages Ravine and Bear Mountain	264	Mount Washington, MA; Salisbury, CT	Strenuous	3.9 mi, 915 ft	2.5-3.0 hours

Fee	Good for Kids	Dogs Allowed	X-C Skiing	Snow-shoeing	Trip Highlights
	✓	✓	✓	✓	truck-sized glacial boulders
	✓	✓		✓	serene and scenic Upper Goose Pond
		✓		✓	magical rocky cleft, ancient evergreens
		✓			picturesque summit of quartzite boulders
	✓	✓	✓	✓	bucolic pastures, lovely views
	✓	✓		✓	former granite quarry artifacts
		✓		✓	cascading brook, beaver pond
	✓	✓		✓	scenic pond and splendid long views
		✓		✓	splendid views, rocky cleft
	✓	✓	✓	✓	meadows, views of mountain ridges
	✓	✓	✓	✓	towering trees, early settlements
	✓	✓	✓	✓	woods with wild feel, Otis Reservoir
		✓		✓	Massachusetts' most spectacular waterfall
		✓		✓	wonderful series of waterfalls, fabulous ridgtop views
		✓		✓	Guilder Pond laurel bloom, picturesque mountain summit
		✓		✓	tri-state vistas
	✓		✓	✓	rolling hay meadows, magnificent vistas
$	✓			✓	great biodiversity, panoramic view
		✓			charming chasm, roaring brook, views

ACKNOWLEDGMENTS

I WOULD LIKE TO THANK PETER TYSON, former publisher of AMC Books, for asking me to take on this second edition, and Victoria Sandbrook Flynn, Project Editor at AMC Books. I enjoyed working with Belinda Thresher, who edited this second edition. Thanks also go to copyeditor Maya Mackowiak Elson, and mapmaker Ken Dumas. A significant number of individuals from nonprofit conservation organizations, state agencies, and other walks of life reviewed drafts of narratives for hikes on properties under their management or for which they have particular knowledge. Collectively they constructively pointed out both errors of commission and omission.

This group of reviewers includes Steve Antil, Park Interpreter, Pittsfield State Forest; Joanna Ballantine, Regional Director—West, The Trustees of Reservations; Rebecca Barnes, Facility Supervisor, Mt. Greylock Complex; Jim Caffrey, Superintendent—Windsor/Williamstown, The Trustees of Reservations; David W. Carlow, Regional Coordinator, Tolland Complex; Cosmo Catalano, Jr., AMC Berkshire Chapter, AT Management Committee; Shep Evans, Laurel Hill Association; Becky Ferguson, Superintendent, Stockbridge Management Unit, The Trustees of Reservations; Pat Gamelli, Forest and Park Supervisor II, Department of Conservation and Recreation (DCR); Alec Gillman, Forest and Park Supervisor III, Mt. Greylock State Reservation; Dustin Griffin; Drew Jones, Hopkins Forest Manager, Center for Environmental Studies, Williams College; Mike Leavitt, Trails and Outreach Coordinator, Berkshire Natural Resources Council; Scott Lewis, Director, Williams College Outing Club; David B. MillerField Operations Team Leader, Mohawk State Forest Complex, DCR; Adam Morris, Field Operations Team Leader, Beartown Complex, DCR; Chris Pryor, Director of Forest Stewardship, New England Forestry Foundation; Leslie Reed-Evans, Executive Director, Williamstown Rural Lands Foundation; Dennis Regan, Berkshire County Director, Housatonic Valley Association; Ken Smith, Becket Land Trust; Rene Wendell, Conservation Ranger, Bartholomew's Cobble, The Trustees of Reservations, and Ruth Wheeler, Kennedy Park Committee.

Although I am grateful to all these folks for their time and efforts, any errors that remain are my sole responsibility.

My companion on many of these hikes through the years has been my wife of 40 years, Christyna M. Laubach. Chris's assistance and encouragement has made this journey that much more enjoyable. I remain indebted to her.

Finally, this book would not have been possible were it not for all the hard working people who protect open spaces and construct and maintain the wonderful system of trails that we are so fortunate to have in the Berkshires. Thank you all!

—René Laubach

INTRODUCTION

TO ME, WALKING IS THE MOST NATURAL THING THAT WE DO. We were born to walk. Walking is how we get from point A to point B, although increasingly less so at this point in human history. Yet there is a distinct difference between simply placing one foot in front of the other and hiking. Walking is merely locomotion; hiking generally implies walking with a purpose, often on a dirt path through a natural or naturalized environment. For me, as for many others, hiking is exercise, therapy, meditation, discovery, education, and joy. The end point—be it a lofty summit, an enchanting waterfall, a particularly massive tree, or a cascading brook—draws me to the trailhead. Yet it is the soothing rhythm of placing one foot in front of the other and in essence being one with nature that make it so rewarding.

After living and working in the environmental field in the Berkshires for 30 years, I thought knew the area well. How surprised I was to learn there were many wonderful places and trails of which I had little or no knowledge. This project has enabled me to stretch my legs, as it were, and embark on a pilgrimage of discovery. A significant number of hikes included in this guide were admittedly new to me, and I am grateful for having had the opportunity to experience them. It is truly amazing how many exceptionally beautiful, biologically rich, and accessible properties there are.

The Berkshires are for the most part a rather settled region, so it may surprise some to learn that there remain wild, untamed pockets of woodland and wetland where one can feel far away from it all. Yet, there is enough of a veneer of civilization even in the wildest locations to give one comfort. So in some ways, the Berkshires offer the hiker the best of two worlds. One world provides security, and the other provides the adventure and connection to nature that we all need. I sincerely hope you enjoy these excursions as much as I have.

I would ask but one thing of you: Please do your part to protect these very special places. We are the beneficiaries of these gifts from those who came before us. They were people who took the long view. Let us join them in ensuring that these places remain for future generations to enjoy and learn from as well.

—René Laubach

HOW TO USE THIS BOOK

WITH 50 HIKES TO CHOOSE FROM, you may wonder how to decide where to go. The locator map at the front of this book will help you narrow down the trips by location, and the At-a-Glance Trip Planner that follows the table of contents will provide more information to guide you toward a decision.

Once you settle on a destination and turn to a trip in this guide, you will find a series of icons that indicate whether the hike is good for young kids, whether dogs are permitted, whether snowshoeing or cross-country skiing is recommended, and whether fees are charged.

Basic information follows: location, rating, distance, elevation gain, estimated time, and maps. The ratings are based on the author's perception and are estimates of what the average hiker will experience. You may find them to be easier or more difficult than stated. The estimated time is also based on the author's perception. Consider your own pace when planning a trip.

The elevation gain is calculated from measurements and information from USGS topographic maps, landowner maps, and Google Earth. Information is included about the relevant USGS maps as well as where you can find trail maps. The bold-faced summary provides a basic overview of what you will see on your hike.

The Directions explain how to reach the trailhead by car, and GPS coordinates for parking lots are also included. When you enter the coordinates into your device, it will provide driving directions. Whether or not you own a GPS device, it is wise to consult an atlas before leaving your home.

In the Trail Description, you will find instructions on where to hike, the trails on which to hike, and where to turn. You will also learn about the natural and human history along your hike as well as information about flora, fauna, and any landmarks and objects you will encounter.

The trail maps that accompany each trip will help guide your hike, but it would be wise to also take an official trail map with you. They are often—but not always—available online, at the trailhead, or at the visitor center.

Each trip ends with a More Information section that provides details about the locations of bathrooms, access times and fees, the property's rules and regulations, and contact information for the place where you will be hiking. A Nearby section includes information about where points of interest, restaurants, or shops can be found near the trailheads.

TRIP PLANNING AND SAFETY

AN OUNCE OF PREVENTION IS WORTH A POUND OF CURE—an old adage to be sure, but so true. Although there is no actual wilderness in the Berkshires, there are remote locations that are miles from the nearest paved and well-traveled road.

Weather, fatigue, injury, a lost trail—all can put you and your hiking companions at risk. Therefore, even for easy hikes of short duration, be sure to carry enough clothing, water, food, and emergency items should you have to spend extra time or even an overnight in the woods for any reason. You will be more likely to have a safe and enjoyable hike if you plan ahead and take proper precautions. Before heading out for your hike, consider the following:

- Select a hike that suits everyone in your group. Match the hike to the abilities of the least capable person in the group. If anyone is uncomfortable with the weather or is tired, turn around and return to complete the hike another day.
- Plan to be back at the trailhead before dark. Before beginning your hike, determine a turnaround time. Don't diverge from it, even if you have not reached your intended destination.
- Check the weather. The weather in New England is highly variable, and the Berkshires are no exception. If you are planning a ridge or summit hike, start early so that you will be off the exposed area before the afternoon hours when thunderstorms most often strike, especially in summer.
- Bring a pack with the following items:
  - ✓ Water: Two quarts per person is usually adequate, depending on the weather and the length of the trip. On extended day hikes, consider carrying some method of water purification so you can refill your water bottles en route.
  - ✓ Food: Even if you are planning just a one-hour hike, bring some high-energy snacks such as nuts, dried fruit, or snack bars. Pack a lunch for longer trips.
  - ✓ Map and compass: Be sure you know how to use them. A handheld GPS device may also be helpful, but is not always reliable.

✓ Headlamp or flashlight, with spare batteries

✓ Extra clothing: waterproof/breathable rain gear, synthetic fleece or wool jacket, hat, and mittens or gloves

✓ Sunscreen

✓ First-aid kit, including adhesive bandages, gauze and tape, nonprescription pain relievers, moleskin, and personal prescription medications at a minimum

✓ Pocketknife or multitool with a blade

✓ Waterproof matches and a lighter

✓ Trash bag

✓ Toilet paper and hand sanitizer

✓ Whistle

✓ Insect repellent

✓ Sunglasses

✓ Cell phone: Be aware that cell phone service is unreliable in rural areas. If you do have a signal, use the phone only for emergencies to avoid disturbing the trail experience for other hikers.

✓ Trekking poles (optional)

✓ Binoculars (optional)

✓ Camera (optional)

- Wear proper footwear and clothing. Wool or synthetic hiking socks will keep your feet dry and help prevent blisters. Comfortable, waterproof hiking boots will provide ankle support and good traction. Avoid wearing cotton clothing, which absorbs sweat and rain and contributes to an unpleasant hiking experience. A synthetic or wool base layer (t-shirt, or underwear tops and bottoms) will wick moisture away from your body and keep you warm in wet or cold conditions. Synthetic zip-off pants that convert to shorts are popular. To help avoid bug bites, you may want to wear synthetic pants and a long-sleeve shirt.

- If you hike ahead of the rest of your group, wait at all trail junctions until the others catch up. This avoids confusion and keeps people from getting separated or lost.

- If you see downed wood that appears to be purposely covering a trail, it probably means the trail is closed due to overuse or hazardous conditions.

- If a trail is muddy, walk through the mud or on rocks, never on tree roots or plants. Waterproof boots will keep your feet comfortable, and sticking to the center of the trail will help prevent erosion.

- Inform someone you trust about your itinerary and expected return time. If you see a logbook at a trailhead, be sure to sign in when you arrive and sign out when you finish your hike.
- Poison ivy is always a threat when hiking. To identify the plant, look for clusters of three leaves that shine in the sun but are dull in the shade. If you do come into contact with poison ivy, wash the affected area with soap as soon as possible.
- Biting insects such as mosquitoes, black flies, deer flies, and no-see-ums are present during late spring and summer months. These can be a minor or significant nuisance, depending on seasonal and daily conditions. A variety of options are available for dealing with bugs, ranging from pump and aerosol sprays and lotions that include the active ingredient N-diethyl meta-toluamide (commonly known as DEET), which can potentially cause skin or eye irritation, to more skin-friendly products containing picaridin, citronella, or eucalyptus. Head nets, which often can be purchased for less than a can of repellent, are useful during especially buggy conditions.
- One serious concern with biting insects is the eastern equine encephalitis virus (commonly referred to as EEE), a rare but potentially fatal disease that can be transmitted to humans by infected mosquitoes. The threat is greatest in the evening hours, when mosquitoes are most active.
- After you complete your hike, check your clothes, skin, and hair for deer ticks, which carry the dangerous Lyme disease.
- Wear two items of blaze-orange clothing in hunting season. For specific dates of Massachusetts hunting seasons, contact the Massachusetts Division of Fisheries and Wildlife at mass.gov/eea/agencies/dfg/dfw/ or 508-389-6300.

LEAVE NO TRACE

THE APPALACHIAN MOUNTAIN CLUB (AMC) is a national educational partner of Leave No Trace, a nonprofit organization dedicated to promoting and inspiring responsible outdoor recreation through education, research, and partnerships.  The Leave No Trace program seeks to develop wildland ethics—ways in which people think and act in the outdoors to minimize their impact on the areas they visit and to protect our natural resources for future enjoyment. Leave No Trace unites four federal land management agencies—the U.S. Forest Service, National Park Service, Bureau of Land Management, and U.S. Fish and Wildlife Service—with manufacturers, outdoor retailers, user groups, educators, organizations such as AMC, and individuals.

The Leave No Trace ethic is guided by the following seven principles:

1. **Plan Ahead and Prepare.** Know the terrain and any regulations applicable to the area you're planning to visit, and be prepared for extreme weather or other emergencies. Small groups have less impact on resources and on the experiences of other backcountry visitors.

2. **Travel and Camp on Durable Surfaces.** Travel and camp on established trails and campsites, rock, gravel, dry grasses, or snow. Good campsites are found, not made. Camp at least 200 feet from lakes and streams, and focus activities on areas where vegetation is absent. In pristine areas, disperse use to prevent the creation of campsites and trails.

3. **Dispose of Waste Properly.** Pack it in, pack it out. Inspect your camp for trash or food scraps. Deposit solid human waste in catholes dug 6 to 8 inches deep, at least 200 feet from water, camps, and trails. Pack out toilet paper and hygiene products. To wash yourself or your dishes, carry water 200 feet from streams or lakes and use small amounts of biodegradable soap. Scatter strained dishwater.

4. **Leave What You Find.** Cultural or historical artifacts, as well as natural objects such as plants and rocks, should be left as found.

5. **Minimize Campfire Impacts.** Cook on a stove. Use established fire rings, fire pans, or mound fires. If you build a campfire, keep it small and use dead sticks found on the ground.

6. **Respect Wildlife.** Observe wildlife from a distance. Feeding animals alters their natural behavior. Store your rations and trash securely.

7. **Be Considerate of Other Visitors.** Be courteous, respect the quality of other visitors' backcountry experiences, and let nature's sounds prevail.

AMC is a national provider of the Leave No Trace Master Educator course. AMC offers this five-day course, designed especially for outdoor professionals and land managers, as well as the shorter two-day Leave No Trace Trainer course, throughout the Northeast. For Leave No Trace information, contact the Leave No Trace Center for Outdoor Ethics, 800-332-4100 or 303-442-8222; lnt.org. For a schedule of AMC Leave No Trace courses, see outdoors.org/education/lnt.

1

NORTHERN BERKSHIRES

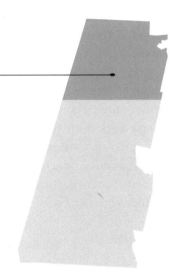

THE NORTHERN BERKSHIRES comprise some of the highest and most remote lands in the county. The area boasts the only true boreal forest in Massachusetts, the only summits above 3,000 feet elevation, craggy outcrops yielding splendid vistas, and sphagnum-filled bog lands. Seventeen of the excursions in this guide are located in this section. Mount Greylock State Reservation is the centerpiece and includes a sizable piece of the Appalachian Trail as well as miles of blue-blazed side trails. This section beckons the hiker with many fine trails ranging in difficulty from easy to strenuous.

Hikes located in this northern section run along the spine of the Taconic Range, including Hopkins Memorial Forest and Taconic Crest Trail (Trip 3). Berlin Mountain (Trip 5) borders New York. Trail-rich Greylock Range (Trips 7, 8, 9, 10, 14, 15, and 16) boasts the state's loftiest peak. The Hoosac Range, including Hoosac Range Trail to Spruce Hill (Trip 11) and Spruce Hill via the Busby Trail (Trip 12), is east of the marble valley. The northernmost hikes, including The Dome (Trip 1) and Pine Cobble and East Mountain (Trip 4), are an extension of Vermont's Green Mountains. This section contains the longest, most arduous hikes, but also a moderate walk to the Cheshire Cobbles and Gore Pond (Trip 17) and a stroll through bucolic Field Farm (Trip 6).

TRIP 1
THE DOME

Location: Pownal, VT
Rating: Moderate
Distance: 5.2 miles
Elevation Gain: 1,715 feet
Estimated Time: 3.5 hours
Maps: USGS Pownal, VT

Although just over the state line in Vermont, The Dome is a familiar natural landmark for Williamstown residents. This out-and-back route to its summit is in fact accessible only from Williamstown. Quite unlike any mountaintop in the area, The Dome's rounded quartzite summit, boggy wetlands, and spruce-fir forest are tantalizingly reminiscent of northern New England or Canada.

DIRECTIONS
From the intersection of US 7 and MA 2 at the rotary in Williamstown, follow US 7 north for 1.5 miles to Sand Springs Road on the right. Turn right on Sand Springs and follow it for approximately 0.2 mile to a three-way intersection. Stay to the right and drive another 0.3 mile more to White Oaks Road. Turn left onto White Oaks Road and drive 1.4 miles to the second wide, graveled pull-off on the right, approximately 0.3 mile north of the Massachusetts–Vermont border (the pavement ends at the state line). There is space for approximately six vehicles. *GPS coordinates*: 42° 44.918′ N, 73° 11.258′ W.

TRAIL DESCRIPTION
Walk around a cable to follow an old roadway marked by rectangular red blazes. The rocky road leads easily uphill under sugar maple, ash, several species of birch, and towering white pines. After oaks appear, enter a small meadow filled with goldenrod, a few black-eyed Susan, and Saint-John's-wort, which has starry yellow blossoms in summer. You'll soon reach a road on the right blocked by earth. American beech sprouts form a thick sapling layer below the oaks and sugar maples, and a low rock wall runs adjacent to the old road and then turns right. You'll encounter a number of detours or reroutes made by all-terrain vehicles along the route.

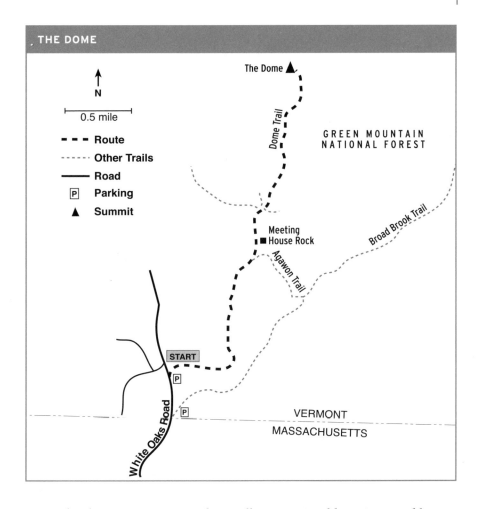

THE DOME

The Dome ▲

Dome Trail

GREEN MOUNTAIN
NATIONAL FOREST

N

0.5 mile

- - - Route
----- Other Trails
——— Road
P Parking
▲ Summit

Meeting
■ House Rock

Agawon Trail

Broad Brook Trail

START

P

P

White Oaks Road

VERMONT
MASSACHUSETTS

As the slope steepens somewhat, walk past spring-blooming wood betony and twining hog peanut, a legume with three leaflets that looks a bit like poison ivy. Level out and continue past another blocked road where the trail bears left. The narrow, eroded path is lined with quartzite bedrock and ascends gently. Chunks of milky white quartz also protrude. Water and other impurities color the otherwise clear quartz. In spring and early summer, listen for the flutelike song of Vermont's state bird, the hermit thrush, which is a common breeder along this route. Note the dead American chestnut sprouts killed back by the blight when the trees attain about 5 inches in diameter. But live root sprouts with long-toothed leaves remain as an identifier. This forest is markedly drier than what you began walking through and what lies ahead. Knee-high sassafras saplings with mitten-shaped leaves, low-bush blueberry, huckleberry,

While vegetation has largely obscured the distant views once possible from its summit, standing atop the evergreen-crowned Dome is still a rewarding experience.

mountain azalea, and bracken fern all hint at the dry, acidic nature of the soils under the oaks of this young forest.

The path climbs moderately, and soon gets rougher. Quartzite bedrock is fractured at sharp angles and paves the treadway. Besides red and white oaks (white oaks have rounded lobes), chestnut oak, with wavy leaf margins, is also present on this sunny, south-facing slope. The thin soil is ochre—high in limonite, a low-grade iron ore. After walking 1.2 miles, yellow-blazed Agawon Trail joins from the right. This steep, downhill trail serves as a 0.7-mile-long connector to Broad Brook Trail and leads north to the Appalachian Trail or south back to near where you parked. Note, however, that this 1.3 miles longer route requires fording a substantial, high-flow brook without the aid of a bridge or stones.

Bear left and continue on the trail past a monolithic quartzite boulder known as Meeting House Rock halfway to the summit. When you reach another reroute, remain on the wider path. Berry bushes, azalea, low sheep laurel, shadbush or juneberry, bilberry, and nannyberry form a dense vegetative cover. Tiny cow-wheat plants with lance-shaped leaves and light yellow blossoms, as well as wintergreen and trailing arbutus, line the path through these fairly dry and open oak-red maple woods. After the grade eases, note the red spruce, and then hobblebush shrubs with heart-shaped and paired leaves thriving under a deciduous canopy.

Arrive at a major T intersection where a long-abandoned truck lies just ahead. Dome Trail, 1.7 miles from the trailhead here, turns right and continues to follow red blazes. The road splits almost immediately, with one fork diverging left. Continue straight and uphill on an equally rough track. Soon, you will reach another split and this time, bear left (note arrow on tree). Continue on and notice that the track divides again. Follow the red blazes upslope, not left. A luxuriant layer of hay-scented ferns graces the level woodland floor—the first in a series of benches interspersed between steeper climbs. You will notice a difference as you proceed through a northern hardwood forest of yellow birches, American beeches (many succumbing to beech bark disease), black cherries (note the black, scaly bark likened by some to burnt potato chips), and red maples that shade thicket-producing hobblebushes.

Some decaying logs are entirely encased in a thick mat of mosses that serve as nurseries for yellow birch seedlings. Patches of sphagnum moss fill wet spots trailside, and small plants with shiny dark green leaves called goldthread because of its orange roots thrive here also. Continue through a low, boggy area colonized by cinnamon fern and red spruces. Hobblebushes produce showy white blossoms in May. Climb easily as you stride over tilted quartzite bedrock on an increasing gradient. A jutting benchlike outcrop is a fine spot for a rest. Canada mayflower and *Clintonia* bloom in spring along the margins. The sweet perfume of balsam fir fills the air.

Begin a steep climb over a treadway cushioned by conifer needle duff. Tiny dogwoods of the heights—bunchberries—enliven the walk in late spring, but goldthread and Canada lily are more numerous and spikemoss forms fuzzy mats. As you zigzag around and over the crest of a ledge outcrop, you enter the true boreal forest zone of red spruce and balsam fir. The trail corridor permits light to reach the ground for blueberries to find a niche. Little grows in the stifling shade of the evergreens. Boggy spots are interspersed between the erosion-resistant quartzite outcrops. The trail levels out in a bedrock opening surrounded by 25- to 30-foot-high spruces. It's easy to imagine that you are standing in northern New England or perhaps even on the Canadian Shield.

The Dome is 2,748 feet above sea level (a sign verifies the elevation). Mountain holly (with small elliptical and waxy leaves), huckleberry, and a few versatile red maples (at home in swamps or dry earth) maintain a hardscrabble existence. The red blazes end on the rounded dome summit at 2.6 miles from the trailhead; no trail has been cut farther into the forest. This whale-size rock is light gray and decorated with rusty hues. Nearby, a section of rock has cleaved, creating a shallow basin that fills with rainwater and serves as a bird-bath and watering hole.

Six-inch-long dark-eyed juncos—gray and white members of the sparrow family—trill from spruce tops in summer, but nest on the ground, while yellow-rumped warblers and golden-crowned kinglets also call the boreal zone home. On a clear day, you may enjoy the limited views of Pine Cobble due south, with the Greylock Range beyond. The spruces are rapidly diminishing the view shed, but no matter; this is a unique and gorgeous summit even without any views at all. When ready to start back, retrace your steps down the mountain, being sure to turn left at the old truck (note the double red blaze on the tree to the left).

DID YOU KNOW?

The governor of the Province of New Hampshire, Benning Wentworth, named the Town of Pownal in colonial times for his fellow governor and friend, Thomas Pownall of the Province of Massachusetts. But when the town was chartered in 1760, the second "l" was dropped from its name.

MORE INFORMATION

Trail open dawn to dusk. Access is free. Green Mountain National Forest, Manchester Ranger Station, 2538 Depot Street, Manchester Center, VT 05255; 802-362-2307; www.fs.usda.gov/greenmountain. The trail is maintained by the Williams Outing Club, 39 Chapin Hall, Williams College, Williamstown, MA 01267 (413-597-2317; wso.williams.edu/orgs/woc/).

NEARBY

The 1753 House, a historically accurate replica of a "regulation house," is located within the MA 2 rotary (intersection of Water Street and MA 2) in Williamstown. It was constructed for Williamstown's Bicentennial with tools and materials used in 1753, including oak timbers from nearby White Oaks. Regulation required settlers to build a house at least 15 feet by 18 feet, and 7 feet high, and clear 5 acres of land in order to gain title.

TRIP 2
MOUNTAIN MEADOW PRESERVE

Location: Williamstown, MA; Pownal, VT
Rating: Moderate
Distance: 4.0 miles
Elevation Gain: 430 feet
Estimated Time: 2.0–2.5 hours
Maps: USGS Williamstown; trail map available online

Straddling two states, this string of small loop trails begins with one of the most evocative panoramic views in the Berkshires. Greylock Range and the Taconics are a stunning backdrop to a meadow that in summer is filled with colorful wildflowers and butterflies. A few short, steep climbs and the ruins of former habitations add interest.

DIRECTIONS

From the intersection of US 7 and MA 2 in Williamstown, follow US 7 north for 1.7 miles, crossing the Hoosic River and Broad Brook along the way. Turn right onto gravel Mason Street and follow it 0.1 mile to where it terminates at a ten-spaces parking area. *GPS coordinates*: 42° 44.314′ N, 73° 12.452′ W.

TRAIL DESCRIPTION

A kiosk complete with large trail map stands just beyond the parking area; trail maps may also be available here. Trail intersections are signed. Follow the mowed Niles Trail across a field of goldenrod, yellow hawkweed, and robin plantain bordered by autumn olive, apple trees, honeysuckle, and dogwood. Autumn olive, now considered an invasive exotic, was planted to control erosion. Its yellowish blossoms fill the air with a sweet perfume in late spring. The trail rises into a wooded strip, and then enters another small field. Quaking aspen and cottonwoods line the left perimeter. As the trail steepens, young white ashes with compound leaves and white pines appear.

Turn right at the trail split to continue to follow the mowed path along the margin of a large meadow, the preserve's namesake. At this low end of the hillside meadow, various field flowers add dashes of color from late spring to fall. The path soon bears left and climbs the modest slope. The panoramic vista of the Greylock Range to the right is without doubt the highlight of this hike.

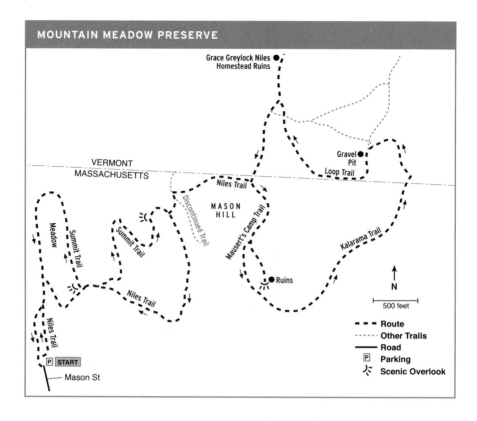

MOUNTAIN MEADOW PRESERVE

Grace Greylock Niles
Homestead Ruins

Gravel
Pit

Loop Trail

VERMONT
MASSACHUSETTS

Niles Trail

MASON
HILL

Discontinued Trail

Mauser's Camp Trail

Kalarama Trail

Meadow

Summit Trail

Summit Trail

Ruins

N

500 feet

Niles Trail

Niles Trail

P START

Mason St

- - - Route
----- Other Trails
——— Road
P Parking
Scenic Overlook

Glance over your shoulder and be treated to a view of the Taconic Range. This 20-acre grassland is alive with a bountiful array of butterflies in summer. The little wood satyr, a small brown butterfly with a row of black bull's-eye spots, is abundant in late spring.

Turn right to enter the forest and cross a trickling flow on a short boardwalk. Note the yellow-painted blazes and metal-diamond tags on tree trunks. At the trail junction, turn left off of Niles Trail onto Summit Trail. White pine, red maple, witch hazel, and striped maple predominate. Oaks are present too. Reach and parallel a low stone walls of water-tumbled quartzite to your left. The climb on a narrow trail becomes steeper and passes a spreading white oak with three trunks. Note that white oak leaves have rounded lobes, unlike the bristle-tipped lobes of red and black oaks. White oak acorns are sweet and mature in the fall of their first year, unlike the two years required for red and black oaks. The trail then climbs the slope with the aid of switchbacks. The last 200 yards are at quite an acute angle. Wild geraniums bloom pink in late spring along the ridgeline path. Only a limited view is possible from the summit at 1,120 feet due to encroaching trees. This U-shaped hill is the result of glacial

The Taconic Range along the Massachusetts-New York border forms a backdrop to the 20-acre meadow encircled by the footpath.

deposition. An interesting small tree here is a multitrunked hophornbeam, a tree with thin, light brown, shredding bark. Its wood is extremely hard and durable.

Bear right and descend to an intersection on the left. Turn left and descend past low maple-leaved viburnum shrubs under a canopy of oaks and red maples. At a junction with a wood road, bear left onto the roadway to continue on Niles Trail, then almost immediately right at the preserve's boundary, in the direction of the preserve's Vermont parking area. Mature red pines, characterized by scaly pinkish bark, were probably planted along the road, which skirts Mason Hill, during the Great Depression. Enjoy treading the wide path that parallels the Vermont state line for a brief time. You'll soon reach a green metal gate along the property boundary, but continue straight ahead. Soon reach another green metal gate, and walk around it to reach a T intersection with another wood road. Turn right to explore the ruins of Mausert's Camp.

During damp conditions in late spring and summer, be alert for fiery orange-red efts traversing the road. This creature, the terrestrial stage of the aquatic red-spotted newt, spends between two and seven years roaming woodlands before returning to ponds as a breeding adult. The red skin warns potential predators that they are poisonous when eaten. Saplings, pole-sized trees, and decaying stumps speak of past logging here. Watch for a patch of wild geraniums in late spring on the left. Bear left at the intersection with the Kalarama Trail; you'll return here shortly. Ahead stands a stone chimney at the end of a clearing. A second fireplace sits on the opposite side. The camp was destroyed by fire in the 1970s. The views of Greylock are partially obscured. Indigo buntings nest along the edge of the clearing.

Retrace your steps to the intersection with the Kalarama Trail and turn left onto it. Descend on this old roadway cut into the side slope, past a gravel borrow pit. Black birches and oaks with lowbush blueberries below dot the rising slope. A couple of beech trees on the right show faint black scars from having been climbed by bears that relish the nuts. Cross a pile of quartzite cobbles ("cobble" is a New England word for hill) gathered during field clearing and marvel at the huge twin-trunked oak on the right that exhibits the scars of four strands of wire. A bit of poison ivy borders the path before it bisects a handsome patch of spinulose woodfern. Stroll easily downhill.

Look for a cluster of delicate maidenhair fern on the left shortly after the trail climbs again. Before long, you'll reach a junction on the right with a narrow trail. Leave the road and continue on Kalarama Trail. A couple of dogwood trees sport large, white, four-petaled blossoms in spring at this intersection. But young white birches are generally more noticeable near the trail. Descend into a shallow hemlock ravine cut by a modest brook. Reach a wood road and bear left to remain on Kalarama Trail, and soon turn right to cross the flow. After the brook crossing, a yellow marker on the right indicates the boundary of Williamstown conservation land. A massive white pine towers behind it.

Bear left and climb past nearly 5-foot-tall bracken fern to an intersection with another wood road at the end of Kalarama Trail. You are now in Vermont. Bear left and follow the old road, cut into the slope, toward the gravel pit. Arrive at the clearing and bear left through the former gravel pit where gravel was removed for road and railroad bed construction in the 1950s and '60s. White pines and quaking aspens colonized the edge of the pit, now carpeted by grass. Reenter the woodland of oaks and a variety of birches on a gravelly track. This was once a multilayered forest dominated by white pine and American chestnut. Pass through a small gravel pit and by a glacial boulder on the left, along Loop Trail, before emerging into a meadow where bluebirds nest in boxes provided for them. Follow the mowed path across it.

At a T intersection with Niles Trail, turn right for a brief walk to the old concrete foundation of the Grace Greylock Niles Homestead on the left and then retrace your steps to the intersection. Continue straight ahead this time and arrive back at the intersection with the trail on the left leading to Mausert's Camp. Turn right on Niles Trail to retrace your steps back to Massachusetts along the base of Mason Hill and turn right to climb back to the intersection just below the summit. But rather than return to the summit, turn left to descend moderately along the ridgeline under a canopy of oaks. White pines soon become numerous above a sapling layer of maple, beech, and birch. In summer, listen for the sweet, languid trill of pine warblers high in the pine boughs.

Continue walking steadily downhill, steeply at times on Niles Trail, and bear right to level out in closely spaced pine groves. Pass the path on the right leading to the summit, and when you reach the large meadow, turn right to explore the north end of the field. Here you have a second chance to admire the stunning views and perhaps observe tawny-coated, white-tailed deer in summer, as well as more butterflies. A rusty hayrack sits idly along the path. Follow the mowed treadway around the field's perimeter. When you reach the trail intersection, bear right to return to your vehicle.

DID YOU KNOW?

Botanist and author Grace Greylock Niles, a Pownal native, wrote *Bog Trotting for Orchids* (1904) and *The Hoosac Valley: its Legends and History* (1912). She died in 1943 at the age of 78.

MORE INFORMATION

Open sunrise to sunset, daily, year-round. Free access; membership in and donations to The Trustees of Reservations are welcomed. Dogs permitted, but must be on leash at all times. Mountain biking, horseback riding, motorized vehicles, hunting, and firearms are not permitted. The Trustees of Reservations, Western Regional Office, 193 High Street, Holyoke, MA 01040 (413-532-1631; westregion@ttor.org; thetrustees.org).

NEARBY

Boat access to the nearby Hoosic River is at Lauren's Launch in Williamstown. Paddlers can travel 4.8 miles north (downstream) to Clayton Park in Pownal. From the Williamstown rotary, follow US 7 for 1.2 miles to an unnamed road on the left at a sign for Hoosic River Access. Follow the unnamed road 0.2 mile, across railroad tracks, to a sign for Lauren's Launch. Park in the pull-off opposite the entrance to the transfer station. There are some tricky rips along the route (hoorwa.org/recreation/paddling-the-hoosic/north-adams-to-hoosic-falls).

TRIP 3
HOPKINS MEMORIAL FOREST
AND TACONIC CREST TRAIL

Location: Williamstown, MA; Petersburg, NY; Pownal, VT
Rating: Strenuous
Distance: 10.4 miles
Elevation Gain: 1,650 feet
Estimated Time: 5.5 hours
Maps: AMC Massachusetts Trail Map #1: B1; USGS North Adams, MA and Berlin, NY; trail map available online

This excursion features monumental hardwood trees, babbling brooks, thrilling vistas, and a geologic curiosity: Snow Hole.

DIRECTIONS

From the intersection of US 7 and MA 2 at the rotary in Williamstown, follow US 7 north for a short distance to Bulkley Street on the left. Drive down Bulkley Street for 0.75 mile to gravel Northwest Hill Road. Turn right and drive for 0.1 mile, bearing left onto the gravel drive to enter Hopkins Memorial Forest (at the carved wooden sign). Park in the small gravel lot on the left, which has room for eight vehicles. *GPS coordinates*: 42° 43.408′ N, 73° 13.402′ W.

TRAIL DESCRIPTION

Amble up the gravel drive between apple trees and a small meadow, where tree swallows and bluebirds nest in boxes that provide housing for cavity-nesting birds. The Rosenburg Visitor Center (once a carriage house) serves as forest headquarters. Excellent trail maps are available at the kiosk that features a posted trail map and historical information. Bear right past Buxton Garden onto a gravel carriage road. The relocated former Moon Farm barn stands on the left.

Tread beneath a canopy of sugar maple, black locust, and white ash, passing by the Williams College Outing Club cabin. A bit beyond stands a maple sugar shed. An adjacent field hosts the forest's main weather station. Numerous research projects are under way on the property's 2,600 acres, and visitors are asked to stay on trails and not interfere with research plots. Ford Glen Brook soon reveals itself 60 feet below to your right. The forest changes after the road

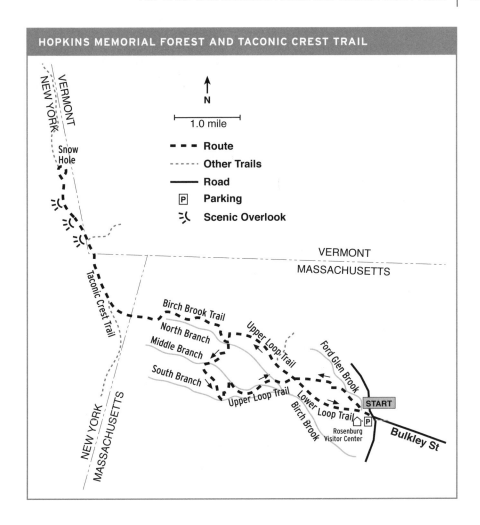

bears left, with the addition of black birch, beech, oaks, and hophornbeam—easy to identify by its flaky, tan bark.

As you bear right, a canopy walkway may be partially visible. The walkway enables scientists to reach a world usually hidden from human eyes. Soon, gigantic oaks dating from the 1860s tower above; it is 40 feet to their first branches. Some were toppled by high winds in 2012. As you continue your stroll, beech, yellow birches, and black birches increase in an obviously younger forest. Starflower and Canada mayflower bloom here in spring, while lowbush blueberry, prince's pine, and shining and cedar clubmosses spread largely by runners in the acidic soil. Watch for pink ladyslipper orchids in June just before the four-way intersection outfitted with a stone bench.

Immediately upon entering the cool, damp fissure known as the Snow Hole, you'll feel a radical drop in temperature, especially during summer.

Turn onto the right most fork for Upper Loop Trail. On your ramble to Birch Brook, ignore several side paths. As you climb gently, a forest of red maple changes to one dominated by oak. Tiny lowbush blueberry shrubs thrive beneath the oaks. Notice that a significant number of oaks have more than one trunk—a sure sign that these woods were logged. Don't mistake the yellow paint on trees for blazes, as these demarcate forest study plots. At the North Branch of Birch Brook, bear right onto signed and blue-blazed Birch Brook Trail. From here, you'll walk 1.5 miles up to meet the Taconic Crest Trail (TCT).

Now the real hiking begins. Stride past the end of a fallen stone walls indicating former pasturing. Then, bear right and past knee- to waist-high blueberries and huckleberries. The grade of this old wood road increases under mixed northern hardwoods and oaks. On a more moderate slope, notice the dying paper birches—pioneering trees that followed the ax and were later shaded out by species whose seeds required less sunlight to germinate. About three-quarters of the way to the ridge, you'll cross into New York State.

Log steps help you ascend the eastern slope past glades of yellow-green ferns—most notably hay-scented or boulder fern. This prolific species characteristically forms solid stands. Hopkins Forest researchers are trying to determine whether it secretes a substance that inhibits the growth of competing species. Finally, reach the obviously well-trodden and undulating TCT. The

TCT is blazed by a white diamond in a blue square for 35 miles along the spine of the Taconic Range. From the intersection, it is 1.6 miles north to the Snow Hole. Turn right. Up here, where soils are shallow, the forest is reduced in height but with a thick sapling layer—especially American beech, which is a prolific sprouter.

Enter an area where much of the small, woody vegetation has been cut, ,creating an early successional habitat for species not able to live in dense woodland. At a **Y** intersection in a waist-high fern glade, continue straight. Shortly after the trail leaves Hopkins Memorial Forest property and passes onto New York State Forest land, you'll arrive at the first of three shrubby clearings where scenic vistas abound. Gaze out upon rolling hills running toward the western horizon. Close at hand, shiny-leaved bilberry shrubs thrive in the sunny gap, as do a few red spruces. Bilberries and less common huckleberries fill a second clearing offering additional views, but the third is arguably the best. Back in the forest, you can't help but notice the many beech trees with black bark lesions. Most are inflicted with beech bark disease. Less than 10 minutes after leaving the third clearing, reach the first of two signed and red-blazed side trails on the right. These are the ends of a short loop leading to a geological and meteorological wonder—the Snow Hole.

Continue to the second red-blazed path; turn right past patches of shining clubmoss, and walk downhill about 250 feet to the entrance on the right. Old graffiti—some dating to 1865—is carved into the relatively soft phyllite bedrock near the entrance. You will want to descend into the crevice to explore it from within, but watch your footing, as the rock may be slick. Immediately you'll feel a radical drop in temperature, especially during the summer months. Mosses, wood sorrel, and ferns soften the tilted, wafer-thin layers of phyllite, while yellow birches clutch the rim. It feels a bit as though you're walking into a giant terrarium. The promise of the Snow Hole held true for me on a steamy July 4 visit as a small pile of dirty snow and ice remained within.

When ready to continue, you can walk back the way you came in or continue on the short loop; both lead back to the Taconic Crest Trail. Be sure to turn left when you join the main trail, and watch for the easy-to-miss Birch Brook Trail on the left to retrace your steps downhill to the junction with Upper Loop Trail at the bridge over the brook. Turn right to cross the brook on a wooden bridge. This woodland contains all four common birch species—white, gray, black, and yellow, all separable by unique bark true to their names. Soon reach Middle Branch of Birch Brook, lumpy with mossy stones, and cross it via another wooden span. Descend easily on a wide path.

Bear left in an arc to drop down close to South Branch of Birch Brook—the third tributary. Shade-casting hemlocks—some sizable—populate the slope. In summer, shade-tolerant woodland butterflies like the northern pearly-eye may make an appearance, although they may be difficult to locate when they alight. This eye-spotted species rarely visits flowers, preferring to sip tree sap and other fluids. Soon meet Middle Branch again, crossing a wooden bridge. The old roadway continues brookside under oaks, beeches, birches, and maples.

Gaze into the depths of clear pools to spot native brook trout. This stream has cut its way through a phyllite bedrock layer cake. A significant number of monumental oaks populate this woodland—a 3.5-foot-diameter specimen stands on the right. Cross over North Branch on a bridge built to accommodate vehicles and climb easily back to the four-way intersection with the stone bench. Turn right to walk back on the south side of Lower Loop Trail along the dividing line between two watersheds—Ford Glen Brook and Birch Brook.

Pass through more fern glades, where an interpretive panel describes the possible chemical warfare waged by hay-scented fern against its competitors. Another informs readers that clubmosses are more common in earth formerly pastured. All four local and aptly named species—prince's pine, shining clubmoss, cedar clubmoss, and staghorn clubmoss—can be seen on this hike. Although capable of reproducing via spores, slow-growing clubmosses rely mostly on cloning themselves. Stride past a dark stand of Norway spruces planted by the U.S. Forest Service, which operated the forest from 1935 to 1968.

Pass an ancient oak with rotting heartwood as you amble downhill. Exotic plants along the margins presage your return to the Rosenburg Center.

DID YOU KNOW?

The Taconic Mountains, a narrow, 150-mile-long range, and one of North America's oldest at 440 million years, runs from Brandon, Vermont, to the Hudson Highlands of New York. The Taconic Crest Trail follows this ridgeline for 35 miles from Hancock, Massachusetts, to Petersburg, New York. Taconic is a derivation of an American Indian word meaning "in the trees."

MORE INFORMATION

Open dawn to dusk, daily, year-round. Access is free. Public restrooms and drinking water are available at the Rosenburg Center; hours: 7 A.M. to 6 P.M. All pets must be leashed. Hunting is prohibited, except deer hunting by special permit in the Massachusetts portion of the property. All vehicles, including mountain bikes, are prohibited. Collecting fauna and flora is prohibited; do not disturb research sites. Hopkins Forest Manager, Center for Environmental Studies, Williams College, P.O. Box 632, Williamstown, MA 01267 (413-597-2346; williams.edu/ces/hmf).

NEARBY

The fine Williams College Museum of Art, not as well known as the larger Clark Art Institute, is located on the college campus and houses 13,000 objects that span the history of art. It is a teaching museum, open daily to the public, free of charge; hours: 10 A.M. to 5 P.M., closed Wednesdays and major holidays. Located at 15 Lawrence Hall Drive, Suite 2, Williamstown, MA 01267 (413-597-2429; wcma.williams.edu).

TRIP 4
PINE COBBLE AND EAST MOUNTAIN

Location: Williamstown and Clarksburg, MA
Rating: Moderate
Distance: 4.8 miles
Elevation Gain: 1,340 feet
Estimated Time: 3.0 hours
Maps: AMC Massachusetts Trail Map #1: B3; USGS Williamstown

A partial-loop hike up the sunny oak- and sheep laurel–covered slopes of East Mountain, the southern terminus of the Green Mountains, to a quartzite- and pitch pine–studded summit and some of the most stunning views in the region.

DIRECTIONS

From the Williamstown rotary (at the junction of MA 2 and US 7), follow MA 2 east for 0.6 mile to Cole Avenue on the left. Follow Cole Avenue for 0.75 mile (crossing the Hoosic River en route), and turn right onto Hoosac Road. Drive for 0.4 mile to Pine Cobble Road on the left and follow Pine Cobble Road for 0.1 mile to a gravel parking area on the left (space for six or seven vehicles). A sign urges hikers not to leave valuables in their car and to lock it. *GPS coordinates*: 42° 42.963′ N, 73° 11.116′ W.

TRAIL DESCRIPTION

From the parking area, cross Pine Cobble Road diagonally, walking uphill for about 100 feet to the signed trailhead on the right. The path initially parallels the road and passes a wooden sign on the left erected by the Williams Outing Club that indicates that this blue-blazed trail leads 1.6 miles to Pine Cobble summit, 2.1 miles to the Appalachian Trail (AT) junction, and 3.4 miles to the Vermont border. Turn left into an oak woodland. White and red oaks predominate, but black cherry, red maple, American beech, black birch, ironwood, tulip tree, and hophornbeam all add diversity. Distinguish white oak by its flaky light gray bark. Rounded quartzite boulders litter the trail.

Striped maples appear as you gently climb. Soon, chestnut oak appears, along with smooth-skinned black birch and multitrunked witch hazel. The trail steepens, and lowbush blueberry thrives in the acidic soil under the tannin-rich oaks. The level bench you are on is thought to be the ancient

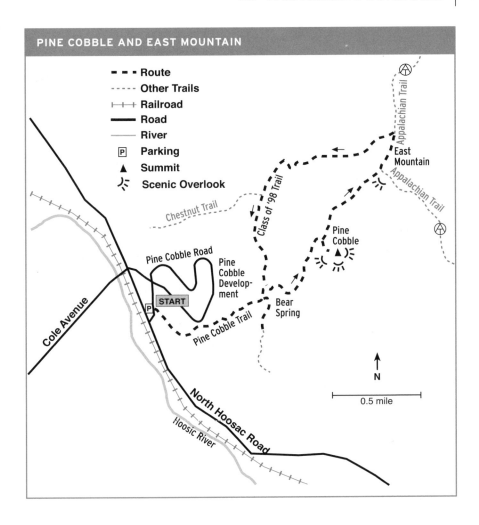

shoreline of glacial Lake Bascom. To the north, its waters were once 500 feet deep. Two-foot-high sheep laurel, another indicator of acid soil, first shows up near here, becoming abundant later. It is said to be poisonous to livestock. After another quarter mile, watch for an unmarked side trail on the right by a gray boulder that leads about 300 feet toward a dark green wall of eastern hemlocks and Bear Spring.

Bear Spring, at the base of a resistant quartzite cliff, is the only surface water on this south-facing slope. The cooler microclimate here fosters sapling yellow birch and striped maple, both northern hardwood species. Ferns are more noticeable too, including common polypody on quartzite boulders. Return to the main trail and continue uphill past luxuriant growths of shiny-leaved wintergreen and very soon reach a signpost at the 0.8-mile mark, where

Nestled in the Hoosic River Valley to the east, North Adams is visible from the quartzite summit of Pine Cobble.

the Class of '98 Trail heads left. You'll be returning by this route, but now continue straight. These nutrient-poor soils host a variety of heath family species including blueberries, huckleberry, and the Massachusetts state flower—trailing arbutus, or mayflower. Its leaves have a sandy texture, while its delicate spring flowers are pale pink.

Notice that as you've gained elevation, the stature of oaks and other hardwoods has decreased in height while the shrub layer has thickened. Chestnut oaks, with wavy-margined leaves and deeply furrowed trunks, are now far more common. The trail steepens again as you reach a sign surrounded by a mat of moss proclaiming, "Welcome to Pine Cobble, a unique natural area owned by the Williams Rural Lands Foundation and maintained for hiking and enjoyment of nature." As you pass through a small boulder field of gray, angular hunks of quartzite, notice low sheep laurel shrubs.

Sassafras trees, which do well in sandy soils, become common. Their leaves have one, two, or three lobes and emit a spicy aroma when crushed. Continue the steady climb amid white birches, young red maples, and chestnut oaks. Marvel at the wooden bowl formed by a triple-stemmed oak—the result of cutting long ago—that collects and holds rainwater. After a rocky climb, a signpost indicating the Pine Cobble summit is to the right, and the AT and Class of '98 Trail are to the left. Follow the side trail right, to excellent vista points. The Williams College campus is visible from a perch atop rounded quartzite cobbles on the right. Beyond is the spine of the northern Taconics, with Berlin Mountain (see Trip 5) as its most prominent feature. A bit farther, on the other side of the ridge, are views to the east of nestled North Adams from Pine Cobble summit, at an elevation of 1,893 feet. Due south 6 miles is the summit of Mount Greylock, complete with the Massachusetts Veterans War Memorial Tower.

The smooth, gray stone is Cheshire quartzite. Six hundred million years ago, it was beach sand. The pure silica of this rock type was once the raw ingredient in Sandwich glass. Some broken rock faces show a rusty tinge of iron. When ready, return to the main trail and turn right to continue another 0.5 mile to the AT junction. After mostly level walking through oaks, gray birch, red maple, witch hazel, lowbush blueberries, sheep laurel, and wintergreen, climb moderately over schist rocks. Watch for a metal anchor point in the rock that once helped support a fire tower. Level out through a shrubby growth of birches and leave the forest for an open rocky promontory. The trail is marked with rock cairns and blue blazes on stones.

The views improve as you climb higher (especially after leaf fall). This boulder field is the perfect place to enjoy the Taconic panorama. The surrounding pitch pines are mostly 12 feet tall. Taller, longer-needled white pines are also present. Even a few red spruces stand among the light gray quartzite slabs. Follow the rock-strewn treadway to its junction with the AT at 2.1 miles (2,050 feet elevation) marked by a signpost on the summit of East Mountain. A mountain azalea shrub stands to the left. Turn left onto the AT and soon reach blue-blazed Class of '98 Trail. Follow it left and downhill through deciduous woodland. Dense understory and stumps indicate fairly recent logging. A caution sign marks a tricky descent over talus, but after a set of stone steps there are fewer rocks. Now parallel angular quartzite boulders— some capped by ferns until you reach the Y junction with Chestnut Trail. Turn left to remain on Class of '98 Trail. Before long, a dramatic 40-foot-high cliff catches your eye. Be sure to follow the blue blazes past side trails until you reach Pine Cobble Trail. Turn right to return to your vehicle.

DID YOU KNOW?

Glacial Lake Bascom, which inundated the Hoosic River Valley from to-day's Cheshire, Massachusetts, to the Vermont border for 800 years, and Bascom Lodge on Mount Greylock are both named for John Bascom

(1827–1911). He was a Williams College alum and faculty member, and one of the first Greylock Reservation Commissioners, appointed in 1898.

MORE INFORMATION

Open daily, year-round; no access fees. There are no restroom facilities. Pine Cobble Trail traverses lands owned by Williams College, Williamstown Rural Lands Foundation (WRLF), P.O. Box 221, Williamstown, MA 01267 (wrlf.org/properties-trails/properties/pine-cobble/); the Massachusetts Division of Conservation and Recreation, MassParks West, 740 South Street, Pittsfield, MA 01202 (413-442-8928); and private owners. The trail is maintained by members of the Williams Outing Club, 39 Chapin Hill Drive, Williamstown, MA 01267 (413-597-2317) and WRLF.

NEARBY

The highly acclaimed Sterling and Francine Clark Art Institute is set on a 140-acre campus of expansive lawns, meadows, and walking trails. The museum is best known for its extraordinary collection of French Impressionist paintings. Closed Mondays and major holidays. There is an admission fee June through September. Located at 225 South Street, Williamstown (413-458-2303; clarkart.edu).

CAT O' TALL TALES

At the peril of leaping, figuratively at least, from the tangible to the mysterious, consider the controversy surrounding the presence, real or imagined, of mountain lions in the Berkshires. Sighting reports surface regularly, though hard proof—a body or bona fide photograph—is still lacking. But the possibility that these big cats once again roam the region exists. Although not having the good fortune to observe one myself, I know folks who are convinced they have done so. Some reports are doubtless simple cases of mistaken identity. Some may even be hoaxes. Yet as someone who has observed more than a few bobcats, I can't imagine anyone mistaking one for the other.

A colleague of mine, who takes a no-nonsense, scientific approach to nature, spotted one crossing a road in front of him as he rounded a corner on his bicycle while coasting down a hill at Quabbin Reservoir. And scat found at a predator-deer kill from the same "accidental wilderness" tested positive for mountain-lion DNA in 1997. Quabbin, in central Massachusetts, is only 40 miles east as the crow flies.

Mountain lion, cougar, puma, panther, or catamount—this fabled creature has many names. Local place names (such as the Catamount Ski Area) hark back to a time when catamounts did indeed inhabit western Massachusetts. The last one shot in the wild in the Commonwealth (in Hampshire County) was way back in 1858, when the extent of forested landscape was significantly less than it is today. The mounted form of that mountain lion now resides at Mass Audubon's Arcadia Wildlife Sanctuary in Easthampton.

Scanning published distribution maps reveals the nearest population of the predator to be no closer than the Florida Everglades, although verified reports do exist from elsewhere along the eastern seaboard. The catamount's chief prey item is deer. Certainly a large and thriving regional deer population would provide ample sustenance to support at least a few animals. And black bear and moose have reclaimed much of their former range in southern New England.

If indeed a wild population exists, and that is yet unproven, the question of origin remains. Some claim that escaped pets are the genesis of local cougar sightings. That may indeed be correct, but could there be more to it than that? In 2011, a driver in southwestern Connecticut struck and killed a mountain lion. DNA detective work traced this young male lion's origin all the way to South Dakota's Black Hills!

TRIP 5
BERLIN MOUNTAIN

Location: Williamstown, MA; Berlin, NY
Rating: Strenuous
Distance: 4.7 miles
Elevation Gain: 1,545 feet
Estimated Time: 2.75 to 3.25 hours
Maps: AMC Massachusetts Trail Map #1: C1; USGS Berlin

A challenging loop route, straight up the east face of the Taconic Range to its highest peak in Massachusetts. Views of Mount Greylock from Berlin Mountain's flat summit are particularly pleasing, and an enchanting little waterfall adds to your enjoyment at the end of the hike.

DIRECTIONS
From the intersection of MA 2 and US 7 in Williamstown, take MA 2 west for 0.3 mile to Torrey Woods Road on the left. Follow Torrey Woods Road (where the pavement ends, it becomes Berlin Mountain Road after approximately 0.5 mile) for 2.1 miles to a small gravel parking area on the left (space for three or four vehicles). *GPS coordinates:* 42° 42.153′ N, 73° 16.231′ W.

TRAIL DESCRIPTION
Small wooden signs at the parking area read "Class of '33 Trail" and "WRLF Loop Trail." Williams College Outing Club students cut the trail that year. A newer sign reads "Class of '33 (Berlin Mount) Trail, Blue Blaze, Berlin Mount Summit 2.5" and points into the forest, where you will emerge later. Instead, walk back down the gravel road that you just drove on for approximately 300 feet and look for a sign on a white birch tree on the right. You will enter a forest of white and yellow birches, red spruce, red maple, and striped maple; follow blue blazes as you descend easily. The trees in this forest are mostly young. Oaks and American beech soon join in.

As the downhill walking becomes steeper, you'll hear Haley Brook, a clear, fast-flowing stream that, according to an interpretive sign, is home to native brook trout and the rare Appalachian brook crayfish.

After crossing the brook, advance uphill under northern hardwoods. Soon arrive at a signed intersection. Turn left to remain on the initially level

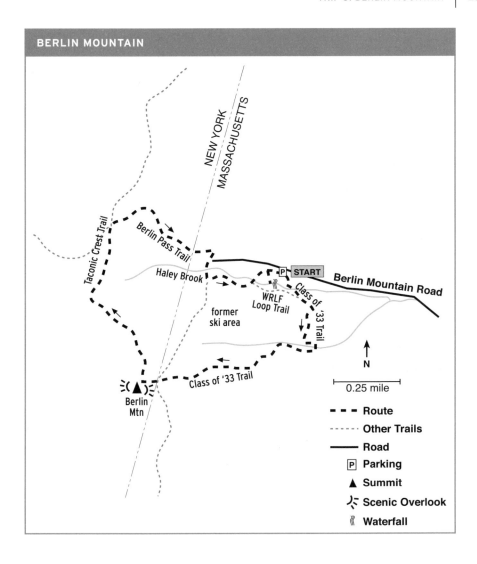

Class of '33 Trail (the Williamstown Rural Lands Foundation [WRLF] Loop Trail turns right). The abundance of pole-sized timber indicates fairly recent harvesting, and the remnants of former logging roads are still visible. Soon the grade increases and follows a trenchlike former skid road with scattered hemlocks and spruces. Some of the hemlocks are considerably older than the hardwoods—beech, birch, and oak. Most of the beeches suffer from the bark disease that is killing beech trees throughout the region.

The path bears left away from the road and winds down rather abruptly. As you level out among mature yellow birches and hemlocks, note the overturned privy ruins on the left—the Williams College Outing Club Berlin Cabin once

Hikers pass through a lush hay-scented fern glade just below the flat summit of Berlin Mountain.

stood here. An intertwined hemlock and yellow birch represent a curiosity on the right. Turn sharply right at the sign and follow along the contour under hemlocks for a short, sloping descent to a nameless brook that has exposed phyllite bedrock. Use caution when crossing on the slick, wet stones, and give the stinging nettles wide berth.

Follow an old road initially. The next mile or so represents one of the most challenging ascents of any hike covered in this guide. A nearly relentless series of steep climbs is moderated only by an occasional less exhausting grade, permitting you to catch your breath. When you stop, note that the upslope to your left has more mature timber than that below you to the right. Plenty of neotropical migrant birds feel right at home on this eastern face of the Taconics, including the 5.5-inch-long, black and yellow Canada warbler. Others include black-throated green warbler, ovenbird, and rose-breasted grosbeak.

At one point, you'll stride past a fallen hemlock. Once you see the root ball, it's easy to envision how heavy rain and high winds might have separated its shallow root network from the bedrock. The sunny gap created enables shade-intolerant species to gain a foothold. Hay-scented ferns have colonized other light gaps. The trail continues to be challengingly steep and well blazed with blue through dense northern hardwoods as you finally reach the unmarked junction on the right with the old Williams College Ski Trail at the border with New York State. This trail is not maintained and is even steeper than the one you just ascended, so it is not recommended for a return. Bear left to gain the mostly flat open summit of Berlin Mountain at 2,818 feet elevation and 2 miles from the trailhead.

The views of the Greylock Range, only 7 miles to the southeast, are splendid, but summit trees are growing taller and vistas are limited. Red spruces ring the circular open area where a fire tower once stood. Crumbling concrete footings are all that remain. Sunshine has encouraged raspberry, bilberry, and lowbush blueberry to proliferate.

The return route follows the Taconic Crest Trail (TCT), blazed by a white diamond in a blue square, as well as round blue plastic discs in New York, to Berlin Pass. It is obvious that this trail is heavily utilized by ATVs. Follow the wide, rocky track downhill to the right, passing through numerous fern glades. White or paper birch trees look especially attractive in this setting of yellow-green ferns. The wide path, steep at times and filled with lots of loose stones, is eroded to phyllite bedrock. As a result, side trails have been created. Juneberry or shadbush trees are among the members of the low-stature ridgeline forest, producing white flowers in April—before their leaves emerge.

After experiencing moderately steep descents alternating with level stretches along the wooded crest for 1.2 miles, you'll arrive at an obvious four-way intersection in a shrubby depression or saddle called Berlin Pass. The TCT continues straight, toward Petersburg Pass, but you'll need to turn right onto the signed but unblazed Berlin Pass Trail. Opposite this trail, the old Boston to Albany Post Road descends to Berlin, New York. The treadway is wide, rutted, and damp in spots, but easy to follow. There are excellent examples of the wafer-thin, layered phyllite bedrock in the trail. This rock began as clay deposits, rich in mica, in a shallow sea, and was then metamorphosed by great heat and pressure to produce a rock intermediate between shale and schist.

After hiking downhill for a while, the dry south-facing slope to your left sports lowbush blueberries, mountain azaleas, and a little snapdragon family member bearing modest yellow trumpetlike flowers in summer with the intriguing name of cow-wheat. It draws its nourishment from the roots of oaks. And as you proceed rather steeply down the rocky trail, oaks indeed become more common. Haircap moss meanwhile softens the margins. Finally, bear right in an arc and emerge into a graveled clearing where the trail meets Berlin Mountain Road. You could turn left and walk down the road 0.4 mile to your vehicle, but more fun awaits.

If you decide to continue, turn right. Still visible on the left slope are the runs of the old Williams College Ski Area built in 1960. Follow the gravel to its end, and turn left to head down a grassy track toward the base of the ski slope. Note the wide WRLF footpath to your right, but turn left onto the loop trail. Haley Brook tumbles out of a large culvert and down a ravine on your left. A canopy of maples, ashes, birches, and beeches shades striped maples and patches of delicate maidenhair fern. Blue cohosh, forming solid stands, and wild leek are profligate on this moist, nutrient-rich slope. Wild leek's twin leaves have an unmistakable onion fragrance and wither completely away by the time the leek's globes of white flowers emerge in summer.

At the intersection, turn left, amble down to the stream, and cross it. The trail is marked by blue diamond WRLF blazes. Briefly ascend a steep slope through deciduous woodland and bear right. At a wooden bridge outfitted with a wire mesh treadway, turn right onto a side trail that leads steadily and then more steeply down, past a beech snag on the right pitted with big pileated woodpecker excavations, to a small viewing platform constructed of recycled plastic lumber. The falls is enchanting and consists of cascades and a horsetail for a total drop of at least 30 feet. The auditory aspect of this experience is to be appreciated as well. In late spring and early summer, listen for the exuberant song of the winter wren. After returning to the main trail, turn right and cross the wooden span. Berlin Mountain Road and your vehicle are a short distance ahead.

DID YOU KNOW?

To obtain use of a 41-acre site at the end of Berlin Road for a ski run, Williams College exchanged portions of a farm between MA 2 and Berlin Road with Williamstown, which wanted the farm acreage for campsites. The ski team now trains at Jiminy Peak in Hancock.

MORE INFORMATION

There are no restroom facilities or potable water along this route. Property crossed by this route is owned by Williamstown Rural Lands Foundation the town of Williamstown, Williams College, the New York Department of Environmental Conservation, and private owners. Taconic Crest Trail is maintained by the Taconic Hiking Club, 39 Campagna Drive, Albany, NY 12205. Class of '33 and Berlin Pass trails are maintained by the Williams College Outing Club, 1004 Baxter Hall, Williamstown, MA 01267 (413-597-2317; woc.williams.edu/). The WRLF Loop Trail is maintained by the Williamstown Rural Lands Foundation, 671 Cold Spring Road, Williamstown,

MA 01267 (413-458-2494; wrlf.org/properties-trails/properties/berlin-road/) and the New York Department of Environmental Conservation, Division of Lands and Forests, 50 Wolf Road, Albany, NY 12233 (518-457-2475; www.dec.ny.gov).

NEARBY

Sheep Hill, a 50-acre former dairy farm and ski area owned and managed by the Williamstown Rural Lands Foundation, features hillside trails offering expansive views of Mount Greylock and surrounding features. The entrance is located approximately 1.2 miles south of Williamstown Center at 671 Cold Spring Road (US 7/MA 2). The property is open year-round for passive recreation and public programs on natural history and rural heritage (413-458-2494; ruraland@wrlf.org).

TRIP 6
FIELD FARM RESERVATION

Location: Williamstown, MA
Rating: Easy
Distance: 2.9 miles
Elevation Gain: 120 feet
Estimated Time: 1.5–2.0 hours
Maps: USGS Berlin; trail map available online

Lying in the valley between the Greylock Range and the Taconics, this Trustees property has an agricultural legacy dating back more than 250 years. Today it beckons hiker, cross-country skier, and snowshoer alike with a fine trail network in a truly bucolic setting offering delightful mountain vistas.

DIRECTIONS
From the intersection of US 7 and MA 9 in Pittsfield (at the Berkshire Athenaeum), follow US 7 north for 16.3 miles to its intersection with MA 43 in Williamstown (a.k.a. The Five Corners). Turn left onto MA 43 for less than 100 feet before turning right onto Sloan Road. Follow Sloan Road for slightly more than 1.0 mile to the signed entrance drive for Field Farm on the right. Drive 0.1 mile to the small gravel parking lot adjacent to the trailhead and maintenance garage/Discovery Room. *GPS coordinates*: 42° 39.931′ N, 73° 15.620′ W.

TRAIL DESCRIPTION
After studying the kiosk, where trail maps are available, turn onto Pond Trail and follow the mowed path through shrubby growth, which includes invasive exotic multiflora rose, Morrow's honeysuckle, and buckthorn.

Soon you'll reach a spring-fed pond adjacent to the former guesthouse, called The Folly. Turn right to follow along the pond shore past a cattail marsh where muskrats—smaller cousins of the beaver—reside. You may have to tread gently over the waterlogged beaver dam and outflow when the water level is high before finding firmer footing beyond.

You'll arrive at the Pond Trail and South Trail intersection. Bear right onto the South Trail and walk among young woody growth draped with vines,

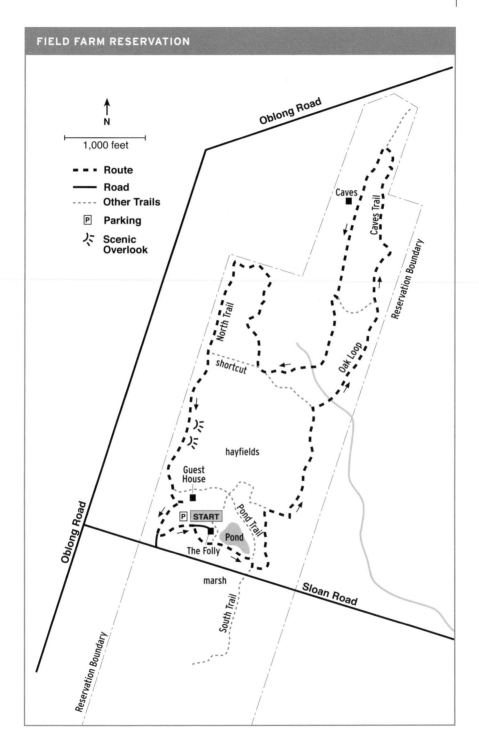

FIELD FARM RESERVATION

Oblong Road

↑
N

1,000 feet

- - - Route
——— Road
- - - - Other Trails
P Parking
Scenic Overlook

Caves

Caves Trail

Reservation Boundary

North Trail

Oak Loop

shortcut

hayfields

Guest House

P START

Pond Trail

The Folly

Pond

marsh

South Trail

Oblong Road

Sloan Road

Reservation Boundary

A tiny brook flows through a deciduous woodland of birch, beech, ash, and oak on its way to join the Green River.

including wild grape, and then turn left onto the connector to North Trail before meeting Sloan Road. Bigtooth aspen, black cherry, white ash, and white pine stand tall. You'll reach a large hayfield at the junction with North Trail; turn right and skirt the meadow's edge. In late spring and early summer, bobolinks nest in the grass, as do red-winged blackbirds. Soon you'll pass through a hedgerow gap on the right; turn left and continue in a northerly direction paralleling the hedgerow.

After leaf fall especially, gaze left to admire the Taconic Range including Berlin Mountain (Trip 5). Pass through a gap in barbed-wire fencing and enter another apple orchard. At the field's far end, follow Oak Loop as it jogs off to the right into a forest of cherry, white birch, ash, and sugar maple. Smaller sinewy ironwood and flaky hophornbeam trees comprise the understory. After crossing a couple of rivulets—one on a wooden span—and another wire fence gap, the path enters a stand of lanky hardwoods—the haunt of the crow-sized pileated woodpecker. Look for its big rectangular excavations in carpenter ant–infested trees and listen for its wild laughing call.

Soon you'll descend wooden steps to cross a bridge over a larger stream. Watch for a massive, columnar black oak, 4 feet in diameter, left of the rather level trail. Its lower section bears what appears to be a lightning strike scar. In season, on private property to the right, you may see hundreds of yards of plastic tubing linking taps placed on sugar maple trees. Leafy clumps of blue cohosh, a spring wildflower of rich woods, dot the forest floor.

You'll reach a **Y** intersection; go right to follow Caves Trail and begin a gradual climb among numerous white birches and hophornbeams, 5 to 10 inches in diameter. One of the first indications of marble bedrock pokes up on the left in the form of a layered boulder capped with mosses and evergreen wood fern. Other indicators of rich woods here are wild ginger and lacy maidenhair fern. When you reach the height of land, follow the contour over rolling topography where a steep drop-off looms to the left. In winter, homes along Oblong Road are visible from this high point as you begin your descent through younger woods.

A livestock barn is visible on the right on private property as the trail bears left. Traffic noise from Oblong Road may be evident as you reach an intersection; bear left to continue on Caves Trail—now an old wood road.

The woods are dominated by bigtooth aspen (named for its leaves), and before long you'll reach a flowing brook on the right that mysteriously disappears beneath the marble bedrock that the trail crosses. Below ground— out of sight—the flow, aided by acid precipitation, dissolves the marble, carving out caves within the rock. To your left rises the rocky spine that you recently walked over. Several examples of these so-called caves appear as you continue south.

The tilted marble outcrops contain excellent den sites for porcupines, a favorite menu item of fishers. After leaving the caves area, the trail bears left and arrives at a junction with Oak Loop. Turn right and pass an up-tilted marble outcrop on the left. Mosses, ferns, and bishop's cap—a spring wildflower with blossoms that resemble snowflakes and seed capsules that look like a bishop's headgear—adorn the rock. The path undulates over flat terrain and approaches a brook babbling through woodland of black and gray birches, beech, ash, and oak. Watch for a patch of primitive horsetails resembling green jointed soda straws before and after you cross the wooden bridge.

Beware of the stout thorns of multiflora rose that fringe the pasture. Both it and the prickly Japanese barberry shrub are sure signs of soil disturbance. A few eastern junipers (a.k.a. red cedar) are also former pasture indicators. Stay right and follow the blazes. This area may be damp as water flows off the slightly higher pasture ahead during wet seasons. When you reach the **T** intersection, turn right on North Trail, and right again at the sign for it (alternately, you can continue straight on the mowed trail, skipping this section and knocking 0.4 mile off the trip distance. The less-traveled route leads among more apple trees, multiflora rose, barberry, and other invasive, exotic shrubs.

You'll turn left where large ash trees display their characteristic cross-hatched bark. After bearing right you'll start a gradual climb and switchback up an easy slope. On the right, stand a few healthy American beeches, their smooth gray trunks unblemished by the *Nectria* fungus. Another large oak—this one red and forked low to the ground—rises as two trunks in a victory sign on the left. Gigantic sugar maples with wire embedded in them stand on the right. A large hickory has barbed wire protruding from a depth of 9 inches.

You'll turn right, reach the pasture corner, and continue straight on a wide, mowed trail. Panoramic views of the Greylock Range and The Hopper (see Trip 8) on the mountain's west face become ever more splendid as you walk on. A lone nest box placed for the declining American kestrel stands like a sentinel out in the field. The Guest House bed and breakfast is visible ahead. Continue through the sculpture garden to the paved drive, turn right, and follow it 150 yards to the roadway that leads left to the parking area.

DID YOU KNOW?

Bobolinks winter on the Argentinian Pampas and arrive back in the Berkshires in May. Males sing their bubbly notes while on the wing above the meadows where the smaller, streaky brown females nest. To ensure their nesting success, mowing after July 15 is recommended—a management practice followed here.

MORE INFORMATION

Open daily, year-round, sunrise to sunset. Free admission, but a donation is suggested for nonmembers over age twelve; members are free. A chemical toilet is situated opposite the map kiosk. Dogs must be leashed at all times. Mountain biking is not permitted. The Trustees of Reservations, Field Farm, Sloan Road, Williamstown, MA 01267 (Western Regional office 413-458-3135; westregion@ttor.org; thetrustees.org).

NEARBY

The mid-century modern Guest House at Field Farm, built in 1948, offers year-round bed and breakfast accommodations. For reservation information, call 413-458-3135 or visit thetrustees.org/field-farm/accommodations. html. Guided tours of The Folly, a mid-century modern building designed by Ulrich Franzen in the mid-1960s, are conducted June through October, upon request.

TRIP 7
GREYLOCK RANGE TRAVERSE

Location: Williamstown, Adams, and North Adams, MA
Rating: Strenuous
Distance: 12.7 miles
Elevation Gain: 2,390 feet
Estimated Time: 6.5–8.0 hours
Maps: AMC Massachusetts Trail Map #1 USGS North Adams; trail map available online

A long, strenuous day hike spanning four summits, including the state's highest peak, and arguably the most sensational panoramic vista in the entire commonwealth—just one of six along the route. The most exhilarating hiking the Berkshires has to offer!

DIRECTIONS
From the Five Corners area of South Williamstown, where US 7, MA 43, Sloan Road, and Green River Road intersect, turn right onto Green River Road and follow it 2.3 miles to Hopper Road and Mount Hope Park on the right. Turn right, cross the Green River, and drive for 2.1 miles (bearing left at Potter Road) to a large gravel parking area on the right at Haley Farm. *GPS coordinates*: 42° 39.323′ N, 73° 12.325′ W.

TRAIL DESCRIPTION
From the parking area at elevation 1,100 feet, follow the cobbled road, past a farm gate and a state forest gate and between stone wallss overhung by sugar maples to Haley Farm Trail on the right; you'll be returning via that trail. A panoramic view of the Hopper is laid out beyond the hayfield. For now, continue past Hopper Trail intersection on your right and descend gently on blue-blazed Money Brook Trail where a dense stand of pale touch-me-not blooms in midsummer, but unlike the predominant orange species in this area, these are lemon yellow. Amble through a grassy stretch via a mowed path that skirts Hopper Brook at the boundary of the Hopper Natural Area. Bear left to cross the clear brook by way of a wooden footbridge and begin an easy uphill walk along the opposite bank.

At a short reroute, where the raging brook has undercut the trail, bear left up stone steps and along the hillside to rejoin the fast-flowing brook. You are

GREYLOCK RANGE TRAVERSE

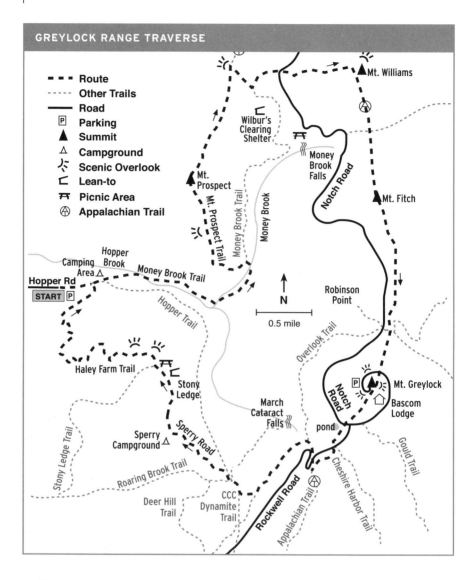

- - - Route
······ Other Trails
——— Road
P Parking
▲ Summit
△ Campground
⚐ Scenic Overlook
⊏ Lean-to
⊓ Picnic Area
Ⓐ Appalachian Trail

Mt. Williams

Wilbur's Clearing Shelter

Money Brook Falls

Mt. Fitch

Mt. Prospect

Money Brook Trail

Money Brook

Mt. Prospect Trail

Notch Road

Hopper Brook
Camping Area △
Money Brook Trail

Hopper Rd
START P

Hopper Trail

N
0.5 mile

Robinson Point

Overlook Trail

Haley Farm Trail

Stony Ledge

Stony Ledge Trail

March Cataract Falls

Notch Road

P

Mt. Greylock

Bascom Lodge

pond

Gould Trail

Sperry Campground △

Sperry Road

Roaring Brook Trail

Deer Hill Trail

CCC Dynamite Trail

Rockwell Road

Appalachian Trail

Cheshire Harbor Trail

walking along the southern flank of Mount Prospect. Sugar maple, white ash, black birch, yellow birch, beech, and oak shield the path. The eroding force of water is evident at another bend in the flow. Soon after a stone-lined cellar hole on the right, tread over a wooden footbridge across cascading Hopper Brook. At a Y intersection, turn left to remain on spacious Money Brook Trail. At this point, the trail parallels Money Brook, a tributary of Hopper Brook, upstream. Magnificent eastern hemlocks rise from the steep slopes as you cross a stream. A wider feeder brook flowing down through the Hopper requires a crossing on rocks; use caution. This is practice for a final crossing on Money Brook via stones a short distance beyond.

Ascend the rocky Mount Prospect Trail. The path turns left at a signed **T** intersection and narrows. The grade soon becomes more challenging and winds along a virtual talus slope of schist requiring some use of hands to negotiate. Caution is called for, especially when the rocks are wet. Soon you bear right under oaks to climb the prominent spine of Prospect, once known locally as the "Hog's Back." Blueberries and huckleberries both offer the hiker sweet morsels in midsummer. Know huckleberry by its rough leaves. The challenging climb is interrupted now and again by more moderate sections, but the overall theme is relentlessly upward. Red maples, shad trees, and mountain azalea join the oaks on this dry, south-facing slope. Reach a vista point on the left where you'll be treated to wonderful long views of the Taconic Range and the Haley Farm. Some moderate uphill stretches remain until the wooded high point where a rock cairn marks the 2,690-foot summit.

An easy-to-moderate descent leads through ferns, under yellow birches, maples, beeches, a few red spruces, and over gneiss (pronounced "nice") bedrock, taking turns leveling out and dropping. One mile beyond the cairn and after passing by dark stands of young spruces, emerge onto bedrock offering fabulous vistas of the northern Taconics and Vermont's Green Mountains beyond. Turn sharply right here to follow the white-blazed Appalachian Trail (AT) south over a needle-cushioned treadway down a spruce-covered east slope until you reach Money Brook Trail. A sign notes Wilbur's Clearing Lean-to is 0.3 mile down the trail to the right. Instead, continue straight and traipse over bog bridges through a damp spruce stand.

Bear right to cross Notch Road and begin your ascent of Mount Williams. Mature spruces are reproducing well here. Later, hobblebush and beech form a dense understory. The ascent becomes more challenging as you climb rocky "steps." But switchbacks make climbing the west slope of Williams manageable. After leveling off in a low-stature wood, the AT bears left to reach the 2,951-foot summit of Mount Williams, named for Ephraim Williams, Jr., the founder of nearby Williams College. Limited views to the northeast are a welcome respite from climbing. When ready to continue, be sure to turn left. The contorted bedrock along the initially level path shows the effects of the tremendous heat and pressure created by continental collision hundreds of millions of years ago.

A steeper and rockier downhill path (opposite a trail to Notch Road) leads to the Bernard Farm Trail junction on the left. Remain on the AT to begin an easy climb to Mount Fitch, where you may detect the aroma of balsam firs.

You will most likely have crested the 3,110-foot summit of Mount Fitch and dropped slightly in elevation again before you realize that you have passed over it. The roughly 3 miles of trail between Williams and Bellows Pipe Trail wend through pleasant woodland. More than a mile beyond Mount Fitch, the Bellows Pipe Trail (Trip 10) goes left. It's only another 100 yards to the steep Thunderbolt Trail—one of the Northeast's pioneering downhill ski runs—on the left. Just beyond Thunderbolt Trail, a side path leads right, to Notch Road and Robinson Point, but continue up on the AT, which in May is festive with wildflowers.

Blackberry canes fill a linear gap through which the trail passes on its somewhat rocky ascent past low beech, birch, and cherry trees. If not obscured by clouds or fog, you'll have your first glimpse of the globe atop the Massachusetts Veterans War Memorial Tower here. Tread up railroad ties and then flagstone steps to paved Notch Road. Look back to view a spectacular panorama that includes the rocky spine of Ragged Mountain and the Hoosic River Valley. Cross the asphalted road and climb over bony outcrops to arrive shortly at the renovated Thunderbolt Shelter. The summit, topped by the iconic granite tower, rises just a short distance ahead. A web of trails encircles the summit, which is enlivened by the clear plaintive whistles (*Old-Sam-Peabody-Peabody-Peabody*) of white-throated sparrows in summer.

For fabulous views eastward, bear left at the Y split. A universally accessible path leads to an overlook where all promontories are identified on a granite tableau. Restrooms and drinking water are available at Bascom Lodge, a real gem, built in 1938 by the Civilian Conservation Corps (CCC). When ready to depart, pick up the AT beyond the tower (where a unique roadside bronze relief map of the Greylock Range is situated) and cross the road. Stroll through bluish conical firs and cross the paved road again near the lofty radio antenna where three composting toilets are situated. The AT descends steeply over rock amid red spruce and firs. When you reach the paved road, turn right, walk 100 feet, and reenter the woods on the right. A brief descent brings you via bog bridges to a scenic human-built pond—once the lodge water supply and headwater for Hopper Brook. At the Y split, leave the AT and stay right, heading downhill on blue-blazed Hopper Trail toward Sperry Road. Bear right at paved Rockwell Road and descend on a wide, rocky path, turning left at the junction with Overlook Trail on the right.

The grade is moderate as you contour down the slope under a canopy of beech and birch trees with red spruces mixing in. After leveling out and passing by a shielded spring on the right, turn right at a T intersection to follow Hopper Trail down more steeply along an unnamed brook to gravel Sperry

Beyond the summit of Mount Prospect, hikers emerge onto bedrock offering fabulous vistas of the northern Taconics and Vermont's Green Mountains beyond.

Road. Turn right and stroll down through the campground, passing junctions for several other trails, including Hopper Trail on the right. But remain on the roadway, passing toilet facilities. The road begins to climb, easily at first then moderately, through mixed forest. The road loops and ends at Stony Ledge (elevation 2,560 feet), where, in my opinion, the most breathtaking vista in the state awaits.

Directly across the 1,500-foot-deep chasm of the Hopper and 1,000 feet higher, is Greylock. From left to right, an expansive view encompasses all the peaks you scaled today—Prospect, Williams, Fitch, and Greylock. Picnic tables invite a long pause. Hopper Brook is audible and the flutelike voices of thrushes spiral up from the extensive forest below in late spring and summer. When ready to continue, find the Stony Ledge Group Site sign at the trailhead on the far end of the gravel turnaround. At the **Y** split, follow the sign left for Stony Ledge and Haley Farm trails, past an outhouse on the left and the brown shelter on the right on a blue-blazed path. The drop is fairly steep amid hardwoods and spruce to the junction with blue-blazed Haley Farm Trail, where you turn right.

A final splendid vista, this one north toward Williamstown and Vermont's Green Mountains, is yours at the end of a short path on the right. Haley Farm Trail descends among the beech, maple, cherry, and yellow birch, and then through the oak-covered slope showing signs of selective logging decades back. Switchbacks lead down quite steeply through two small bowls and continue through a forest of well-spaced large sugar maples, beneath which new growth seeks the sun. Sugar maples thrive in such nutrient-rich soils. Reach level ground at last among birches and arrive at the hayfield you gazed across hours ago at the start of your trek. Mount Prospect looms ahead. Stroll through the meadow and turn left on the old road toward the parking area to end a rewarding day.

DID YOU KNOW?

After Captain Ephraim Williams, Jr. died in battle during the French and Indian War in 1755, his estate provided funds for a free school in West Township—later Williamstown. The school would eventually become world-renowned Williams College.

MORE INFORMATION

Open daily, year-round. Access is free of charge. A parking fee is charged only on the summit May–October. Toilet facilities are located at the trailhead, Bascom Lodge, the campground on Sperry Road, and Stony Ledge. Carry in, carry out rules apply. Mount Greylock State Reservation is managed by Massachusetts Department of Conservation and Recreation. Visitor Center, 30 Rockwell Road, P.O. Box 138, Lanesborough, MA 01237 (413-499-4262; mass .gov/eea/agencies/dcr/massparks/region-west/mt-greylock-state-reservation-generic.html).

NEARBY

According to the Williams College archives, Captain Ephraim Williams, Jr., supervised the completion of Fort Massachusetts in 1745, which was strategically situated by the Hoosic River, between the future towns of North Adams and Williamstown. Today, a plaque in the Price Chopper supermarket parking lot along MA 2 in North Adams marks the site.

TRIP 8
HOPPER TRAIL TO MOUNT GREYLOCK SUMMIT

Location: Williamstown and Adams, MA
Rating: Strenuous
Distance: 9.0 miles
Elevation Gain: 2,390 feet
Estimated Time: 5.0–6.0 hours
Maps: AMC Massachusetts Trail Map #1; USGS North Adams; trail
map available online

Arguably the most scenic route to the summit of the state's highest peak and among those requiring the greatest elevation gain, the Hopper Trail leads from Haley Farm through lush woodland to the Campground on Sperry Road, to the Appalachian Trail (AT), the state's only true boreal forest, and the summit. The descent is via Overlook Trail and Money Brook Trail for added variety.

DIRECTIONS
From the Five Corners area of South Williamstown, where US 7, MA 43, Sloan Road, and Green River Road intersect, turn right onto Green River Road and follow it 2.3 miles to Hopper Road and Mount Hope Park on the right. Turn right, cross the Green River, and drive for 2.1 miles (bearing left at Potter Road) to a large gravel parking area on the right at Haley Farm. *GPS coordinates:* 42° 39.323′ N, 73° 12.325′ W.

TRAIL DESCRIPTION
A trail map is posted at the kiosk; copies may be available as well. A chemical toilet is situated to the right. A view of the Hopper—so named because of its resemblance to a grain hopper—greets you from the very beginning. Follow the farm road past machinery, livestock, hayfields, and pastures of the functioning Haley Farm—a bucolic setting for a trailhead to be sure. The angular mound of Mount Prospect rises off to your left. Shortly, you'll pass a sign with park regulations and a brown metal barway. The cobbled roadway is lined by stone wallss and overarching sugar maples. Blue blazes mark the route.

When you reach Haley Farm Trail on the right, step out into the hay meadow for a fabulous view of the Hopper, but then continue straight on Hopper Trail. A bit farther, Hopper Brook Loop Trail leads off to the left.

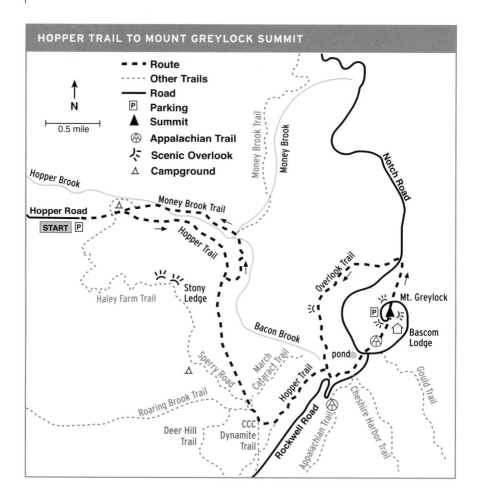

HOPPER TRAIL TO MOUNT GREYLOCK SUMMIT

- - - Route
···· Other Trails
— Road
P Parking
▲ Summit
Ⓐ Appalachian Trail
Scenic Overlook
△ Campground

N
0.5 mile

Hopper Brook

Money Brook Trail

Money Brook

Notch Road

Hopper Road

Money Brook Trail

START P

Hopper Trail

Haley Farm Trail

Stony Ledge

Overlook Trail

Mt. Greylock

P

Bacon Brook

pond

Bascom Lodge

Sperry Road

March Cataract Trail

Hopper Trail

Cheshire Harbor Trail

Gould Trail

Roaring Brook Trail

Deer Hill Trail

CCC Dynamite Trail

Rockwell Road

Appalachian Trail

Continue straight to the Hopper Trail intersection and bear right on a narrow path up through prickly Japanese barberry, multiflora rose (which blooms in June), and honeysuckle shrubs—all invasive exotics characteristic of human disturbance. Before long, you'll enter a maple and white birch woodland and traverse bog bridges across seepages. Hopper Brook is audible. If you're wearing shorts, give a wide birth to stinging nettles lining the path. A steeper climb over a rocky path begins soon after you enter the Hopper—a 1,600-acre National Natural Landmark.

You'll reach the cutoff trail to signed Money Brook Trail on the left. You'll be taking this trail upon your return, but continue uphill now. Shiny schist with high mica content litters the trail through sugar maple, white ash, and American beech woodland. Work your way up a grade that exceeds 25 degrees in places. Yellow birch, another northern hardwood forest indicator, becomes

At the Haley Farm Trail intersection, step out into the hay meadow for a fabulous view of the Hopper, a National Natural Landmark.

numerous. Take a moment to appreciate the abundant bird life in this forest. In late spring to midsummer, male black-throated blue warblers, black-throated green warblers, ovenbirds, American redstarts, red-eyed vireos, and hermit thrushes sound off to attract mates and announce their claims to nesting territories.

Alternately, level out and climb under sugar maples with an understory of sapling beeches, striped maple, and hobblebush. Sharp-needled red spruce becomes a dominant species as you approach the campground along gravel Sperry Road at elevation 2,400 feet and 2.4 miles from the trailhead. The road was named for William H. Sperry, the longest-serving Greylock Reservation Commissioner (1900–1938). Turn left onto the road (a chemical toilet is located along the road in the other direction) and pass another gravel road on the right that leads to Roaring Brook Trail, and Deer Hill Trail and Shelter. Slate-gray-and-white dark-eyed juncos trill sweetly from the tall spruces, but nest on the ground. Opposite the entrance station is the path to March Cataract Trail. A wayside panel relates the history of the Civilian Conservation Corps (CCC), which at its zenith employed 100,000 men in 68 Massachusetts camps. Based here from 1933 to 1942, crews of 200 men rotated every six months. We continue to benefit from their fine work.

Bear right and follow the road over two gushing high-gradient streams—the first bounces over schist steps. About 100 yards past the entrance station, turn left to continue on Hopper Trail. Native stone steps indicate the route up through mixed woods of beech, birch, and spruce to a T intersection with an old carriage road—Deer Hill Trail. Turn left, on a gentle grade, past the source of a spring below. Striped maple and hobblebush, with paired, heart-shaped leaves, are abundant. Black-throated blue warblers construct cup nests among the latter's pliable branches. You'll cross a few small flowages and maneuver over bedrock outcrops that are often slick underfoot. The evocative aroma of balsam may soon be apparent.

In some spots, the layered bedrock serves as a handy staircase. At the junction with Overlook Trail on your left, turn sharply right and continue uphill on rocky Hopper Trail. Soon reach Rockwell Road, which ascends the mountain from the visitor center in Lanesborough, but the path bears left away from the asphalt. Before reaching Rockwell Road again, turn left to follow the signed path to the AT. The narrow path climbs into the balsam fir zone—part of the circumspect boreal forest in this state. Here, at 3,000 feet above sea level, among the stunted yellow birches and firs, blackpoll warblers breed. This small, black-capped, black-and-white bird is abundant in the vast boreal forests of Canada, but is virtually restricted to upper Greylock in Massachusetts. Its sibilant, vibrating notes are insectlike.

Soon you'll merge with the white-blazed AT and continue straight ahead following a line of bog bridges to a serene pond that once supplied drinking water to Bascom Lodge. If clouds do not obscure the summit, the 200-foot-tall radio tower with a 70-foot TV antenna visible across the pond indicates that the summit is but a few hundred vertical feet away. The trail follows the shoreline briefly, leads up over a staircase ledge, and meets Rockwell Road near its junction with Notch Road (leading to North Adams and MA 2) on the left. Turn left and walk about 100 feet (past the intersection) to pick up the AT again on the left.

Your final ascent is through low-stature beech, yellow birch, mountain ash, and young balsams. The soil is thin at this elevation, and the growing season is short. Some trees show signs of stress, from both the harsh climate and acid deposition. Cloud droplets contain an elevated level of atmospheric pollutants—sulphuric acid among them. Although the trail traverses exposed bedrock, *Clintonia* manages to thrive in pockets of soil. Its yellow flowers transform into china-blue berries that confer its other moniker—bluebead lily.

Finally, step out onto pavement near the summit garage. Composting toilets are situated on the right, opposite the TV tower. In winter, chunks of wind-blown ice from the structure can be hazardous to anyone below. Rustic Bascom Lodge, constructed in the 1930s, mostly by the CCC, stands a short distance to the right. The lodge offers restroom facilities, meals, and accommodations. A water spigot at the back of the building is for hikers' use. John Bascom was an original member of the Greylock Commission. Walk straight, cross the access road, and continue on the AT through clumps of firs to the Massachusetts Veterans War Memorial Tower, erected in 1932. A bronze relief model of the Greylock Range invites examination just after you cross the roadway again at the entrance to the summit parking area. Ahead, the 93-foot-high granite tower may be ascended via a spiral metal staircase (closed for renovation in 2015 and scheduled to reopen in 2016). From a paved path on the other side of the tower, enjoy excellent views north, east, and south, including the bare summit of Mount Monadnock in New Hampshire. Bronze plaques interpret key landmarks. In summer, listen for the signature plaintive whistle of the white-throated sparrow—*Old-Sam-Peabody-Peabody-Peabody*—at these heights.

From the summit, retrace your steps and bear right, around the end of the TV tower to the blue-blazed Overlook Trail. Descend under the dense shade of low spruce and fir. Listen for Swainson's thrush and golden-crowned kinglets in early summer. The trail becomes rutted and passes shrubby mountain maples on its way to crossing paved Notch Road. The path leads easily down past gnarled and diseased beech trees. Many mature yellow birches hug the trail. Hobblebush covers the slope and lines the trail. Hermit thrushes may be heard here. Reach a wide spot in the path where a spur leads right 80 feet to a view west to the Hoosic Valley and the Taconics beyond, and north to nearby Mount Prospect and ridgelines in Vermont. Back on the mostly level Overlook Trail, tread bog bridges until you hear the sound of flowing water.

Cross narrow Hopper Brook above March Cataract Falls and ascend fairly steeply for a short distance to the familiar junction with Hopper Trail. Turn right and retrace your steps through the campground and down Hopper Trail back to the blue-blazed Money Brook Trail (which you passed on your ascent) on the right. Turn right and amble downhill fairly sharply under a canopy of sugar maples and ashes. Sharp-lobed hepatica (one of the earliest bloomers in April), red trillium, baneberry, jack-in-the-pulpit, mitrewort, and foamflower make this a fine wildflower trail in spring. Maidenhair fern adds to this trail's charms in summer. Red oaks appear as you descend toward rushing Bacon Brook. The trail turns left at a flat spot under hemlocks. Pass large oaks and descend to Bacon Brook, but first cross a shallow feeder stream on stones.

Bear left, walk 90 feet, and turn right to cross Bacon Brook on a fine wooden bridge. Bear left again on a short, level path to Money Brook Trail.

Follow the trail left (labeled Hopper Road) over another wooden span. At the **T** intersection on the far side, turn left (notice the large white ash on the bank), following energetic Money Brook and blue blazes briefly downstream to its confluence on the left with Bacon Brook. The merged streams flow west together as Hopper Brook. An old cellar hole on the left is all that remains of a former farmstead. Red-flowering raspberry thrives in a seepage area and blooms in late June. This old wood road, adjacent to Hopper Brook (on Money Brook Trail), winds downhill easily over stones—a pleasing finale to this mountain excursion.

The erosive force of flowing water is evident where the stream has cut deeply into the bank. Reach and cross another wooden span over the brook. Soon pass through a couple small, grassy clearings where low-impact camping is permitted. There is an outhouse on the left in the first field. Re-enter woods and walk gradually up, soon rejoining Hopper Trail on the left; continue straight, back to your vehicle.

DID YOU KNOW?

A small population of Bicknell's thrush once bred on Mount Greylock, wintering on the Caribbean island of Hispaniola. Never exceeding two dozen, they dwindled to only a handful by the 1960s. The last one was found in 1972. Degradation of their wintering habitat, climate change, and a catastrophic storm may have played a role in the bird's disappearance from Greylock.

MORE INFORMATION

Open sunrise until dusk, daily, year-round. Access for hikers is free. The Massachusetts Veterans War Memorial Tower is open 9 A.M.–5 P.M. daily from Memorial Day to Columbus Day, weekends only mid to late-May (closed in 2015 for repairs). Bascom Lodge is open mid-May to mid-October. Dogs permitted, but must be on a maximum 10-foot leash. Visitor Center, 30 Rockwell Road, P.O. Box 138, Lanesborough, MA 01237 (413-499-4262; mass.gov/eea/agencies/dcr/massparks/region-west/mt-greylock-state-reservation-generic.html).

NEARBY

The Williamstown Historical Museum, founded in 1941 and located in the David and Joyce Milne Public Library at 1095 Main Street, offers an interesting glimpse into local history. The museum is open Tuesday–Friday, 10 A.M.– 3 P.M., and Saturday 10 A.M. to noon. Admission is free (413-458-2160; williamstownhistoricalmuseum.org).

OLD-GROWTH CHAMPIONS

The recognized guru of old-growth forest in Massachusetts is an amiable, soft-spoken native North Carolinian named Robert Leverett. Leverett has, more than once, bushwhacked up and down just about every rugged hillside that could possibly hide ancient trees. To be sure, almost all old-growth stands occur on steep, virtually inaccessible slopes that defy logging. Finding them has been a career-long challenge and a labor of love for Leverett, who is executive director of the Eastern Native Tree Society and president and cofounder of Friends of the Mohawk Trail State Forest, where many of the ancient ones reside.

In Massachusetts, approximately 2,700 acres of old-growth forest remain out of a statewide forested expanse of 3 million acres. The two largest stands are only 200 acres each. Most are far smaller, some hardly bigger than a rural backyard. To be considered old growth, a stand must cover at least 5 acres and hold at least eight trees per acre that are a minimum 150 years old. It's not a high threshold to meet, one would think, but in Massachusetts, which was 75 percent deforested by the mid-1800s, meeting even those standards is not an easy proposition.

The largest Berkshire stand is in the Hopper, a federally designated 1,600-acre National Natural Landmark on the western flanks of the Greylock Range. Those 115 acres and another 60 in Mount Greylock State Reservation still hold 200-year-old red spruce. Six parcels totaling almost 100 acres remain in southwestern Berkshire County, in the Mount Washington and Mount Everett State Forests, including Bash Bish Falls (Trip 44), Mount Race (Trip 45), Sages Ravine and Bear Mountain (Trip 50), Alander Mountain (Trip 47), and Mount Everett (Trip 46). Additionally, several stands of 20 acres or more exist in Monroe State Forest, including Dunbar Brook (Trip 13).

But old-growth forest is much more than old trees sporting eye-popping statistics. An old-growth is a climax forest type; by definition, that means it is self-perpetuating. In order for that to occur, the old trees must be regenerating themselves. Otherwise, the entire stand would eventually succumb to old age. Trees have natural life spans. For eastern hemlock, that is about 600 years, and for red spruce, about 400. In addition to trees of every age class, old-growth forests host a myriad of other species. There is nothing like standing in the dim light beneath 150-foot-high old-growth giants listening to the ascending flutelike notes of a Swainson's thrush.

TRIP 9
STONY LEDGE VIA HALEY FARM TRAIL

Location: Williamstown, MA
Rating: Moderate to Strenuous
Distance: 5.6 miles
Elevation Gain: 1,460 feet
Estimated Time: 2.5–3.0 hours
Maps: AMC Massachusetts Trail Map #1: D4, USGS Adams

A short but fairly steep hike to arguably the most scenic panorama in the entire Commonwealth. The return is by way of one of the reservation's most popular trails along the southern slope of the bowl-shaped Hopper.

DIRECTIONS
From the Five Corners area of South Williamstown, where US 7, MA 43, Sloan Road, and Green River Road intersect, turn right onto Green River Road and follow it 2.3 miles to Hopper Road and Mount Hope Park on the right. Turn right, cross the Green River, and drive for 2.1 miles (bearing left at Potter Road) to a large gravel parking area on the right at Haley Farm. *GPS coordinates:* 42° 39.323′ N, 73° 12.325′ W.

TRAIL DESCRIPTION
Walk past the barn and by a farm gate bordered on both sides by hayfields and then around a state forest gate. Tread along an old cobbled lane and under a canopy of sugar maples for a couple hundred yards to the signed Haley Farm Trail intersection on the right and a fine easterly view into the Hopper. Turn right and follow the blue-blazed path through a hayfield and up into the forest. The path is level initially in the shade of maples, birches, and white ash, and then steepens before bearing left on the first of a series of four major switchbacks that take you up the slope. It becomes steeper and rougher.

The first of numerous patches of maidenhair fern graces the verge after a right turn. You'll proceed at quite an incline; diagonal trenches (water bars) shunt water off the treadway. Under sugar maples—characteristic of rich woods—a profusion of ferns flourish including spinulose wood, Christmas, glade, and maidenhair. A series of stone steps lead up the most aggressive section of the route and to a small saddle before turning left and continuing

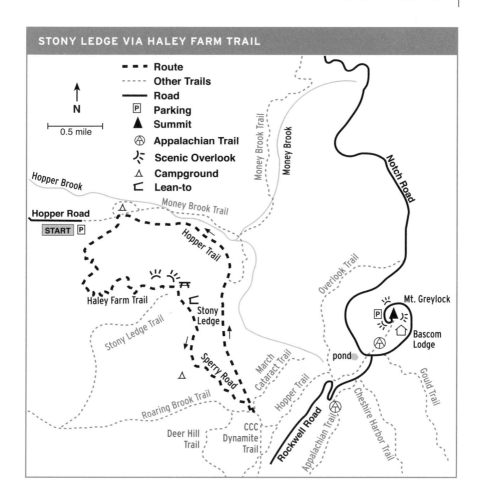

STONY LEDGE VIA HALEY FARM TRAIL

- ■ ■ ■ Route
- ┄┄┄ Other Trails
- ─── Road
- P Parking
- ▲ Summit
- Ⓐ Appalachian Trail
- 𝄞 Scenic Overlook
- △ Campground
- ⊏ Lean-to

N
0.5 mile

Hopper Brook
Hopper Road
START P

Money Brook Trail
Money Brook
Notch Road

Money Brook Trail
Hopper Trail

Haley Farm Trail
Stony Ledge
Stony Ledge Trail

Overlook Trail
Mt. Greylock
P ▲
Bascom Lodge
pond

Sperry Road
March Cataract Trail
Hopper Trail
Roaring Brook Trail
Cheshire Harbor Trail
Gould Trail

Deer Hill Trail
CCC Dynamite Trail
Rockwell Road
Appalachian Trail

the climb. Lots of pole-sized timber here is a clue to past logging, as are the rotting stumps you encounter farther on. Oaks and American beech now join the deciduous woodland mix. A few hemlocks make an appearance amid rockier ground. Under a predominance of oaks, the grade eases, but gone are the lush ferneries in this drier environment. Wild sarsaparilla and prince's pine instead enliven the forest floor.

Pass through a small cleft in a low ledge and enter northern hardwoods again—sugar maple and yellow birch. The dominants are joined by a small understory tree—hophornbeam. At the end of a narrow col, turn right and continue ascending over rocks and a network of surface roots. Hobblebush's paired, palm-sized, and heart-shaped leaves morph from green to maroon in late summer. Its coral-red berry clusters ripen to blue-black. Easy switchbacks lead through woodland with abundant undergrowth and to a fine vista point

Stony Ledge, once called Bald Mountain, offers arguably the most spectacular vista in Massachusetts.

on the left where you'll enjoy the views of farm fields and the buildings of Williams College, all backdropped by southern Vermont's verdant ridges. The rounded mass of the Dome (Trip 1) is clearly visible. Note the deep green patch of conifers ringing its summit.

Continue on a relatively easy grade up through dense fern growth. Note the outcrop on the right cushioned by a thick mat of yellow-green sphagnum moss. Just beyond, the first short red spruces appear. Level out under deciduous trees and arrive at a signed **T** intersection with Stony Ledge Trail, a former ski trail built by the CCC in the 1930s. Turn left and proceed up a steep section toward Stony Ledge Shelter and Stony Ledge. The wooden lean-to group shelter stands on the left just before you emerge from the shade of the forest at a brown metal bear box into the open at Stony Ledge (elevation 2,560 feet), where a spectacular view of the Greylock Range and Hopper awaits. From left to right, Mounts Prospect, Williams, Fitch, Greylock, and a portion of Saddleball are all visible. From a nearby bench or picnic table, you can hear the distant roar of March Cataract Falls and Money Brook flowing wildly some 1,000 feet below you.

To continue, you'll follow gravel Sperry Road through the picnic area and to the primitive campground under spruces, and native hardwoods for about 1 mile—an easy downhill jaunt. Pass two composting toilets opposite a wooden picnic shelter just prior to reaching Hopper Trail at the signed intersection on the left. This is your return route. The level, blue-blazed path leads through young spruce growth, but the woods are mostly deciduous, with an abundance of hobblebush. The grade increases as you drop down along the southern flank of the Hopper. The sound of flowing water is much more evident than it was from Stony Ledge.

The path's angle of descent becomes more acute and rockier. Eastern hemlocks are more numerous on this north-facing slope, which in turn, lowers the temperature. After leaf fall, a fine view through the trees on the east side of the Hopper is possible as the flowing water gains volume. Reach the first of three large, fallen trunks across the trail. The descent eases, and soon you'll reach the Money Brook Trail on the right. Remain on Hopper Trail as it leads under a canopy dominated by sugar maple, with some white ash. Copses of stinging nettle and yellow jewelweed alternately impinge on the path; avoid contact with the former.

You'll cross a few intermittent drainages, level out, and soon traverse a series of bog bridges. After the last set, invasive Japanese barberry—a sign of human disturbance—makes an unwelcome appearance. You'll walk through a small clearing and reach the cobbled roadway that began your hike. Turn left to return to your vehicle, passing the Haley Farm Trail junction along the way.

DID YOU KNOW?

The Haley and Greene families sold their farmland to the Commonwealth in 1990, protecting the access and approach to the scenic and biologically significant Hopper. The Department of Conservation and Recreation and the Williamstown Rural Lands Foundation together created the Haley Farm Trail as a shorter route to Stony Ledge in 1997.

MORE INFORMATION

The Reservation is open daily, sunrise until dusk, year-round. Access for hikers is free. Dogs are permitted, but must be on a 10-foot-maximum leash, and the owner must have a current rabies vaccination certificate in their possession. Mount Greylock State Reservation Visitor Center, 30 Rockwell Road, P.O. Box 138, Lanesborough, MA 01237 (413-499-4262; mass.gov/eea/agencies/dcr/massparks/region-west/mt-greylock-state-reservation-generic.html).

NEARBY

Mount Hope Park in Williamstown—located where you turned from Green River Road across the concrete bridge over the river onto Hopper Road—is a scenic and pleasant place to have a picnic after your hike, or to do some fishing (if licensed). The high-gradient and coldwater Green River is a trout stream that tumbles and gushes over rocks as it flows through the small, well-kept park.

TRIP 10
MOUNT GREYLOCK AND
RAGGED MOUNTAIN VIA BELLOWS PIPE TRAIL

Location: North Adams and Adams, MA
Rating: Strenuous
Distance: 8.8 miles
Elevation Gain: 2,140 feet
Estimated Time: 5.0 hours
Maps: AMC Massachusetts Trail Map #1: D5; USGS North Adams;
trail map available online

**Spring wildflowers grace the mixed woodlands along this historic
route followed by Henry David Thoreau in 1844. A side path leads
to Ragged Mountain and a magnificent view of Greylock's east face.**

DIRECTIONS
From MA 8 (State Street) and MA 2 in downtown North Adams, follow MA
2 west (West Main Street); travel approximately 1.1 miles and turn left onto
Notch Road (note the brown and white Mount Greylock State Reservation
sign here). Follow Notch Road for 1.2 miles to where Notch Road makes a
sharp left near the Mount Williams Reservoir and turn left. Continue straight
ahead into a small gravel parking area with room for about six vehicles.
GPS coordinates: 42° 40.404′ N, 73° 08.325′ W.

TRAIL DESCRIPTION
Stride easily up an old gravel road under an inviting canopy of sugar maples.
Planted Norway spruces stand darkly on the left. This initial portion of the
route passes through North Adams Watershed land. Impressive red oaks and
white ashes border the raised roadbed that likely follows a road initially built
by pioneering farmer Jeremiah Wilbur in the late 1700s. Notch Reservoir can
be seen down to your left. The road soon crosses a feeder stream confined to
a culvert. In all, there are some twenty water crossings (some merely a trickle)
in the first 2.0 miles, but none pose a problem for the hiker. Wildflowers such
as wild ginger, foamflower, false Solomon's seal, and jack-in-the-pulpit grace
the verge.

Three mills once operated along Notch Brook down to the left. Old trees
now border the roadway's left flank. Iconoclastic naturalist and transcendental

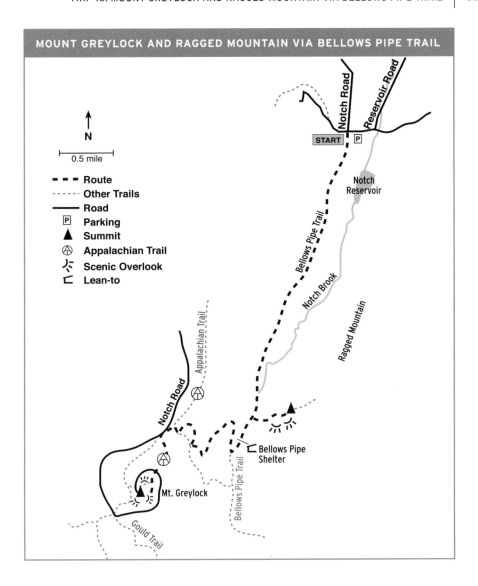

thinker Henry David Thoreau tramped this route toward the summit just days after his 37th birthday. Of it he wrote, "My route lay up a long and spacious valley called the Bellows, because the winds rush up or down it with violence in storms, sloping up to the very clouds between the principal range and a lower mountain." That lower mountain is Ragged Mountain. Trees now hem in Thoreau's "spacious valley." In his day, the landscape was virtually devoid of trees and the "half pipe" shape of the Bellows would have been much more discernable.

The scar produced by the 1990 landslide on Greylock's eastern face seems relatively close at hand from a perch on Ragged Mountain.

After a time, the path steepens and becomes rockier. Some of the feeder streams have carved out small ravines. In spring, the lacy leaves and white, heart-shaped flowers of squirrel corn are common. This plant is the original version of the cultivated plant bleeding heart. False Solomon's seal is also numerous among the ashes, maples, and birches. With the continued ascent, trees of a typical northern hardwood forest soon appear—American beech and yellow birch, with striped maple in the understory. Wildflowers grow lush in these rich woods, blooming in spring—among them miterwort, named for the traditional Bishop's headdress; *Clintonia*; and wild sarsaparilla. The tongue-shaped leaves of trout lily (adder's tongue) blanket the steep slopes. In spring, sections of the trail may be wet. More wildflowers—Solomon's seal, rose twisted stalk, Indian cucumber-root, violets of various hues, and Canada mayflower—are a delight to the eye. The path soon becomes narrower and more eroded. You'll notice wildflowers that have begun to set seed in the valley, such as red trillium, are in full bloom at this elevation. You've literally followed spring up the mountain. The trail splits briefly, immediately after you cross a flowing stream, and turns sharply left. A mill once stood at the head of the brook. Do not follow the more eroded path. Watch out for the stinging nettle that borders the footpath.

Note that the trees are of shorter stature here due to the harsher growing conditions and less fertile soils. There is another temporary trail split (stay left). Spring beauty, with five delicate pink-veined whitish petals, blooms in profusion here. As the slope moderates, young deciduous growth is common. Planted spruces and red pines are present too. After a brief, steep climb, reach the 0.5-mile-long side trail to Ragged Mountain South Peak on the left—just before a remnant stone walls. This intersection can be easily missed. Turn to follow a narrow woodland path under Norway spruces. The undulating trail reaches a stone walls and turns left to parallel it for a short stretch. This stone fence once bordered sheep pasture. Bear left and commence climbing quite steeply through semi-open birch, beech, and maple woods.

You'll reach a schist ledge on the right, perhaps 15 to 20 feet high. Stunted trees, mountain ash, and azaleas convey the effects of elevation. At the upper end of the ledge, watch for the sharp turn to the right that takes you up the steep and rocky trail via switchbacks, as it's easy to miss. Shiny fragments of schist litter the path. After the second hard right, an attention-getting view of the Greylock's east face presents itself—especially after leaf fall. Notice the flaky brown rock tripe lichen attached to the outcrop a bit farther on the right. Watch for a side path on the right that leads 40 feet to open lowbush blueberry fringed ledge, where a truly stunning view of the Greylock massif awaits! Ahead lies the Hoosic River valley.

Retrace your steps to Bellows Pipe Trail and turn left on the mostly level old road. Jewelweed carpets the forest floor in late spring. Yellow birch with brassy and peeling bark dominates, as do sugar maple and gray birch. Reach a signed intersection and turn right to leave the Bellows Pipe and ascend moderately. From here, it is 1.0 mile to the Appalachian Trail (AT) and 2.0 miles to the summit on a rockier path via the lean-to shelter on the right. Continue past it. In spring, watch for small native white butterflies—West Virginia white and mustard white. The trail alternately steepens and levels out. Soon, the angle becomes more serious and you'll find yourself stopping to catch your breath. In May, white-blooming hobblebush brightens this slope traversed by switchbacks.

Among the stunted gray beeches and rock outcrops, the golden stars and glossy leaves of trout lilies glorify the hillside in spring, along with abundant spring beauties and red trilliums. At the Y trail intersection with the AT, take the left fork (actually more or less straight ahead). On the left is a shed for Thunderbolt Ski Trail first-aid supplies. Shortly, arrive at intersections with Thunderbolt Trail (the pioneering downhill ski trail) on the left and a short trail leading to Notch Road on the right, but continue straight ahead and ever uphill on the white-blazed AT. The treadway is firm, and the sweet spicy aroma of balsam fir permeates the mountain air.

The beacon on the top of the Massachusetts Veterans War Memorial Tower comes into view ahead, appearing as a huge crystal sphere. Stone steps lead you up to Rockwell Road. Cross it and climb the last angular section over ledge to the restored Thunderbolt Shelter on the right. Follow the paved path to skirt the summit parking area and find yourself among 15- to 20-foot-tall-pyramidal balsams and arrive at the granite tower on the Commonwealth's highest summit at 3,491 feet. A web of summit paths, with the tower at their center, lead to various lookout points that offer views northeast to New Hampshire's Mount Monadnock and many other points 60 miles or more distant. At Bascom Lodge, water, restrooms, meals, and trail merchandise are available. The Civilian Conservation Corps (CCC) constructed the lodge in the 1930s. Note that hikers are asked to fill water bottles from a spigot around the back of the building, rather than from the drinking fountain inside.

The plaintive, whistled *Old-Sam-Peabody-Peabody-Peabody* of white-throated sparrows is emblematic of this bit of boreal forest. Yellow-rumped warblers and dark-eyed juncos (sparrows that are slate-gray above and snowy white below) also breed at these heights. When ready to return, walk back to the Thunderbolt Shelter and the AT to begin the descent along the same route. Enjoy the lofty view of Ragged Mountain after you cross the road.

DID YOU KNOW?

The Thunderbolt Ski Trail, built in 1934 by the CCC, was one of America's premier expert downhill ski runs. Its 2,175-vertical-foot drop served as the site of numerous sanctioned races until the mid-1950s. A few years ago, a group of Thunderbolt aficionados reinstated an annual ski race.

MORE INFORMATION

Open sunrise until dusk, year-round. Access is free. The tower is open 9 A.M.–5 P.M. daily from Memorial Day to Columbus Day, weekends only mid- to late May. It is closed for renovations in 2015 and scheduled to reopen in 2016. Bascom Lodge is open mid-May to mid-October. Mount Greylock State Reservation, Visitor Center, 30 Rockwell Road, Lanesborough, MA 01237 (413-499-4262 or 413-499-4263; mass.gov/dcr/parks/mtGreylock/).

NEARBY

Open in 1999, the Massachusetts Museum of Contemporary Art (Mass MoCA) has since become one of the world's premier centers for making and showing modern art. With annual attendance of 120,000, it ranks among the most visited institutions in the United States dedicated to cutting-edge art. It's housed in a sprawling nineteenth-century mill complex on 13 acres. There is an admission fee. Located at 87 Marshall Street, North Adams, MA 01247 (413-662-2111; massmoca.org).

PINE CONE JOHNNIES

As you hike Berkshire trails, you can't help but be impressed by the work of the Great Depression-era Civilian Conservation Corps (CCC). The Corps was one of President Franklin Delano Roosevelt's enduring legacies. Created during a time of national economic calamity, the CCC gave meaningful employment to thousands of young men. They built roads; countless trails, ponds, and dams; various park facilities; and even such noteworthy structures as Bascom Lodge atop Mount Greylock (constructed between 1933 and 1937). Much of their handiwork is still serviceable today. Certainly our public lands have never seen such an infusion of manpower directed at creating and improving recreational facilities before or for that matter since.

At the height of the CCC's involvement in Massachusetts, some 51 camps employed up to 10,000 men. Of these camps, fourteen operated in the Berkshires. Monuments to their work are everywhere, which is especially amazing because it has been more than 75 years since they left the woods.

At the Sperry Road Campground in Mount Greylock State Reservation and at the Benedict Pond dam in Beartown State Forest, wayside exhibits relate some of the fascinating history made by the recruits. We owe these "Pine Cone Johnnies," as they were known, a debt of gratitude.

In his fascinating book *Berkshire Forests Shade the Past*, local historian Bernard A. Drew relates the tale of two CCC companies that operated in Beartown State Forest on one site from June 1937 until October 1941. According to Drew, each camp was assigned some 200 men, most in their early 20s and all hailing from Massachusetts. Fort Devens, northeast of Worcester, served as their boot camp. The U.S. Army was responsible for the operation of the camps, while the U.S. Forest Service was charged with overseeing the work. Local men were hired to act as foremen. At Beartown, their accomplishments included building and fortifying roads, adding 6 miles of trails, and construction of two dams—one of which expanded the size of Benedict Pond to 35 acres. In fact, the Beartown companies were among the most active in all of New England.

TRIP 11
HOOSAC RANGE TRAIL TO SPRUCE HILL

Location: North Adams, MA
Rating: Moderate
Distance: 5.4 miles
Elevation Gain: 540 feet
Estimated Time: 2.5–3.5 hours
Maps: USGS North Adams; trail map available online

**A largely out-and-back hike on a portion of fabled Mahican
Mohawk Trail that follows the spine of the Hoosac Range to a
stunning vista atop Spruce Hill. This is a longer but less
traveled option to Spruce Hill than via Busby Trail (Trip 12).**

DIRECTIONS
From the intersection of MA 8 and Center Street opposite the main entrance
to Mass MoCA in downtown North Adams, turn right onto Center Street, go
right, and then left at a traffic light to follow MA 2 (Mohawk Trail) east, up to
and past the Hairpin Turn for a total of 4.7 miles (0.9 mile beyond the Hairpin
Turn) to the top of the hill and an ample gravel parking area on the right.
GPS coordinates: 42° 41.789′ N, 73° 03.886′ W.

TRAIL DESCRIPTION
The route begins at an elevation of more than 2,000 feet at a wooden kiosk complete with a large trail map. Walk up into the fern-rich forest of northern hardwoods—American beech, red maple, birch, and oak. The path is demarcated
by red on white blazes on trees. Hobblebush (viburnum) is abundant in the
understory along the mostly level trail. There are a few damp spots along the
path, and oaks soon become dominant. It's an interesting mix of forest types;
northern hardwoods versus oaks with southern affinities. Goldthread, lowbush
blueberry, and other northern forbs grace the forest floor. Notice also the small
spruces; oddly, they are the only ones along the entire route.

Begin a gradual ascent over a treadway set with a few protruding quartzite
rocks. Virtually all the beech trees (many appear young) show signs of disease—
their normally smooth, gray trunks are disfigured by a fungus. The 4-inch-
tall, bottle-brush-like stalks of shining clubmoss form soft mats beneath. This

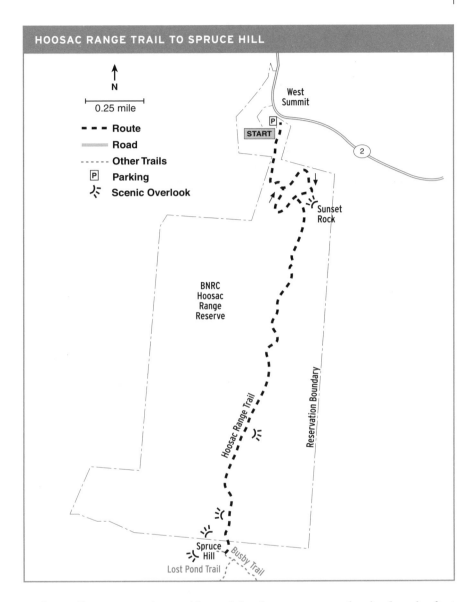

trail is well constructed, as evidenced, by the stone steps that lead to the first switchback. After 0.5 mile, reach a signed intersection. It hardly matters which path you choose because both lead to Sunset Rock vista point in 0.3 mile. Stay straight for the most direct route to the view. You'll return via the other later.

Yellow birch joins the beech and red maple. The path is littered with chunks of schist, a metamorphic rock that glistens due to high its mica content. As you near the ridge top, the trees become shorter. Hedge bindweed, with white and

Just before reaching the Spruce Hill summit hikers enjoy an expansive vista westward beyond the Hoosic River Valley to the Greylock Range.

pink morning glory–like flowers in summer, and raspberry canes blanket the forest floor under breaks in the canopy. In shady spots, some tree trunks are cushioned with mosses. More stone steps and easy switchbacks bring you to Sunset Rock (2,253 feet) and a nearly 180-degree view—from west to northeast—of the Hoosic River valley, downtown North Adams, and the rolling hills beyond. A stone bench offers a nice place for a snack. When ready, continue about 100 feet to a signed intersection and turn left on Hoosac Range Trail toward Spruce Hill, 1.9 miles distant.

Amble up through woodland marked by open patches nearly smothered in bindweed and raspberries. You'll catch a glimpse through foliage gaps of wind turbines along a ridgeline to the left. Wind up the modest slope under more hardwoods, including black cherry. Beech sprouts form a fairly dense understory. Parasitic flowering plants called beechdrops draw nourishment from beech roots and produce inconspicuous purple-brown, orchidlike blossoms in early fall. For nearly the rest of the route, the path undulates, utilizing stone steps, through a low-stature forest with occasional canopy breaks. A notable old yellow birch—hollow at the base—fronts a 100-foot-plus-long moss-adorned ledge that walls in the treadway.

Bear left away from this ledge, but you'll encounter more later on. Yellow birches are adept at gaining a foothold, and mosses cushion the hard stone. One on the left is flecked with rock tripe, a leafy lichen. A short wooden span leads over an intermittent brook, the only one along this ridgeline route. The walking is easy as you stroll past expansive patches of shining clubmoss and hobblebush. The paired heart-shaped leaves of hobblebush turn shades of maroon in late summer, and its berry clusters are crimson. Reach a signed intersection with a 250-foot-long side trail to a vista point on the left. It's worth a look and affords a view of rolling hills to the east. Continue on the well-built trail past even more ledge outcrops.

You'll emerge into a narrow, linear clearing—a power line cut. You are standing directly above the Hoosac Tunnel, a quarter mile beneath your feet! Reenter forest, walk past more ledge outcrops, and arrive at an unsigned intersection with a trail on the left, but continue straight on blazed Hoosac Range Trail. Soon you'll reach another intersection, this one on the right, that quickly leads to an expansive vista across bedrock—bordered by blueberries and hay-scented fern and rimmed with mountain ash—westward across the valley to the Greylock Range. Mountain ash glows with coral-red berry clusters in late summer. Return to the main trail and turn right for the last 0.2 mile to Spruce Hill.

After walking through two more small clearings, past more ledges, you'll arrive at a point on the right where a couple of well-worn paths lead steeply up over bedrock to the summit (use the wider second path). From here, the route (now Busby Trail) is blazed blue. Look back for a view of two sets of wind turbines on a ridgeline several miles away. Bear left to follow a narrow path a short way to the open summit of Spruce Hill, marked by two USGS benchmarks. It offers views in virtually all directions—especially south and west. But watch your footing atop this cliff as you maneuver for that perfect photo. The quarry at the foot of Mount Greylock is brilliant white. Enjoy the views—some of the finest in the area. When ready, scramble down the short, steep bedrock to the main trail, and retrace your steps all the way to within 100 feet of Sunset Rock. When you reach the **T** junction, turn left for a slight route variation (both options are 0.3 mile long) back to the signed intersection. At the major intersection, turn left to walk the 0.5 mile back to your vehicle.

DID YOU KNOW?

The Hoosac Range is a southward extension of Vermont's Green Mountains. And Hoosac (also spelled Hoosic, Hoosick, and Hoosuck) is an Algonquin word that means "place of stones."

MORE INFORMATION

The route traverses lands owned and managed by the nonprofit Berkshire Natural Resources Council, a regional land trust. Hoosac Range Trail is open free of charge during daylight hours. Motorized vehicles, fires, camping, littering, and cutting or removing plant material are prohibited. Open to hunting in season. Berkshire Natural Resources Council, 20 Bank Row, Pittsfield, MA 01201 (413-499-0596; bnrc.net). Spruce Hill summit is in Savoy Mountain State Forest, 260 Central Shaft Road, Florida, MA 01247 (413-663-8469 or 413-664-4800; mass.gov/eea/agencies/dcr/massparks/region-west/savoy-mt-state-forest-generic.html).

NEARBY

Camping is available mid-May through mid-October at Savoy Mountain State Forest. Reservations suggested for 45 sites (one for groups) and four log cabins that are available for year-round rental. Call the phone number above for more information. From MA 2, drive east less than 0.5 mile and turn right on Central Shaft Road. Travel 2.8 miles to park headquarters, 3.3 miles to the North Pond day-use area, and 3.7 miles to the campground.

TRIP 12
SPRUCE HILL VIA BUSBY TRAIL

Location: Florida and North Adams, MA
Rating: Moderate
Distance: 2.6 miles
Elevation Gain: 670 feet
Estimated Time: 1.5–2.0 hours
Maps: USGS North Adams; trail map available online

**Perhaps the best views after a short hike in the entire region.
An old road leads past an early-nineteenth-century cellar hole to a
rocky perch with stunning views of the eastern face of the
Greylock Range, and the Taconic Range beyond, as well as points
north and south.**

DIRECTIONS

From the intersection of MA 8, MA 2, and MA 8A in downtown North
Adams, follow MA 2 (Mohawk Trail) east for approximately 5.1 miles
(via the hairpin turn). Turn right onto Central Shaft Road just after the
Florida town line. Stay to the right at each of the next two forks and drive an
additional mile (passing the Savoy Mountain State Park headquarters on
the right) to a wide gravel pull-off area on the right with space for some
ten vehicles. *GPS coordinates*: 42° 39.477′ N, 73° 03.351′ W.

TRAIL DESCRIPTION

From the kiosk, where trail maps may be available, walk up into a young forest
of birch, maple, and beech, with a few red spruce. After about 150 feet, reach
Busby Trail, a dirt road that suffers from off-road vehicle traffic in spite of their
prohibition. Turn right onto the level, blue-blazed path bordered and shaded
by sugar maples, white and gray birches, striped maple, and hobblebush shrubs.
Before long, you'll find yourself in a power line easement filled with raspberry
canes, gray birches, and sapling red maples. Chestnut-sided warblers whistle
their *pleased, pleased, pleased to meetcha* breeding refrain and nest in shrubs
here from May through July.

Back in the forest, the blue-blazed trail bypasses the rutted and often wet road
to the left for a couple hundred yards. Continue through a northern hardwood
forest of birch, beech, maple, and hemlock. Patches of the Massachusetts state

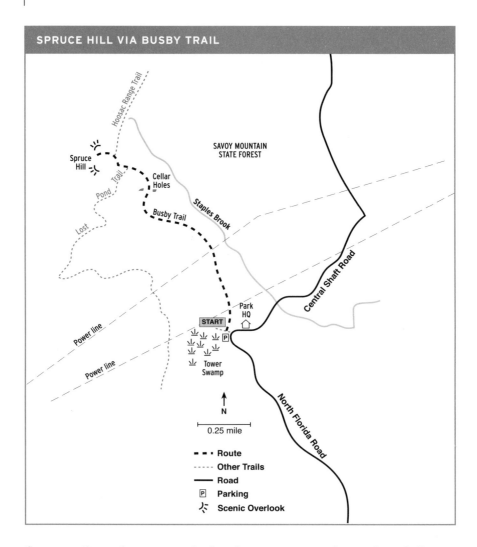

SPRUCE HILL VIA BUSBY TRAIL

Hoosac Range Trail

Spruce Hill

SAVOY MOUNTAIN
STATE FOREST

Cellar
Holes

Trail

Pond

Busby Trail

Staples Brook

Lost

Central Shaft Road

Power line

Park
HQ

START

Power line

Tower
Swamp

North Florida Road

N

0.25 mile

- - • Route
----- Other Trails
——— Road
P Parking
⅄ Scenic Overlook

flower, trailing arbutus, grace both sides at one point, their pale pink flowers emerging for a short time in early May. More common, however, are the little paired leaves of partridgeberry and the heart-shaped leaves and spike of tiny white blossoms of Canada mayflower. Soon the roadway rises a bit and becomes drier and more pleasant.

Traverse another power line cut filled with arrowwood (note the straight branches), bilberry, raspberry, and birch. The cut—devoid of trees—reveals the lay of the land as it dips and then rises to a ridgeline on the right. Ignore the narrow roadway that joins Busby Trail from the right a bit farther along, and begin a gradual ascent. So far, you've had to expend little effort. During the 1930s, the legendary Civilian Conservation Corps planted groves of Norway spruces here and at many other locations. These trees are now maturing and provide habitat for birds and mammals that prefer conifer stands such as fiery orange, black, and white Blackburnian warblers and impish red squirrels that feast on bird's eggs as well as spruce seeds and fungi. There are virtually no spruces on Spruce Hill itself and virtually all those that you encounter along the trail have been planted.

Listen for the sound of flowing water to your right and soon gaze upon a small brook. The stone remnants of former bridge abutments are visible along the far bank, as is a stone walls. You'll find white ash trees here, identifiable by their cross-hatched bark, that do well in moister ground. In fact, other than the spruce plantations, deciduous trees predominate. Continue an easy climb, bear right, and cross a narrow drainage—wet in spring. The clean white trunks of paper birch here are most attractive. At one point, flowing water has eroded a gully, exposing rock and forming a modest falls during wet seasons. Watch your step.

A bit farther, tread up and over bedrock steps; the remains of an un-mortared wall stand on your left. The old road becomes rockier before you arrive at a jumble of rectangular cut blocks of schist on the left that indicate a former foundation. A few feet farther and on the opposite side gapes a well-preserved cellar hole. A yellow birch threatens to cleave apart stones of the right wall. It's interesting to contemplate what farm life would have been like here some two hundred years ago.

Busby Trail now turns sharply left, where the shiny, pointed leaves of trout lily carpet the ground profusely in late spring, and begins to climb. The treadway becomes briefly sandy under a canopy of black cherry, ash, birch, and beech, and here is where you'll finally have to exert yourself. The sand sparkles with flecks of the mineral mica. Soon cross a stone walls built of good-sized schist blocks—moving them into place would have been no easy chore. A bench sits on the right. Continue straight up the slope. A luxuriant growth of skunk currant about 18 inches high fills the sunny forest floor where you turn left, and shining clubmoss forms a patch of green "bottle brushes" on the right.

The path winds up through attractive woodland. Listen for the lisping *beer, beer, bee* songs of tiny black-throated blue warblers in late spring and early summer as you approach ledge outcrops. They nest low among the wiry branches of hobblebush, which in spring are lovely with bunches of white flowers resembling doilies. At the trail split (note the arrow carved into the bark of a small beech), turn right through a swale.

Soon reach a steep but well-built stone staircase that leads up the ledge. A bouquet of exquisite painted trillium—three petals, three leaves—clamors for attention partway up in May. Bear left and continue a more moderate climb under stunted beech trees into a wonderful spring wildflower garden. *Clintonia* (bluebead lily), bunchberry (a tiny, ground-hugging dogwood), wild oats, and lowbush blueberry have turned this into a fairyland forest. The paired heart-shaped leaves and flat, white flower clusters of hobblebush are abundant. The tiny, fertile flowers produce red berries, and in fall, the leaves turn lovely shades of maroon.

After a few short switchbacks, reach the end of the Hoosac Range Trail, which joins Busby Trail and leads 2.7 miles to MA 2 (Trip 11). Turn left for one last ascent over a ledge outcrop, and emerge into the open. Follow the blue blazes left over bedrock and through a hobblebush thicket for the best views from exposed, slanted schist bedrock at an elevation of 2,566 feet. What a fantastic vista from this perch on the Hoosac Range! The Greylock Range is sprawled out to the west, with Ragged Mountain lying at its feet, and the Taconics stand beyond Greylock. North Adams lies in the Hoosac Valley to your right, with Pine Cobble poking up beyond. To the left is the town of Adams. At your feet, lowbush blueberry plants crowd the perimeter and show creamy bell-shaped blossoms in spring, while a few wind-trimmed mountain ashes hold forth to the right.

You'll want to linger here and soak in all the stunning scenery. The fall foliage spectacle in October is a great reason to visit then. When ready to return, retrace your steps 1.3 miles back to where you left your vehicle.

DID YOU KNOW?

If you are fortunate enough to have planned your hike for mid-September to early November, be on the lookout for migrant hawks passing by from right to left. You are most likely to observe broad-winged hawks (sometimes in "kettles" of dozens of birds in September), sharp-shinned and Cooper's hawks, rocking, black turkey vultures, and ospreys.

MORE INFORMATION

Open 8 A.M. to dusk, year-round. Busby Trail access is free. Pets must be on a 10-foot-maximum leash and attended at all times. Must have proof of current rabies vaccination. Motorized off-road vehicles and alcoholic beverages are prohibited. Savoy Mountain State Forest, 260 Central Shaft Road, Florida, MA 01247 (413-663-8469; mass.gov/eea/agencies/dcr/massparks/region-west/savoy-mt-state-forest-generic.html).

This farmstead cellar hole along the Busby Trail creates an opportunity for reflection on farm life here two centuries ago.

NEARBY

Natural Bridge State Park holds a true natural phenomenon—one of only two marble arches in the world formed by water erosion. Open 10 A.M. to 6 P.M., Memorial Day to Columbus Day. From MA 8, follow McCauley Road to parking. P.O. Box 1757, North Adams, MA 01247 (413-663-6392; mass.gov/eea/agencies/dcr/massparks/region-west/natural-bridge-state-park-generic.html).

TRIP 13
DUNBAR BROOK

Location: Florida and Monroe, MA
Rating: Moderate to Strenuous
Distance: 6.25 miles
Elevation Gain: 1,010 feet
Estimated Time: 4 hours
Maps: USGS Rowe; trail map available online

Old-growth trees, massive boulders, and a roaring flow make the Dunbar Brook Trail a path of superlatives. A steep slope leads to a stretch of graveled woodland roads that enable a great loop through wild uplands at the northeastern edge of the Berkshires. Fording the brook during high flows can be difficult.

DIRECTIONS

From the intersection of MA 2 and MA 8 (opposite Mass MoCA) in North Adams, follow MA 2 east up to the Hairpin Turn, Western Summit, and Whitcomb Summit to Whitcomb Hill Road on the left at 7.5 miles. Follow Whitcomb Hill Road (staying right at the intersection with Monroe Road) for 2.5 miles to the junction with River Road. Turn left and drive on River Road across railroad tracks (active rail line—exercise caution when crossing) at the Hoosac Tunnel and continue another 4.0 miles to a gravel parking area (day-use only) on the left, across from the Dunbar Brook Picnic Area. *GPS coordinates*: 42° 42.275′ N, 72° 57.161′ W.

TRAIL DESCRIPTION

From the parking area, where a stylized map and recreation area rules are posted, follow the rough track up the inclined power line corridor for about 150 feet to a footpath on the right where you enter a dark hemlock wood. Blue blazes mark the trail. Do not follow the wooden staircase fitted with railings down to the small concrete dam that spans the brook.

Amble along the hill's contour beneath shade-casting hemlocks along a rocky slope. Yellow birches rise from the gneiss boulders they firmly grasp. As you descend toward the untamed flow, you'll be struck by the sheer size of some of the boulders in the streambed. But the sound of water cascading over rocks is what first captures your attention. Dunbar Brook, an evocative

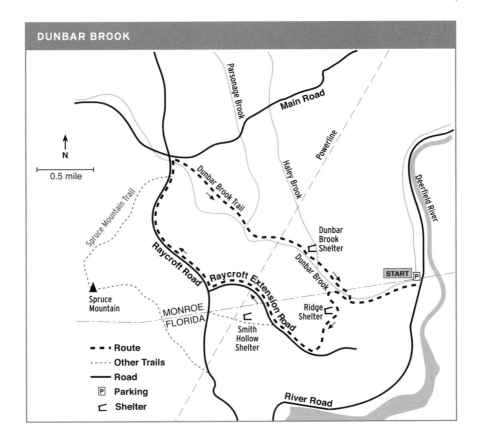

DUNBAR BROOK

Parsonage Brook

Main Road

Powerline

Haley Brook

Deerfield River

N

0.5 mile

Spruce Mountain Trail

Dunbar Brook Trail

Dunbar
Brook
Shelter

Dunbar Brook

START P

Raycroft Road

Raycroft Extension Road

Spruce
Mountain

MONROE
FLORIDA

Ridge
Shelter

Smith
Hollow
Shelter

- - • **Route**

----- **Other Trails**

—— **Road**

P **Parking**

⊏ **Shelter**

River Road

tributary of the nearby Deerfield River, flows below. The brook, as well as the forest, has a wild, untamed appearance.

A bordering outcropping drips moisture from its mossy sphagnum coat. More boulders—some the size of trucks—protrude from the slope; others, rounded by flowing water, litter the stream. Yellow birches soon become more numerous. Along the path, foamflowers send up frothy white heads of modest flowers in late spring. Its leaves resemble those of geranium. The shrub with white blossoms earlier in spring and paired heart-shaped leaves is hobblebush. Soon bear left and climb rock steps, then gradually higher above the brook into a mixed forest. A towering white ash, with cross-hatched bark, stands sentinel-like on the right. Bigtooth aspen, red maple, and beech join the deciduous mix when you drop closer to Dunbar Brook. Early yellow violet, red trillium, baneberry, jack-in-the-pulpit, starflower, and wild ginger are among the woodland wildflowers you may spot in spring.

When you reach an intersection where stone steps lead down to the brook bank, bear left instead to ascend the steep slope (you'll be crossing the brook

Dunbar Brook pours over gneiss boulders polished to a fine patina by the abrasive actions of the swift current.

in this vicinity on stepping stones to close the loop later). Blue blazes lead in both directions. The path undulates, then slants up the steep incline and finally bears right toward the height of land. You'll experience nearly two-thirds of the hike's total elevation gain here. Some impressive trees—sugar maples, yellow birches, and white ash that escaped the ax thanks to the slope's acute angle—dot the slope.

Reach Ridge Shelter on the right, bearing left just before it. A privy is located 100 yards farther along this old wood road on the right. Blazes are a bit spotty here, but the path is easy to locate on this somewhat level stretch. A pond on the left, transitioning to a bog, has virtually filled in with fallen leaves and branches. Arrive at gravel Raycroft Extension Road (a snowmobile corridor) and bear right. Although a road, it is more of a wide, nearly level path through pleasant deciduous woodland that now includes oaks and American beech. Because you're far from the roaring waters of Dunbar Brook, the voices of neotropical songsters such as scarlet tanager, American redstart, ovenbird, red-eyed vireo, and rose-breasted grosbeak are audible in late spring and early summer.

White birch—one of the most attractive of our northern trees—is numerous along the roadway, and red spruce soon becomes common at this elevation. If you reach the unsigned intersection with a wood road bearing left down to

Smith Hollow Shelter in late spring and early summer, listen carefully for the ascending flutelike song of Swainson's thrush, a species found only at high elevation in Massachusetts. Continue on Raycroft Extension Road through mixed woods dotted with big gneiss boulders, and then traverse a bright power line right-of-way. Back in the forest, plantations of Norway spruce and red pine were established in the 1930s. Note the 6-inch-long cones of this exotic spruce littering the ground. Some trees have been harvested, allowing deciduous growth—cherry, birch, and raspberry—to fill the sunny void. Canada mayflower and *Clintonia* flower in spring along the roadway.

Arrive at a T intersection with unsigned gravel Raycroft Road and turn right onto this route—more traveled by motor vehicles. Potentially heavy ATV traffic on summer weekends (despite being illegal here) is a good reason to plan your hike for a weekday. Sugar maples and light green hay-scented ferns line the mostly level road, while gneiss boulders protrude from the forest floor. The road begins an easy descent and then becomes rougher. Large, platy-barked yellow birches bear little resemblance to youthful, brassy skinned individuals. Two brooks flow through culverts under the roadway. Cabin-sized boulders—one characteristically serving as an anchor for a yellow birch on the left, are eye popping. After a short rise, continue the descent, sometimes steeper and in the dense shade of hemlocks, and bear right. On the left, a narrow blue-blazed path leads up to the wooded summit of Spruce Mountain.

As you continue downward on Raycroft Road, the sound of flowing water becomes apparent. More monumental boulders appear—one with a sheer face toward the road; reach a flat pullout area on the right adjacent to Dunbar Brook. The roadway soon crosses it on a wide wooden bridge. Blue-blazed Dunbar Brook trailhead is to the right immediately after you cross. Enter a mixed forest of hemlock, beech, and yellow birch. The roaring, cascading stream gushes through tight squeezes between and over rocks, creating an evocative scene. But be careful if you move closer for a better view, as the rocks are slippery and the current unforgiving! Note how eons of flow have abraded and sculpted the bedrock. Between here and where you parked, the brook drops some 700 vertical feet.

The path is a bit difficult to follow initially, but that improves. It's difficult to miss the stone ruins of a millrace on the left, where diverted water once turned a millwheel. Look for blue blazes that lead across a feeder stream's rocky tumble where foot-tall American yew bushes (a favorite of deer) thrive. Its needles resemble hemlock but are longer and a lighter shade of green. Climb up under a canopy of large hemlocks and northern hardwoods away from Dunbar Brook on a needle-cushioned treadway. Bear right when you reach a narrow wood road that traverses mature woodland dotted with more boulders. One on the right is the size of a cottage where the treadway narrows further. There is little undergrowth except where big trees have fallen to admit light. Look for the cloverlike leaves of wood sorrel. In June, its five-petaled, pink-veined blossoms resemble those of spring beauty.

Now temporarily out of sight of the brook, the needle-cushioned path climbs under hemlocks, undulates, and then follows the grade downward, sometimes with moderate steepness. Glimpse Spruce Mountain through a screen of trees to your right. Watch for the large pink slippers of the moccasin flower during early June in the acidic soil. Red spruce is regenerating very well here, as evidenced by the abundant seedlings and small trees. No doubt the most imposing boulder along the route—verdant with moss and capped by polypody ferns—lies where the trail turns sharply right and skirts its over-arching face. Other boulders are a veritable nursery for hemlocks and spruces. Tiny, orange-throated Blackburnian warblers sing their lisping refrains from high in the evergreens during the breeding season.

As you continue a steady and sometimes rather steep descent, the sound of rushing water becomes evident again. Level out just above the brook and bear left to parallel it. The rocky streambed, cascades, and crystalline pools beckon the photographer. Walk over level ground where red-backed salamanders hide under logs by day and search for tiny morsels by night, while poisonous (to eat) red efts wander blissfully in broad daylight. Watch for piles of moose droppings. Cross Parsonage Brook on a log bridge. The delightful trail widens under a leafy canopy on the far bank and turns right. A boulder with a thick milky quartz intrusion on the right just before the power line cut may catch your eye.

Raspberry, bush honeysuckle, meadowsweet, interrupted fern, birch, and red maple fill the linear light gap. Back in mixed woodland, you'll be awed by a pair of massive white pines—one twin-trunked—on the right. Tiny prince's pine, a clubmoss, and lots of ground-hugging partridgeberry, with coral-red berries, create a miniature woodland beneath. The old roadway was built up on the down slope side to create a fine footpath. Descend; soon Haley Brook joins in from the left. A mammoth split white ash towers on the left. Indian cucumber root (which has an edible tuber), false Solomon's seal, and red trillium thrive in the rich soil as you reach Dunbar Brook Shelter. Turn left and walk about 100 feet to cross a wooden bridge over Haley Brook. Native stone abutments indicate that a bridge of higher capacity once spanned the stream. Continue to parallel the brook's course.

Watch for an old millstone in Dunbar Brook just before you arrive at another pair of mammoth, straight-boled, 100-plus-foot-tall white pines. Not surprisingly, Monroe State Forest is known for its old-growth pines. Soon bear right to cross Dunbar Brook on rocks. Use caution, as the stones may be slippery. A shallow water crossing may be available 175 feet downstream. After crossing, gain the trail above the brook and turn left on the trail that you tread earlier, back to the parking area. Near the end where the trail splits, be sure to take the right fork uphill.

DID YOU KNOW?

Old-growth forest in Massachusetts is limited to approximately 2,700 acres statewide. To qualify as old growth, a forest must not have been significantly disturbed for at least the last 150 years. In Monroe State Forest, some 270 acres meet those criteria, including pockets of old-growth hemlock, white pine, red spruce, and associated hardwoods—yellow birch, American beech, and white ash.

MORE INFORMATION

Open 6 A.M.–9:30 P.M., daily, year-round. Free access. Chemical toilets are available at Dunbar Brook Picnic Area across River Road. Privies are available at shelters along the route. Carry in, carry out all trash. Snowmobiling permitted when conditions allow. All-terrain vehicles and alcoholic beverages not permitted. Monroe State Forest, Tilda Hill Road, Monroe, MA (413-339-5504 [Mohawk Trail State Forest]; mass.gov/eea/agencies/dcr/massparks/region-west/monroe-state-forest-generic.html). Trailhead parking area and restroom facilities at Dunbar Brook Picnic Area are owned and managed by USGen New England, Inc., P.O. Box 9, Monroe Bridge, MA 01350 (413-424-7229).

NEARBY

The Hoosac Tunnel was an engineering marvel when completed in 1875. At 4.75 miles long, it remains the longest active transport tunnel east of the Rockies. It was built at considerable cost in dollars and human lives (193 died during its construction, which began in 1848). The eastern portal in Florida can be glimpsed on the left as one drives up to the trailhead. This freight line is still active—do not linger near the tunnel entrance or tracks!

Location: Adams, Cheshire, New Ashford, and Williamstown, MA
Rating: Strenuous
Distance: 10.4 miles
Elevation Gain: 1,675 feet
Estimated Time: 6.0–7.0 hours
Maps: AMC Massachusetts Trail Map #1: D4; USGS Cheshire, North Adams; trail map available online

While stopping short of the Mount Greylock summit, this hike has its own delights—a flower-filled hillside meadow offering incredible views and a damp boreal forest atop Saddle Ball Mountain, where sphagnum moss carpets the ground.

DIRECTIONS

From the south: From MA 8 in Pittsfield at Allendale Center, drive north on MA 8 for 9.1 miles into Cheshire and turn left onto Fred Mason Road. Follow it north for 2.9 miles (it becomes West Road after approximately 1.0 mile) to West Mountain Road on the left. Turn left and follow West Mountain Road 1.6 miles, past parking for Gould Trail to the Cheshire Harbor trailhead.

From the north: Take MA 8 south to Adams and turn right at the President McKinley monument onto Maple Street. Follow Maple Street 0.9 mile, and turn right onto West Mountain Road. Follow it for 1.6 miles to the trailhead. *GPS coordinates:* 42° 36.635′ N, 73° 9.399′ W.

TRAIL DESCRIPTION

Park in the gravel lot at road's end, at an elevation of 1,560 feet. Follow the gravel roadway to your right (northwest) that leads into a meadow. Except in summer, Greylock's summit looms above a gap in the tree line as you make your way past a small sign: "Old Adams Rd. to Cheshire Harbor Tr. to Summit 3.5 mi." Reach a map board at the woodland edge. Just before a metal forest gate, a sign on the right reads "To Cheshire Harbor Trail." A short path cuts the corner off the rutted road. Bear right and follow the rocky roadbed up along stone wallss in a forest of sugar and red maples, black and gray birches, young red spruce, and hemlock. Green-trunked striped maple and American beech fill the understory. Hay-scented fern, New York fern, and spinulose woodfern

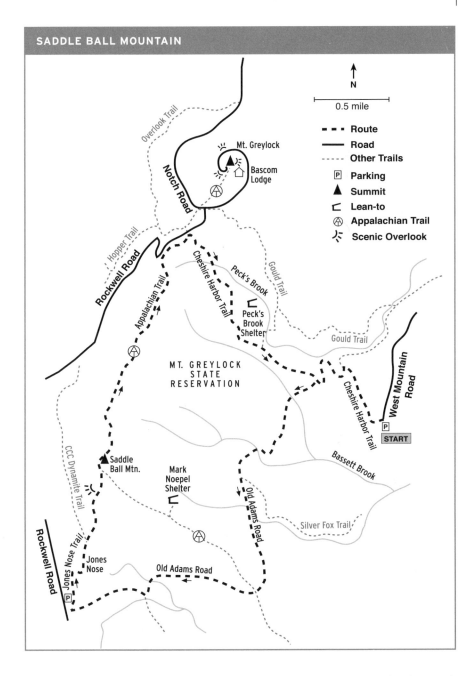

SADDLE BALL MOUNTAIN

border the road. Bits of rusty barbed wire embedded in trees hint that livestock grazed what was once a grassy hill.

Parallel the slope's contour lines uphill; you soon stride across intermittent brook beds. Ancient steel culverts held together with rivets are artifacts of

A small ledge outcrop on Saddle Ball ridge offers panoramic views south to the Central Berkshire Lakes, Lenox Mountain and New York's distant Catskills.

a bygone age. As you curve sharply left, a blue-blazed path appears on the right—Gould Trail. There is a major split in the roadway here, but they quickly rejoin. Several "switchbacks" lead up the slope, where you'll find the first balsam firs. At the 1.0-mile mark, reach Old Adams Road on the left. Turn left onto this predominantly level route as it contours along the lower slopes of Saddle Ball Mountain. These rich woods are fertile grounds for wildflowers, including Indian cucumber-root, sessile-leaved bellwort, Canada mayflower, red trillium, and *Clintonia* (bluebead lily).

Stream crossings are an enjoyable feature of this trail. In short order, an unnamed tributary of Bassett Brook is crossed via wide, wooden bridge. The brook wends through a rocky ravine, producing small cascades en route. Mixed woodland has reclaimed these slopes. Hobblebush shrubs along with spindly goosefoot (striped) maple and beech saplings dominate the understory, while hay-scented ferns soften the road shoulders. Arcing through a deeply cut bank brings you to a hemlock ravine offering a glimpse of a staircase of gushing cataracts—another Bassett Brook headwater. On the right, a small vernal pool hosts wood frogs and salamanders that play out an ages-old breeding ritual in early spring. Cross another wide vehicle bridge and relish a small cataract and horsetail falls a few feet upstream.

Enjoy the easy grade and soon junction with Silver Fox Trail on the left. Remain on wider Old Adams Road. Trees with multiple trunks and pole-sized and sapling growth belie former logging. A third brook crossing, the final Bassett Brook feeder stream, lacks the drama of the previous two. Vehicles have gouged muddy swales in the road, which winds through forest dominated by beeches and other hardwoods. Near the intersection with Red Gate Trail on the left, red spruce becomes more numerous—first 6- to 15-foot-tall trees, then mature ones with boles 2 feet across. Continue straight ahead 150 more feet to cross the Appalachian Trail (AT). Old Adams Road leads through mixed woods and past plush, green schist boulders as you head easily downhill.

Note remnants of a stone walls that once bounded a former sheep pasture. After you pass another multitrunked yellow birch, the trail bends left and the descent soon steepens on a rougher track. Cross the modest headwaters of Kitchen Brook on another wooden bridge and arrive at a signed T intersection. Turn right on Old Adams Road and head upward over protruding thinly layered phyllite rock toward Jones Nose.

Here the roadway is cut deeply into the earth. The ascent soon becomes gradual. A few oaks, the first of the day, mingle with beech, birch, maple, and spruce. Lush undergrowth characterizes this young, spacious forest. But soon forest gives way to a shrubby clearing of chokecherry, meadowsweet, steeplebush, raspberry, and birch. A grassy path runs through this early growth, where indigo buntings and common yellowthroats reside in summer. The trail splits where the snowmobile route bears left. Walk around a metal gate and emerge into the open at gravel Jones Nose trailhead parking lot along paved Rockwell Road.

Pick up Jones Nose Trail on the right before the kiosk, which has a map of the reservation. The blue-blazed route leads up a sharply sloping meadow resplendent with blooming shrubs in midsummer. In late July and early August, the hillside is ablaze as fireweed, steeplebush, and meadowsweet all add splashes of pink to the angular hillside, which is said to resemble the profile of a man who once farmed this area. Fireweed colonizes burned sites; their spikes of orchidlike flowers are candy for the eyes. Steeplebush (hardhack) is also well named because this shrub's tiny magenta blossoms form a spire. Meadowsweet, which is related to steeplebush, has pale pink frothy flowers that attract bees and beetles alike.

Chokecherry (with blood-red fruits), goldenrods, and yellow Saint-John's-wort enliven the slope. Scrumptious blueberries may be reason enough to make the climb in midsummer. As you tread the narrow grassy path, glance over your shoulder to take in the ever-expanding view to the south and west. The Taconic Range forms the border between Massachusetts and New York to the west. As the ascent becomes tougher, a switchback leads up over stone steps into sapling, mountain, and striped maples and over bedrock outcrops. A moist glade holds the odd white blossoms of turtlehead, whose leaves comprise the diet of the Baltimore checkerspot butterfly caterpillar. The big, coarse fern with bronzy green fronds is Goldie's. Hobblebush is abundant here.

At a signed Y intersection with CCC Dynamite Trail, take the right fork to the AT, 0.5 mile distant. The climb increases as you near the summit of Saddle Ball. Hermit thrushes can be heard in summer. An outcrop on the right is a veritable rock garden of mosses, ferns, tree seedlings, and flowers. Soon, you'll reach a small bedrock clearing bounded by spruce, mountain ash, and birch. A bit farther, an obvious side path on the left beckons you to a panoramic view; you won't be disappointed. From the schist ledge, views of the central Berkshire lakes, Lenox Mountain, and on a clear day the distant Catskills can be seen. Back on the main trail, bear right at the blue blaze for a detour. Watch your footing over rocks and roots under wet conditions. The fairly steep footpath goes serpentine, rocky, and undulating as you enter the boreal zone of redolent balsam fir just before the signed AT junction.

The AT leads north over the level wooded Saddle Ball summit of 3,247 feet at a rock cairn. The most abundant wildflower along the trail is *Clintonia*; in midsummer, clusters of porcelain-blue fruits top its flower stalks. The spongy ground forms a great seedbed for balsam fir. Milky quartz pops up here and there. The trail alternately rises and falls, crossing a small brook, its flow stained the color of tea by tannins. The erect stems of shining clubmoss poke up in luxuriant patches. At this elevation, fog, cloud droplets, and rain produce near–temperate rainforest conditions. The result: boulders covered with mossy mats. Sphagnum moss, containing dead cells that hold moisture, carpets low areas. Ghostly white Indian pipes rising from the mossy mat lack chlorophyll and so must obtain nourishment from other plants. Thin bog bridges lead through this cool, acidic wetland, past ground-hugging bunchberries adorned with clusters of scarlet berries.

Continue on the AT to where it reaches the S curve on Rockwell Road—a reliable site for nesting blackpoll warblers, found in the Commonwealth only on upper Greylock. Turn right on the AT to reenter woodland. This forest is predominately deciduous—featuring beech—and the trail alternates level spots with steep climbs and descents, soon arriving at unblazed Cheshire Harbor Trail on the right at Rockwell Road. Watch for an intriguing view of Greylock's summit, Bascom Lodge, and the Massachusetts Veterans War

Memorial Tower before the road crossing. Turn sharply right for the final 3.0-mile leg of the hike (sign erroneously indicates 4.5 miles) on this wide, cobbled path under a canopy of northern hardwoods. Begin a moderate-to-steep descent over a well-worn trail that thousands take from Adams to the summit each Columbus Day. Stay right at the split, and soon cross Peck's Brook on a wooden bridge.

Peck's Brook Loop Trail intersects on the left approximately halfway down. You'll level off amid copious hobblebush and then descend in earnest. At the familiar intersection with Old Adams Road on the right, continue straight on Cheshire Harbor Trail, retracing your steps 1.0 mile to the parking area at the end of West Mountain Road.

DID YOU KNOW?

Greylock Glen, a 1,000-acre state-owned parcel on the eastern flank of Mount Greylock, has been the site of a number of controversial commercial development proposals over the years. More recently, in conjunction with environmental groups, the town of Adams, and the state, more modest plans for an eco-friendly development are being considered.

MORE INFORMATION

Open daily, year-round. Access by foot is free of charge. There are no toilet facilities along the route. Carry in, carry out rules apply. Mount Greylock State Reservation is managed by the Massachusetts Department of Conservation and Recreation. Visitor Center, 30 Rockwell Road, P.O. Box 138, Lanesborough, MA 01237 (413-499-4262; mass.gov/eea/agencies/dcr/massparks/region-west/mt-greylock-state-reservation-generic.html/).

NEARBY

The life of a prominent American civil rights leader of the nineteenth century is celebrated at the Susan B. Anthony Birthplace Museum, 67 East Road, Adams. Born here in 1820, Anthony was a social reformer, a pioneering feminist, and suffragist. Open year-round. Memorial Day to Columbus Day, hours are Thursday to Monday, 10 A.M.–4 P.M.; Columbus Day to Memorial Day, hours are Monday, Friday, and Saturday, 10 A.M.–4 P.M., and Sunday, 11:30 A.M.–4 P.M. There is a small admission fee (413-743-7121; susanbanthonybirthplace.com).

TRIP 15
MOUNT GREYLOCK STATE RESERVATION— EAST SIDE

Location: Adams, MA
Rating: Moderate to Strenuous
Distance: 6.6 miles
Elevation Gain: 1,930 feet
Estimated Time: 4.0–4.5 hours
Maps: AMC Massachusetts Trail Map #1: D5; USGS Cheshire, USGS North Adams; trail map available online, at DCR regional office

This is one of the shortest routes to the summit of the state's highest peak, with significant elevation gain, but anyone in reasonably good physical condition should be able to complete the hike.

DIRECTIONS

From the south: From MA 8 in Pittsfield at Allendale Center, drive north on MA 8 for 9.1 miles into Cheshire and turn left onto Fred Mason Road. Follow it north for 2.9 miles (it becomes West Road after approximately 1.0 mile) to West Mountain Road on the left. Turn left and follow West Mountain Road 1.6 miles, past parking for Gould Trail to a circular gravel parking area where the road ends. The trailhead is on the right.

From the north: Take MA 8 south to Adams and turn right onto Maple Street at the statue of President McKinley. Follow Maple Street for 0.4 mile and turn left onto West Road. Follow West Road for 0.6 mile to West Mountain Road on the right. Drive on West Mountain Road for 1.6 miles to a circular gravel parking area where the road ends. The trailhead is on the right. *GPS coordinates: 42° 36.635′ N, 73° 09.399′ W.*

TRAIL DESCRIPTION

Begin at an elevation of 1,560 feet and follow the gravel roadway to your right (northwest) that leads through a field. Make your way past a small sign on the left that reads "Old Adams Rd. to Cheshire Harbor Tr. to Summit 3.5 mi." There is a map board at the woodland edge. Walk past a metal gate and follow the old rocky roadbed right, gradually up along stone wallss and under a canopy of sugar and red maples, black and gray birches, red spruce, and hemlock. Green-trunked striped maple and American beech populate the understory.

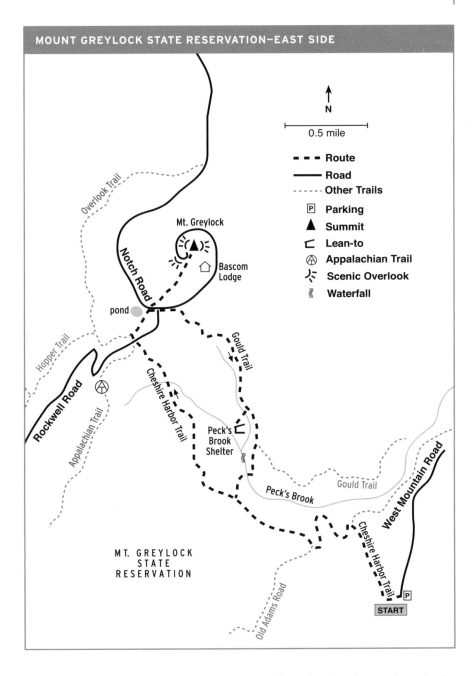

MOUNT GREYLOCK STATE RESERVATION—EAST SIDE

N

0.5 mile

- - - **Route**
——— **Road**
········ **Other Trails**
P **Parking**
▲ **Summit**
⊏ **Lean-to**
⊛ **Appalachian Trail**
⟩⟨ **Scenic Overlook**
≷ **Waterfall**

Overlook Trail

Mt. Greylock

Bascom Lodge

Notch Road

pond

Hopper Trail

Rockwell Road

Appalachian Trail

Cheshire Harbor Trail

Gould Trail

Peck's Brook Shelter

Gould Trail

Peck's Brook

West Mountain Road

MT. GREYLOCK
STATE
RESERVATION

Cheshire Harbor Trail

Old Adams Road

P

START

Hay-scented, New York, and spinulose woodferns border the road, as do the shiny paired leaves of partridgeberry (watch for bright red fruits in fall). Bits of rusty barbed wire embedded in trees prove that livestock once pastured here.

The 93-foot-tall granite Massachusetts War Veterans Memorial Tower, from which five states may be visible, was dedicated in 1933.

Follow the slope's contour; the path curves sharply left. At this point, a narrow path leads down into the forest to Gould Trail, but stay on the wide Cheshire Harbor Trail. It splits briefly here, but rejoins 50 yards farther up. Curving right, you'll note the first red spruces of the hike. After some twists and turns, you will reach a signed intersection with Old Adams Road on the left, at the 1.0-mile mark, but continue straight on Cheshire Harbor Trail. The heart-shaped and paired leaves of chest-high hobblebushes provide nest sites (low to the ground) for black-throated blue warblers. The scoured treadway becomes even rockier, and you'll step over ledge outcrops of metamorphic schist rock. Reach a sign for Peck's Brook Loop on the right (you will return via this way later), but continue straight uphill. The triangular seed capsules of a patch of sessile-leaved bellwort are notable on the right in autumn. A large, shaggy, three-trunked red maple stands on the left where the surface roots of beech lace the trail.

The path now leads up through woods of beech and yellow birch. Although some trees are sizable, this forest is generally young. Beeches sprout from roots and form clones of smooth, gray-barked trees. A 4-foot-long quartz boulder perched on schist to your left will catch your eye. Mountain maple saplings have taken root among the boulders. Distinguish its leaves, which porcupines are fond of, by their saw tooth edges. The sound of flowing water is heard again and the sweet aroma of balsam fir is evident as you reach Peck's Brook. Beware of possible loose and missing boards as you cross it on a wide, wooden snowmobile bridge.

On the far side, the path splits but soon rejoins as it ascends. Evergreens are now more numerous. Reach Rockwell Road. The southbound Appalachian Trail (AT) is on the left, just before the pavement. Cross the road (note sign on tree indicating this is the way to the summit) and follow the AT north over wooden stairs amid a heavenly balsam fragrance. The AT is narrow as it weaves through stunted spruce, yellow birch, and mountain ash, and over bog bridges to reach a **T** intersection with the blue-blazed Hopper Trail on the left. Turn right to continue on the AT over more bog bridges toward the summit.

You'll be walking through a boreal forest zone in the company of spruce and fir trees that generally grow above 2,600 feet elevation in only a handful of locations in Massachusetts. The zone's climate is equivalent to that of interior Canada. Upper reaches of the mountain are often foggy, and the condensing moisture is acidic enough, along with shallow soil and harsh temperatures to negatively impact the growth of woody vegetation. You'll soon reach a scenic spring-fed pond, which once supplied water to the summit lodge. The communication tower on the summit is easily visible from here unless fog-shrouded.

Follow briefly along the shore and shortly reach Rockwell Road again. Turn left, walk about 100 feet, past the intersection with Notch Road, and catch the AT on the left side of Rockwell Road. Follow the signature white blazes over a rocky path and reach an asphalt parking area adjacent to the antenna tower. Composting toilets are located here. From this point, it is only a few hundred feet across the roadway to the 93-foot-high tower on the summit. Attractively rustic Bascom Lodge—where drinking water, flush toilets, meals, and overnight accommodations are available (May–October)—stands to the right. You'll want to explore the summit (3,491 feet) and take in the expansive views on a clear day. Look for the distinctive low pyramid of southern New Hampshire's Mount Monadnock, 60 miles to the west-northwest.

When ready to begin your descent, retrace your steps past the composting toilets and continue south on the AT (beware of wet or loose rocks), soon reaching Rockwell Road. Now return via a more interesting and challenging route, by using a portion of the Gould Trail. Look for the trailhead on the left at a small gravel parking area opposite the intersection with Notch Road. Initially narrow and steep, blue-blazed Gould Trail soon levels off under maple, beech, striped maple, hobblebush, and dense jewelweed. Pass through a stand of yellow birch and balsam fir—I never tire of the fragrance! Raspberry canes flourish in the light gaps. At a junction with an almost unrecognizable overgrown trail, bear left to continue descending. Sugar maples predominate in the now deciduous woodland. Cross a couple of intermittent streambeds, the first over a wooden span. The bedrock channel of the next one is virtually moss-lined. There is much spruce regeneration on the fairly steep slope, and then the trail widens to become a rocky roadway.

At 1.4 miles from the summit, a short, signed trail on the right crosses the brook to Peck's Brook Shelter. The lean-to nestled on the hillside above the tumbling brook is well worth the 3-minute walk, especially for the waterfall flowing during wet seasons. Upon your return to the main trail, turn right and level out under hardwoods. Bear right at a wide overgrown path, as the sign directs, and reach a signed Y intersection with Peck's Brook Loop. The left fork leads down to West Mountain and Gould roads, but turn right toward Cheshire Harbor Trail and Peck's Brook Ravine. The path descends gently as you tread past prince's pine and shining clubmoss and wildflowers such as *Clintonia*, Canada mayflower, and wild sarsaparilla. Bear right and proceed toward the sound. A series of switchbacks down the steep slope deposit you at the exceedingly rocky brook. Follow Peck's Brook downstream briefly, through a narrow ravine. Clear pools provide abodes for brook trout and spring salamanders in this idyllic spot.

Watch for a trail to your right across the brook that ascends the far slope. A blue blaze on a maple on the far side marks the spot. The trail leads steeply up stone steps and via short switchbacks. The already narrow trail has eroded in places. Continue through another hobblebush thicket to the intersection with Cheshire Harbor Trail. You passed this point earlier at the beginning of the hike. Turn left to follow it back to the intersection with Old Adams Road on the right. From here it is 1.0 mile back to your vehicle. Continue straight, and after the series of switchbacks, you'll reach the parking area.

DID YOU KNOW?

The name Cheshire Harbor is an odd one because the trail does not originate at a body of water. Rather, it refers to a former settlement, midway between Adams and Cheshire, reputed to have served as a way station on the Underground Railroad that secreted escaped slaves north.

MORE INFORMATION

Mount Greylock State Reservation is managed by the Massachusetts Department of Conservation and Recreation. Visitor Center, 30 Rockwell Road, P.O. Box 138, Lanesborough, MA 01237 (413-499-4262; mass.gov/eea/agencies/dcr/massparks/region-west/mt-greylock-state-reservation-generic.html). Carry in, carry out rules apply.

NEARBY

Berkshire Outfitters in Adams is a full-service outdoor sports store offering both sales and rentals. Open daily; call for store hours or visit berkshireoutfitters.com; 413-743-5900. Located along MA 8 (Grove Street), 1.2 miles north of the intersection of Fred Mason Road and MA 8; store is on left.

TRIP 16
MOUNT GREYLOCK STATE RESERVATION–
JONES NOSE AND ROUNDS ROCK

Location: Cheshire and New Ashford, MA
Rating: Easy to Moderate
Distance: 2.6 miles
Elevation Gain: 235 feet
Estimated Time: 1.5–2.0 hours
Maps: USGS Cheshire; trail map available online

A delightful ramble along Greylock's midslopes features stunning vistas, prolific blueberry barrens, and a small plane crash site from the late 1940s; easily one of the most fascinating and enjoyable walks on the mountain.

DIRECTIONS

From Park Square in the center of Pittsfield, drive north on US 7 (North Street) for a total of 6.6 miles to North Main Street in Lanesborough. Turn right onto North Main, bearing right at Scott Road at 0.7 mile. The Mount Greylock Visitor Center is 1.0 mile farther along Rockwell Road on the right. Continue past the visitor center an additional 3.8 miles to a large gravel parking lot at Jones Nose on the right. *GPS coordinates*: 42° 36.102′ N, 73° 12.023′ W.

TRAIL DESCRIPTION

After examining the information regarding the history of Jones Nose at the kiosk (elevation 2,420 feet), cross Rockwell Road to blue-blazed Northrup Trail. The mowed path leads through a meadow filled with goldenrod, dewberry, meadowsweet, and steeplebush. All bloom in summer. Clumps of cherry, mountain ash, and gray birch are surrounded by a luxuriant growth of hay-scented fern. Indigo buntings and chestnut-sided warblers sing in summer from treetops and shrubs. At the **T** junction, turn left on Northrup Trail (Stage Trail leads right). You'll descend easily into deciduous woods dominated by sugar maple and white ash. The treadway undulates through fern glades, where the songs of red-eyed vireo, ovenbird, and rose-breasted grosbeak can be heard in spring and early summer.

You'll cross a small brook. American beech and yellow birch—two important northern hardwoods—form a canopy over hobblebush shrubs as you follow the

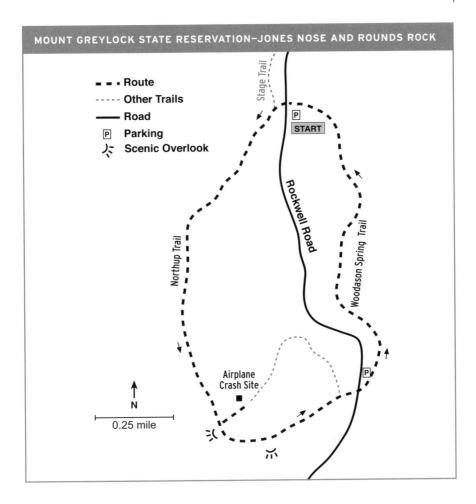

MOUNT GREYLOCK STATE RESERVATION—JONES NOSE AND ROUNDS ROCK

- ▪ ▪ ▪ **Route**
- ----- **Other Trails**
- —— **Road**
- Ⓟ **Parking**
- 𝟅 **Scenic Overlook**

Stage Trail

START

Rockwell Road

Northup Trail

Woodason Spring Trail

Airplane Crash Site

N

0.25 mile

contour of a hillside that drops off steeply on the right. Prickly raspberry canes fill light gaps as you make your way past a garden of wildflowers; red trillium, blue cohosh, and various violets bloom in spring before the forest canopy blocks out the sun. Other raspberries—purple-flowering—don't produce tasty fruit. The mature woodland hosts other summer breeders including hermit thrush and black-throated green and black-throated blue warblers.

After about 0.5 mile, reach a ledge outcrop on the left and a series of angular boulders. One impressive slab is capped by mosses, polypody fern, and sapling yellow birches. The presence of wild ginger, wild leek, and maidenhair fern all indicate nutrient-rich soils. Turn left when you reach a side trail that connects to Rounds Rock Trail. Climb easily under more hardwoods—especially beech, which fills the understory with sprouts and laces the footpath with its roots. You'll cross a series of springs and seeps along this slope before

From the first vista point, a cliff-top perch, hikers enjoy a fine view of the Taconic Range and on clear days, New York's Catskill Mountains beyond.

arriving at Rounds Rock Trail at a signed intersection. Turn left and follow a rockier path and natural schist staircase to ascend an outcropping.

This younger forest is characterized by numerous low, deformed trees just before you reach a blueberry- and fern-filled barren at the **T** intersection with Rounds Rock Loop Trail. Turn left initially; the barren is dotted with clumps of mountain holly, white or paper birch, and mountain ash. After about 250 yards, arrive at the site of the August 12, 1948, airplane crash. An interpretive sign, rusted wreckage, and memorial to the young pilot tell the tragic tale. Return to the intersection and continue straight a short distance to a side path on the right; follow the side path until you reach a view of the Taconic Range, Jiminy Peak ski area, a ridgeline of white wind turbines, and New York's Catskill Mountains beyond.

Return to Rounds Rock Trail and turn right to continue through more blueberries (ripening late July through August), ferns, and pyramidal red spruces. Eastern towhees skulk in the brush. At another side path on the right, you'll walk down some 200 feet to a fantastic view of Lenox Mountain and the central Berkshire Lakes from a clifftop perch. Retrace your steps to Rounds Rock Trail and turn right. Conical red spruces stand sentinel-like amid the blueberries and ferns—a scene reminiscent of Maine. Back in the deep woods, North Country wildflowers like goldthread appear. Beech trees soon replace spruce and Canada mayflower carpets the ground as you reach a gray granite marker, erected in 1912, marking the boundary between New Ashford and Cheshire.

You'll turn left and continue through mixed woods, and a grove of spruces, and under a canopy of yellow birch, black cherry, sugar maple, and spruce with lush undergrowth. You'll pass by the other end of Rounds Rock Loop Trail on the left and continue straight toward Rockwell Road. Soon you'll cross it and pick up Woodason Spring Trail; turn left toward Jones Nose. Creeping partridgeberry blooms in early summer; its coral-red fruits are edible, but virtually tasteless. Many American beech trees in these woods are diseased, their normally smooth gray bark disfigured by the *Nectria* fungus. Beeches sprout prolifically; the understory is predominantly beech, but hobblebush shrubs are numerous and head high. Beneath the trees, *Clintonia*, or bluebead lily; sessile-leaved bellwort; and Canada mayflower thrive.

The winding footpath parallels gurgling Kitchen Brook for a stretch, crosses it and several others in rapid succession, and then enters a forest that appears more recently cut. The forest soon gives way to a savannah with a view of Jones Nose (the southern end of Saddle Ball Mountain). In early to midsummer, enjoy pink fireweed stands just before you return to the parking lot and your vehicle.

DID YOU KNOW?

Jones Nose took its name from local farmer Seth Jones, while Rounds Rock is named for Jabez Rounds. Both worked their mountain farms in the 1790s. Sheep grazed the Rounds Farm. Forty-two farmers once worked the land that is now Mount Greylock State Reservation. The Rounds Farm was added to the state reservation in 1915.

MORE INFORMATION

The reservation is open year-round, sunrise to sunset. Access is free. There is a summit parking fee of $2 per vehicle for Massachusetts residents, $4 per vehicle for nonresidents. Pets are permitted on a 10-foot-maximum leash. Pet owners must have proof of current rabies vaccination and clean up after their pet. Alcoholic beverages are not permitted. Hunting is permitted in season, except in War Memorial Park—a 0.75-mile radius around the tower (413-499-4262; mass.gov/eea/agencies/dcr/massparks/region-west/mt-greylock-state-reservation-generic.html).

NEARBY

Before or after your hike, visit the Mount Greylock State Reservation Visitor Center at the mountain's base. Features include a 13-minute orientation film and exhibits on the cultural and natural history of the mountain. Open year-round; summer hours (Memorial Day–Labor Day): 9 A.M.–5 P.M.; winter hours (September–May): 9 A.M.–4:30 P.M.; closed Thanksgiving, Christmas, and Tuesdays and Wednesdays from November 15 to April 15; 30 Rockwell Road, P.O. Box 138, Lanesborough, MA 01237 (413-499-4262, mass.gov/eea/agencies/dcr/massparks/region-west/mt-greylock-state-reservation-generic.html).

A BEAR IN THE WOODS

Few local creatures engender more trepidation than black bears. I'll readily admit to an elevated pulse every time I see one of these magnificent mammals. You're more likely to come upon one while motoring toward the trailhead, but trail encounters do occur.

Black bears are formidable beings and, indeed, larger than life. An adult male or boar generally weighs in at 250 pounds in Massachusetts, but record-sized individuals have tipped the scales at 600 or more. Although they may be brown or blond, I've never seen any shade other than black in these parts. The considerably larger grizzly bear does not dwell in our woodlands.

Healthy black bears are rarely aggressive. They generally detect our scent or hear us coming and beat a hasty retreat. If you do meet one, remain calm, back off, and allow the bear to retreat. You can thrill to the encounter once the animal has departed. A mother bear with cubs or yearlings merits special concern, but do not panic. Giving the animals a wide berth is the best action.

Some bears unfortunately have learned to associate humans with food, and this is potentially dangerous—usually for the bear. Bears that are coaxed near human habitation by garbage, birdseed, or even deliberate handouts are far more apt to be struck by automobiles, shot, or otherwise treated badly. And a diet of human food is certainly not a recipe for good health. Sadly, as more and more of us choose to live in proximity with bears, the odds that conflicts will result increase.

Black bears are now quite common. While only 100 roamed area woodlands in 1978, in 2014, that number was estimated at 4,000. Several factors seem to be at work. The fact that our woodlands have come of age is probably foremost. A breeding nucleus was always present in northern New England, and as that population increased, competition forced animals south.

If you spend much time on the trail, you will find bear "sign"—a polite word for fecal matter. An ample pile of large diameter, dark, blunt-end droppings is almost certainly of bear origin, especially if major constituents are seeds and berry pits. Coming upon bear scat is a tangible reminder that we share this land with some rather amazing creatures—what conservationists like to refer to as "charismatic megafauna."

TRIP 17
CHESHIRE COBBLES AND GORE POND

Location: Cheshire and Dalton, MA
Rating: Moderate
Distance: 7.6 miles
Elevation Gain: 1,250 feet
Estimated Time: 3.5 hours
Maps: USGS Cheshire

A fantastic vista point and the solitude of a scenic pond are the major rewards of this out-and-back hike along the Appalachian Trail.

DIRECTIONS
From the junction of MA 9 and MA 8 in the Allendale section of Pittsfield, travel north on MA 8 for 7.3 miles to a traffic signal at Church Street in Cheshire. Turn right onto Church Street and follow it 0.4 mile, just past the post office on the right to the expansive Ashuwillticook Rail Trail parking area on the right. *GPS coordinates*: 42° 33.745′ N, 73° 09.399′ W.

TRAIL DESCRIPTION
The first 0.4 mile or so of the route is on pavement. Walk left (north) on the Ashuwillticook Rail Trail, turn right at Church Street and cross the Hoosic River—note the white Appalachian Trail (AT) blazes on utility poles. You'll reach the intersection of Main and East Main Streets. Walk up East Main 150 feet to Furnace Hill Road on the right. Turn right onto Furnace Hill and head up for almost 0.25 mile, at which point the AT turns left into the forest at a private drive.

Immediately begin the ascent following white, rectangular blazes under hemlocks and a few Norway spruces. Hardwood companions include black birch, red maple, and American beech. Cross a short wooden span and stride up railroad ties through a mixed hemlock and hardwood forest. Soon the hemlocks yield to hardwoods, including flaky-barked black cherry. At a clearing, the AT turns sharply right, along an old tote road. Pass through a gap in a fallen stone walls built of tough quartzite, then turn left off the tote road. After leaf fall, the rounded hump of Mount Greylock is visible to the left from the undulating trail. After the AT turns left, white birches appear. Multi-

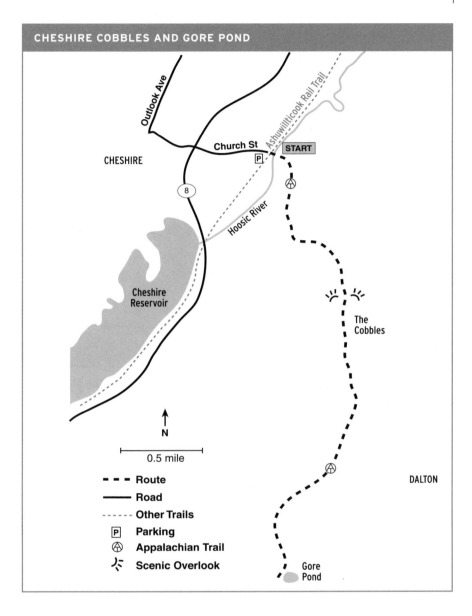

CHESHIRE COBBLES AND GORE POND

Outlook Ave

Ashuwillticook Rail Trail

Church St

CHESHIRE

START

8

Hoosic River

Cheshire
Reservoir

The
Cobbles

N

0.5 mile

- - - Route

——— Road

------ Other Trails

P Parking

Ⓐ Appalachian Trail

⅄ Scenic Overlook

DALTON

Gore
Pond

trunked hardwoods indicate former logging. The tiny evergreen shoots of primitive clubmosses—both prince's pine and shining clubmoss—soften the forest floor.

The path now steepens a bit, crossing a number of old tote roads in the process. White ash, yellow birch, and understory striped maple join the woodland mix with the increasing elevation. Beneath the trees spreads a luxuriant cover of evergreen spinulose woodfern. At a junction with a well-traveled

From the Cheshire Cobbles panoramic views of Ragged Mountain and the six-mile long Greylock Range beyond reward the hiker.

path, the AT turns right to wend up the slope. Constructed water bars, edged with rock, shunt water off the treadway; a jumble of quartzite boulders define the slope. Over eons, the rocks have eroded to sand that now whitens the path. Soon pass by massive boulders on the left—some capped by polypody fern. Crevices between the boulders invite porcupines and other creatures to den, as the iron-stained Cobbles loom ahead. Mountain laurel forms a wreath around their base. The path roughens as you continue past the impressive cliff face and turn left over stone steps to gain the crest. Bear left at a protruding rock on a short blue-blazed side path among laurel and hemlocks, and pass through a sort of "secret passageway" hemmed in by evergreen laurel to emerge onto the exposed bedrock that offers an expansive vista. Watch your footing.

From atop this rocky perch—composed of 500-million-year-old Cheshire quartzite—look southwest to Cheshire Reservoir, northwest to the hamlet of Cheshire just below, and north to Mount Greylock and Ragged Mountain to its right—10 miles distant. The Hoosac Range lies farther right, studded with wind turbines. The Cobbles are a popular destination for hikers, and for good reason. When ready, return to the AT and turn left (south) to begin a moderate ascent through mixed woodland to a USGS marker embedded in the bedrock. The level trail follows along the cliff edge for a distance, passing another brass marker and screened views of the reservoir. The bony ridgeline is flanked by gray birch, blueberry shrubs, and a few mountain ash. Reach an attractive small, grassy clearing dotted with small red maples and reindeer lichen.

Begin an easy descent over glacially grooved bedrock and amble through more hardwoods—birch beech, maple, and cherry. Clumps of hobblebush sport clusters of white flowers in May. The route undulates and crosses a grassy wood road to span a brook on stepping stones. Climb moderately again and cross modest flows three more times in fairly short order. Then, traverse an old logging road and bear left on the AT. White ash becomes numerous as the trail winds among stands of raspberries in light gaps—former pastures. Your climb steepens somewhat and leads into a level landscape of storm-damaged woodland with numerous snags. Traverse a damp, hummocky area under hemlocks with some red spruce and goldthread, a low wildflower sporting shiny rounded leaves, delicate white flowers, and telltale orange roots.

Climb again, steadily up the slope of North Mountain, passing a boulder reminiscent of an overstuffed couch. After cresting the wooded summit at 2,211 feet, begin a descent among numerous white ashes (note their cross-hatched bark) and cross another wood road. The path leads into the shade of a hemlock grove alongside a beaver wetland and turns right to cross Gore Brook over a series of split log bridges and stones. Beaver dams on the left hold back the flow. Follow the AT over a few more split logs to the west shore of Gore Pond on the left. Under the shade of hemlocks, enjoy the pond's tranquil beauty. Look for a beaver lodge off to the left. This is the turnaround for the hike, but you'll probably want to linger a bit before turning back to retrace your steps northward.

DID YOU KNOW?

The Cheshire quartzite of the Cobbles is almost pure quartz and was once used to make glass. A glass industry was established in the local area, but much of it was shipped east to Cape Cod for use in making the renowned Sandwich Glass.

MORE INFORMATION

The U.S. Park Service administers the Appalachian National Scenic Trail. Motorized vehicles and hunting are not permitted within the 1,000-foot-wide AT corridor, but hunting is allowed in season on some adjacent properties. Camping is permitted only at designated sites. Volunteer maintainers of the

Berkshire Chapter of the Appalachian Mountain Club maintain 90 miles of the AT in the state (amcberkshire.org).

NEARBY

A replica of the Cheshire Cheese Press stands at the intersection of Church and School streets, adjacent to the AT message board, just a short walk from the Ashuwillticook parking area. A bronze plaque from 1940 commemorates Baptist Elder John Leland, of Massachusetts and Virginia, who presented the Big Cheshire Cheese, weighing 1,235 pounds, to newly elected President Thomas Jefferson on January 1, 1802. The people of Cheshire had voted unanimously for Jefferson.

2

CENTRAL BERKSHIRES

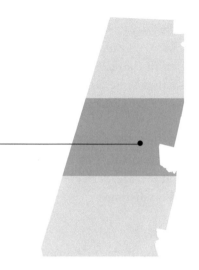

THE CENTRAL BERKSHIRES HOLD THE COUNTY'S MOST POPULOUS CITY, but also the Commonwealth's most expansive state forest. The Taconic Range continues along the border with New York on the west, while to the east, the high, undulating, and sparsely settled Berkshire Plateau stretches for mile after forested mile. Between them, the Housatonic River carves a wide valley through relatively soft marble bedrock.

Sixteen of the hikes in this guide are found in this section. The high points are not as lofty, for the most part, as those in northern or southern Berkshire, but there are fine vistas to be had nonetheless. A number of unusual hiking destinations in this section are far from run-of-the-mill and include the historic destinations of Old Mill Trail (Trip 21) and Shaker Mountain (Trip 22). A significant number have moving or still water as a major focal point. These include spectacular Schermerhorn Gorge (Trip 29), tranquil and scenic Upper Goose Pond (Trip 33), and the little-known gem of Basin Pond (Trip 32). Summit vistas are available too. Among the hikes with a long view are Pleasant Valley Wildlife Sanctuary—Fire Tower Loop (Trip 24), and Pittsfield State Forest (Trip 19). Stevens Glen (Trip 30) contains an enchanting waterfall, while the Ashuwillticook Rail Trail (Trip 18) provides universal access to Cheshire Reservoir and adjacent wetlands teaming with life.

TRIP 18
ASHUWILLTICOOK RAIL TRAIL–
LANESBOROUGH TO CHESHIRE

Location: Lanesborough and Cheshire, MA
Rating: Easy to Moderate
Distance: 7.4 miles
Elevation Gain: 20 feet
Estimated Time: 3.0 hours
Maps: USGS Cheshire; trail map available online

The Ashuwillticook Rail Trail's southernmost section is studded with biologically rich wetlands that host a panoply of birds and ends at picture-perfect Cheshire Reservoir. The moderate rating is based on distance.

DIRECTIONS

From the south: From the intersection of MA 8 and MA 9 in Pittsfield (at Allendale Shopping Center), drive north on MA 8 for 2.5 miles to Berkshire Mall Road on the left. A large paved parking lot straddles the road. The trailhead is located to the right. Visitors are cautioned about leaving valuables in their vehicles and are urged to lock them.

From the north: From the intersection of MA 8 and Maple Street at the statue of president William McKinley in the center of Adams, take MA 8 south for 10.9 miles to Berkshire Mall Road on the right.

GPS coordinates: 42° 29.331′ N, 73° 12.220′ W.

TRAIL DESCRIPTION

This 10-foot-wide, paved, universal-access trail is without doubt the most popular, if unconventional, trail in Berkshire County. Cyclists, inline skaters, walkers, joggers, and birders all share the path amicably. This portion of the rail trail is extremely popular, and the parking lot is often filled with vehicles by late morning. To have the best chance of spotting wildlife, you should arrive early in the morning. Begin by heading north in the direction of a brick restroom building. Just beyond it on the left stands a kiosk where trail maps may be available. A donation pipe is situated near it.

Basic rail trail etiquette mandates that walkers (and other users for that matter) stay to the right. When you stop, be sure not to block the path. Cyclists

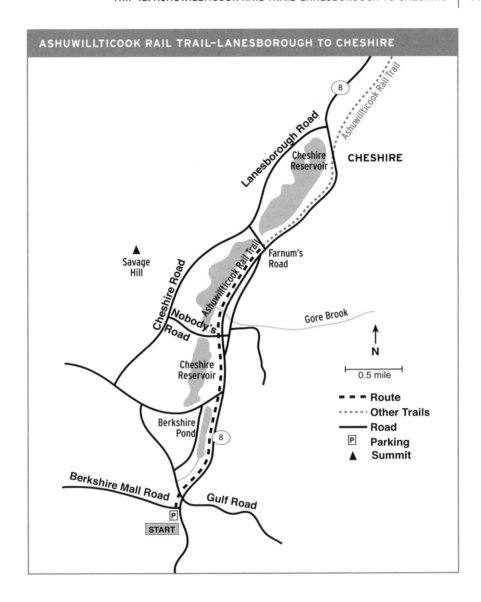

and even inline skaters approaching from behind will call out that they are passing on the left or ring a bell to alert you to their presence. Because courtesy is the rule, there is surprisingly little conflict between user groups on the Ashuwillticook.

Pass through a gap in a green metal gate and immediately peer into a wooded swamp with skeletal white pines and ribbon-leaved cattails on the left—just the sort of habitat favored by many aquatic and semi-aquatic creatures. These are the headwaters of the Hoosic River, a northward-flowing

Cole Mountain borders the northern basin of Cheshire Reservoir as seen from Farnum's Road.

tributary of New York's mighty Hudson. Binoculars are recommended for this hike as the many open wetlands invite wildlife and thus wildlife viewing. During the warm months, you're apt to observe familiar mallards, elegant wood ducks, Canada geese, and perhaps a great blue heron. On a late July visit, I counted 25 different species before walking the first 0.5 mile. Smaller birds to spot include feisty eastern kingbirds, skulking gray catbirds, olive-drab warbling vireos, male red-winged blackbirds flashing red epaulets, and crested cedar waxwings. Look for painted turtles hauled out on logs and various species of camouflaged frogs including bellowing bullfrogs and banjo-plucking green frogs.

There is also smaller game to be sought. Butterflies are numerous in summer. Harder to miss are the darting darners and skimmers—the dragonflies. Some to watch for are common whitetail, ebony jewelwing, and widow skimmer. And don't worry; they are harmless. Extensive patches of bullhead lily pads blanket sections of the marsh. Their yellow flowers never seem to fully open, while their stalks are rooted in the muddy bottom 3 or 4 feet down.

Soon you'll stride beneath an overpass and enter a shaded section of trail bounded by oaks, maples, black birches, ashes, and white pines. Shrub swamps and marshy sloughs continue on both sides of the asphalt. Trees felled by North America's largest rodent, the beaver, are in evidence in the red maple swamp. Red maples are among the most tolerant of trees. They thrive in poor, dry soils as well as in saturated ones, in bottomlands, and on mountaintops. Along a lengthy straightaway, a marshy pond on the left known as Berkshire Pond is filled shore to shore in late summer with both of our native lilies, the aforementioned bullhead species and the exquisite white fragrant lily. Recycled-plastic lumber picnic tables and benches overlook the lily pond.

As you move out of sight of the water, attention shifts to nonflowering plants, including lush fern growth—sensitive and interrupted species—and the green stalks of horsetails. Both these plant groups have existed virtually unchanged on Earth for hundreds of millions of years. Pass a few homes and be alert to a patch of poison ivy on the right before the next road crossing at Old State Road, where you'll walk around green metal gates. Quite handily, trail distances in miles are stenciled on the pavement. Perhaps the last remaining artifacts of the rail line besides the railroad bed itself are cement whistle posts. A large white W adorns the top of each post. The posts told the engineer when to sound his locomotive's whistle. They're situated 0.25 mile on either side of a road crossing.

The first whistle post appears near the Cheshire town boundary marker on your right. At this point, it's obvious that you're walking along a former railroad track bed as it drops off steeply to either side. Pass under utility lines supported by tall, paired wooden poles that cut a swath over the hills to either side. The next road crossing, right after a miniature duck pond with domestic fowl, is the intriguingly named Nobody's Road. The origin of the name is anybody's guess. A panorama of North Mountain lies to the east beyond Route 8. After passing by willows, you'll cross clear Gore Brook. Its flow nourishes an alder and red maple swamp. Savage Hill at 1,924 feet above sea level represents the height of land ahead to the west.

The view becomes expansive moments later as you gain the southern end of the middle lake basin. While cattails and lilies provide habitat and food for aquatic mammals and birds, to the north the surface is more open. Two series of benches and picnic tables face the lake at this especially scenic location. Check out the little pool on the right where bluegills are often visible. Camp Mohawk's beach lies on the opposite shore. Reenter refreshing woodland shade.

Near the lakeshore, young quaking (or trembling) aspens, the favorite food of beavers, may all be sprouts from the same rootstock—a clone if you will, something aspens are apt to do. Their heart-shaped leaves are attached to twigs by means of long, laterally flattened stems, which makes them flex and rustle with the wind. Maple, ash, and oak are more dominant here, and some of the oaks are quite large. After another whistle post, young and medium-aged white ash and giant cottonwoods dominate the scene. The latter are fast-growing relatives of aspen and produce truckloads of minute seeds, each attached to a mass of cottony fluff that enables them to fly on the air currents. Wind carries them far from the parent trees. In summer, cottonwood seeds pile up in windrows.

You'll arrive at Farnam's Road between the familiar green metal gates. A restroom building is located to your left along the shore of the reservoir's upper basin. This is a favorite shore-fishing location. There are more benches and picnic tables here, so this is a nice spot for a relaxing break before you retrace your steps 3.7 miles to the parking area at Berkshire Mall Road.

DID YOU KNOW?

The name Ashuwillticook is derived from the American Indian word for the south branch of the Hoosic River. It means "at the in-between pleasant river," or the pleasant river between the hills, those hills being the Greylock Range to the west and the Hoosac Range to the east.

MORE INFORMATION

Open dawn to dusk, year-round. Access is free of charge. Dogs must be leashed and under control; owners must clean up after their pets. Motorized vehicles (except electric-powered vehicles used by people with disabilities), horses, alcoholic beverages, fires, hunting, trapping, feeding of wildlife, and removal of park resources are prohibited. Accessible restrooms are available at Berkshire Mall Road parking area in Lanesborough and at Farnam's Road at the turnaround point in Cheshire. Massachusetts Department of Conservation and Recreation (DCR), Regional Headquarters, P.O. Box 1433, 740 South Street, Pittsfield, MA 01202 (413-442-8928; mass.gov/eea/agencies/ dcr/massparks/region-west/ashuwillticook-rail-trail.html). DCR's Universal Access Program (413-545-5353).

NEARBY

If you're looking for a takeout meal, cold drink, or cider and donuts (in season) after your hike, try Whitney's Farm Market, a local favorite, at 1775 S. State Street (MA 8) in Cheshire; open Monday–Saturday 9 A.M.–7 P.M., Sunday 9 A.M.–6 P.M. ; fall hours 9 A.M.–6 P.M. daily (413-442-4749; whitneysfarm.com).

TRIP 19
PITTSFIELD STATE FOREST—
LULU CASCADE, BERRY POND, TILDEN SWAMP

Location: Pittsfield, Lanesborough, and Hancock, MA
Rating: Moderate
Distance: 5.0 miles
Elevation Gain: 1,000 feet
Estimated Time: 3.0–3.5 hours
Maps: USGS Pittsfield West, MA, and Stephentown, NY; trail map available online

This triangular loop route boasts a trifecta of water attractions— lovely cascades along Lulu Brook and two of the state's highest natural water bodies—scenic Berry Pond and Tilden Swamp, a former bog turned beaver pond.

DIRECTIONS

From US 7 at Park Square in the center of Pittsfield, turn west onto West Street and travel 0.5 mile to a left turn to continue on West Street. Drive for an additional 2.2 miles to Churchill Street on the right. Follow Churchill Street for 1.7 miles to Cascade Street on the left. Drive 0.7 mile to the Pittsfield State Forest contact station (trail maps available here). From there, continue another 0.7 mile to the Lulu Brook Day Use Area and a spacious gravel parking area on the left. The trailhead is located across paved Berry Pond Circuit Road at an iron gate. *GPS coordinates*: 42° 29.576′ N, 73° 17.927′ W.

TRAIL DESCRIPTION

Walk to the far (north) end of the parking lot and cross paved Berry Pond Circuit Road diagonally to a brown iron forest gate adjacent to where Lulu Brook flows under the road. A sign marks the start of Lulu Brook Trail (not recommended in icy conditions).

After only a couple of minutes of walking, you'll arrive at Lulu Cascade. The path ascends moderately and levels out on a schist ledge above the brook. This is not a large waterfall, but enchanting nonetheless as the brook plunges into a crystal-clear pool surrounded by mossy boulders. Watch your footing. Over the course of the next mile or so, you'll be treated to additional smaller cascades. A big egg-shaped milky quartz boulder, resistant to erosion and

PITTSFIELD STATE FOREST–LULU CASCADE, BERRY POND, TILDEN SWAMP

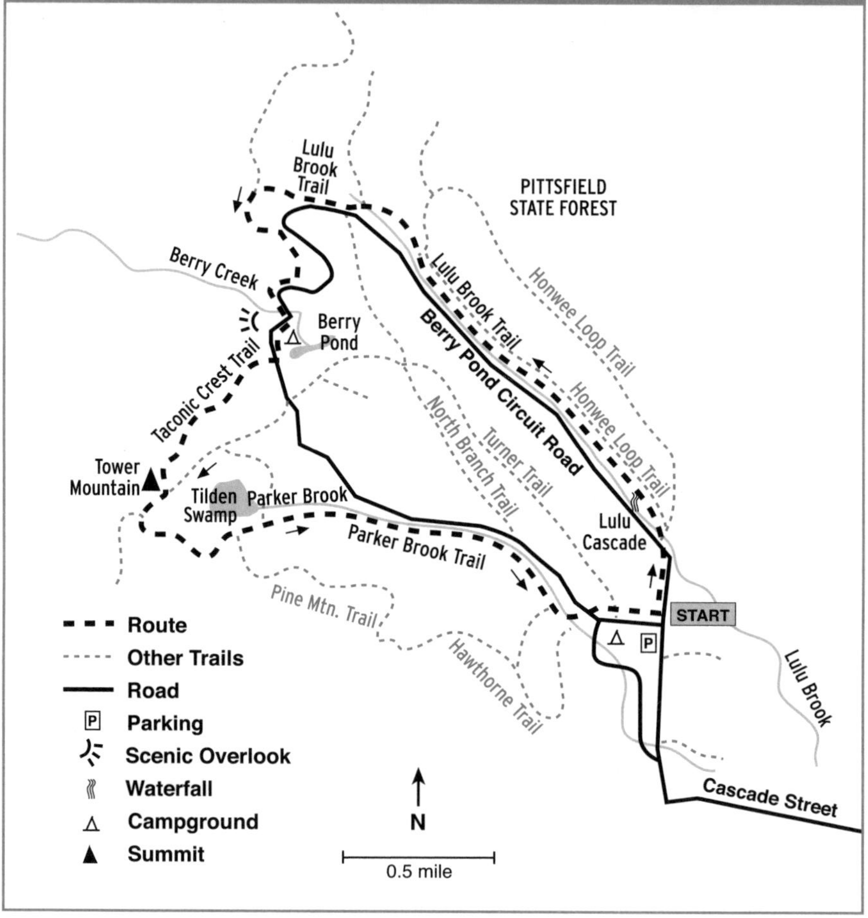
Lulu Brook Trail
PITTSFIELD STATE FOREST
Berry Creek
Berry Pond
Lulu Brook Trail
Berry Pond Circuit Road
Honwee Loop Trail
Honwee Loop Trail
Taconic Crest Trail
North Branch Trail
Turner Trail
Tower Mountain
Tilden Swamp
Parker Brook
Parker Brook Trail
Lulu Cascade
START
Pine Mtn. Trail
Hawthorne Trail
Lulu Brook
Cascade Street
Route
Other Trails
Road
Parking
Scenic Overlook
Waterfall
Campground
Summit
N
0.5 mile

flecked with moss, may catch your eye. Occasional blue plastic triangles mark the trail. You'll walk upstream on an undulating trail through a ravine cut by the stream, under a canopy of hardwoods—oak, ash, maple, birch, and beech, joined by hemlock. Striped maple and hobblebush fill out the understory. Tall meadow rue—spindly stalks with thumbnail-sized leaves topped by starry white flowers—enlivens the banks in summer.

The path alternately climbs along the leafy slope and dips to brook level. Watch for ground-hugging trailing arbutus, the Massachusetts state flower, and partridgeberry along the upper level. At one point along the stream, a tilted schist ledge from which flat slabs have cleaved juts out. On humid summer days, fog may hang above the cold flow. The abundant moisture makes this a verdant place. Climb again and closely parallel Honwee Trail. You'll

Scenic Berry Pond, at 2,150 feet above sea level, is the state's highest natural water body.

soon cross several wooden spans across minor drainages. Arrive at a stone walls composed largely of milky quartz. Tall white pines rise up and create a needle-cushioned treadway as you level out farther from the brook. Soon pass through a red pine plantation. Their trunks are ramrod straight with a pinkish hue. Shortly arrive at a T intersection with an old wood road. Turn left and walk a short distance to a rocky ATV track. Turn left and cross the brook on an ATV bridge to the circuit road. Turn right onto the paved road and walk 150 feet to a blue-blazed trail on the right. Turn right onto it and soon bear left on a narrower path under birches, maples, and beeches. Below them are shiny-leaved clusters of a northern wildflower called goldthread.

At an unmarked intersection, bear left and amble easily along the slope, reaching the Taconic Crest Trail before long at a T intersection. Turn left and climb past plush patches of shining clubmoss. Level out under oaks and beeches. A luxuriant growth of hay-scented fern blankets the ridgeline forest's floor. Pass an empty trail register box on the left. This forest is stunted due to the thin soil and a harsh microclimate. When you arrive at Berry Pond Circuit Road again, turn right, stroll 150 feet to a white-on-blue blaze for the Taconic Crest Trail on the right, at a sign for Azalea Fields. Turn right onto the path that follows the field edge where raspberry canes proliferate. Mountain azalea shrubs bloom pink in late May and offer a delicious aroma.

Enter young woodland with Canada mayflower and ferns and shortly arrive at a level clearing—just feet from the summit of Berry Hill—and a T intersection. Shad trees, red maple, mountain ash, and the shrubs—arrowwood, bilberry, meadowsweet, and lowbush blueberry, in addition to azaleas, thrive atop the bedrock. Turn right and walk gently down through a tunnel of vegetation to a gravel pullout area off the circuit road offering wonderful glimpses into New York State all the way to the Catskills.

After taking in the views, walk downhill along the road's grassy shoulder to the state's highest natural water body—Berry Pond at 2,150 feet. Showy white blossoms of fragrant water lilies dot its surface in summer. Close to shore, look for pumpkinseed sunfish fanning their tails to create circular depressions in which the female deposits her eggs for the male to guard. Continue along the shoreline and follow the gravel roadway straight where the paved road bears right. The gravel leads past campsites to the circuit road again, which you cross to the right.

Taconic Crest Trail continues up the far side into beech, maple, and oak woodland. As you level out among the hardwoods, notice that some red oaks have twin trunks—the probable result of stump sprouting following logging. Begin an easy descent. Small light gaps are now filled with hay-scented fern and raspberries. Delicate maidenhair fern may attract your attention just before some eye-catching milky quartz ledge outcrops softened by emerald green mosses. Flutelike voices of the hermit thrush are often heard under this leafy canopy.

Climb moderately along the slope's flank, taking advantage of a few switchbacks, to reach a shrubby clearing on the summit of Tower Mountain (2,193 feet). Regenerating woody vegetation has obscured this former vista. Abundant lowbush blueberry patches start producing ripe fruit by the end of June—a tasty consolation. No doubt black bears visit here as well. Taconic Crest Trail bears right at this Y intersection, but instead, bear left on a narrow path that leads down through a shrubby growth of wild raisin and raspberry. Descend through fern growth from which young trees—especially black cherry, shad, and red maple—rise up.

Stride past a couple informal trails on the right and arrive at a rutted gravel ATV road under a mix of hardwoods and white pines. Turn right and follow the track a few hundred feet to an easy-to-overlook blue-blazed woodland path on the left that leads toward Tilden Swamp. Follow it through a young, mostly deciduous forest with a fairly dense understory. A few American chestnuts have managed to reach 4 or 5 inches in diameter. These root sprouts are a sad reminder of a species that once dominated the forest community prior to the onset of the chestnut blight in the 1920s. Pass a trail that joins on the right but continue easily down slope. The water's surface is visible through the trees— mostly beech, oak, birch, and white pine.

At the junction with Parker Brook Trail on the right, continue a few more feet to Tilden Swamp. Since the mid-1990s, beaver activity has turned the former swamp (or more accurately bog) into a pond. Here at the pond's south-eastern end, you can inspect the tall, arched dam constructed by the world's second-largest rodent. Yellow bullhead lilies protrude now from the water in summer; this peaceful spot is home to dragonflies, damselflies, pickerel frogs, and bullfrogs. Beaver ponds are part of a natural cycle, and one day a bog may return to Tilden Swamp.

Parker Brook is the outflow from the pond. Retrace your steps to the trail of the same name and turn left to follow it. After just a few steps, unmarked Pine Mountain Trail descends left to a wooden footbridge across Parker Brook. But continue straight to follow the brook downhill under beech, maple, birch, and oak. The narrow, water-cut gorge is quite deep, and the pliable branches of hobblebush are bountiful on its steep side slopes. Colorful wood warblers are a treat for the eyes as they search for leaf-munching caterpillars in the foliage from late spring through summer. One to be found here is the lovely Canada warbler that sports a necklace of black feathers on its citron yellow breast.

Continue a steady descent along a hillside graced with ferns. Eventually, bear right on the blue-blazed path. It later bears right again under a cover of hardwoods. Hemlocks increase in number before you reach an intersection with a trail on the right. Soon you'll come to a junction with an old roadway that runs up to unsigned Hawthorne Trail. Stay straight, pass clumps of win-tergreen and partridgeberry, whose red fruits are eaten by grouse. Head to a four-way intersection and turn left to cross Parker Brook on a wooden ATV span. Before doing so, you should check out the angular schist outcrops along the stream under an umbrella of hemlocks.

Almost immediately beyond the brook, the path meets a trail on the left under oaks and then another on the right. Bear right, walk by more chestnut sprouts and past campsites to the one-way, paved circuit road where rows of depression-era Norway spruces stand. Bear right, walk 50 feet and turn left onto wide gravel Crossover Road heading modestly uphill past a modern, seasonally open restroom building. You'll amble by a number of side paths including unsigned Turner Trail on the left. Mature oak trees tower on the right. After you pass a metal forest gate, you'll reach the paved road and turn left, following it several hundred feet straight back to Lulu Brook Day Use Area and your vehicle.

DID YOU KNOW?

Classic bog species, including the carnivorous pitcher plant and round-leaved sundew, as well as leatherleaf and other bog denizens, once grew profusely in the damp, acidic soils of Tilden Swamp. Since the beaver flooding, however, only a few bog remnants currently survive along the largely inundated shoreline.

MORE INFORMATION

Open sunrise to 8 P.M., daily, year-round. A small day-use fee per vehicle is charged from early May to mid-October. Parking is free for ParksPass holders; vehicles with handicapped, POW, or disabled veteran plates/placard; and seniors 62 and older with the Massachusetts Senior Pass. A restroom building, open seasonally, is also located at Lulu Brook Day Use Area. Picnicking permitted at Lulu Brook Day Use Area. Alcoholic beverages are prohibited on all state lands. Pittsfield State Forest, 1041 Cascade Street, Pittsfield, MA 01201 (413-442-8992; mass.gov/eea/agencies/dcr/massparks/region-west/pittsfield-state-forest-generic.html).

NEARBY

The Berkshire Museum in Pittsfield offers a unique array of art, history, and natural science exhibitions, activities, and attractions. An aquarium of native and exotic creatures is a favorite. Open Monday through Saturday, 10 A.M.–5 P.M., and Sunday, 12 P.M.–5 P.M. Admission is $13 for adults ages 18 and up, $6 for children, and free for members and children under 3. Located at 39 South Street (US 7), Pittsfield, MA 01201 (413-443-7171; berkshiremuseum.org).

TRIP 20
WARNER HILL

Location: Dalton and Hinsdale, MA
Rating: Moderate
Distance: 6.3 miles
Elevation Gain: 430 feet
Estimated Time: 3.0–3.5 hours
Maps: USGS Pittsfield East

This is an enjoyable hike on the Appalachian Trail through northern hardwoods interspersed with evergreens. Warner Hill's partially cleared summit yields a pleasing view of Mount Greylock.

DIRECTIONS
From the intersection of Elm and East Streets in Pittsfield, follow East Street east for 3.0 miles to Division Road at the Dalton town line. East Street becomes South Street in Dalton. Drive north on South Street for 0.85 mile to Grange Hall Road on the right. Follow Grange Hall Road for 1.1 miles and park on the wide gravel shoulder on the left. Parking in winter along Grange Hall Road may not be possible as the road shoulder is not plowed. *GPS coordinates*: 42° 27.391′ N, 73° 09.711′ W.

TRAIL DESCRIPTION
Cross to the south side of the road (be alert for traffic speeding downhill around the curve) and ascend the rather steep slope on the white-blazed Appalachian Trail (AT) lined with white ash, red maple, black cherry, and American beech. Note the interesting steplike gneiss rock outcrop studded with quartz crystals. As you level out, prince's pine and cedar clubmoss—ancient nonflowering plants—add a fairyland quality to the forest floor. On the right stands a fine yellow birch, one of the classic northern hardwood forest indicators.

Come upon the remains of a fireplace chimney built of local stone and mortar left of the path, just before descending into a shallow gully. Norway spruces confirm former human occupation. After a modest climb up the far side, reach a blue-blazed trail on the left that leads to Kay Wood Shelter, where a privy and picnic table are located. A metal box near the structure is designed to keep hikers' food safe from black bears. The shelter's picturesque setting

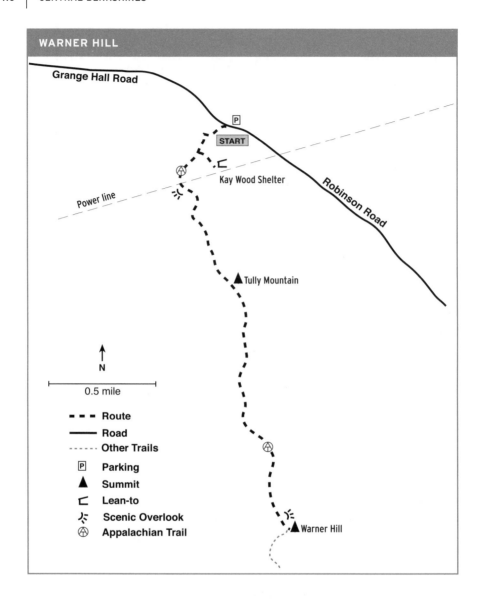

WARNER HILL

Grange Hall Road

P

START

Kay Wood Shelter

Power line

Robinson Road

Tully Mountain

N

0.5 mile

- - - Route
— Road
----- Other Trails
P Parking
▲ Summit
⊏ Lean-to
⚡ Scenic Overlook
Ⓐ Appalachian Trail

Warner Hill

on a moss-and-lichen-covered gneiss outcrop makes the 0.3-mile round trip worthwhile. You'll pass a massive sugar maple on the left en route.

Return to the main trail, turn left, and climb moderately along the slope. Screened views of the Taconic Range's rounded summits to the west are possible after leaf fall. Note the wind-thrown black cherry on the left whose root ball holds stones in a tenacious grasp. Soon negotiate small boulder fields, their stones cleverly utilized in construction of the treadway. This hilltop is grassy. Actually, it's thickly vegetated with sedges, which are similar to grasses but have triangular rather than round stems.

Soon you'll emerge into a power line gash filled with blackberry brambles and meadowsweet shrubs at an elevation of 1,981 feet that makes a nice view of Lenox Mountain possible. The path beyond the right-of-way is straddled by emerald clumps of clubmosses and spinulose woodfern, both of which remain green year-round. Walk over a gently undulating trail under a leafy canopy and through a shallow bowl. A dark green hemlock grove to your left contrasts with the comparatively light green shades of maples, cherries, and beeches. Past a tiny drainage rill, you'll come across an expansive growth of shining clubmoss, which when brushed against in late autumn emits a smoky cloud of microscopic spores. The highly flammable spores once provided the flash for early flash photography.

Traverse damp areas on several series of plank bridges. Modest gray, tight-skinned shad (a.k.a. juneberry) share the damp earth with yellow birch. Be alert for well-camouflaged ruffed grouse that you might encounter here. You'll begin a gradual climb to the level, wooded summit of Tully Mountain at an elevation of 2,085 feet. No long views here. Twin yellow birches stand trailside on the left. Although these two are no longer yellow, young trees with thin, peeling, brassy bark, are especially attractive. As you stride over an exposed chunk of gneiss bedrock, note the 6-inch-thick milky quartz intrusion that filled a fracture when buried deep underground hundreds of millions of years ago.

Along this high-elevation stretch are pockets of boreal evergreens—red spruce. In a damp swale, goldthread and wintergreen bloom in spring and summer, respectively. Both display white blossoms. Those of goldthread are star-shaped while tiny bells adorn wintergreen. Follow along a ledge outcrop, the slope dropping off to the left, and descend into a hobblebush stand. Its big heart-shaped leaves are among the first to reveal their multiple hues in autumn. Conifers become more common now, interspersed with hardwoods. At one point, cross two small streams separated by about 60 feet as the trail continues to undulate easily and then pass through a bowl hemmed in by dramatic gneiss ledges—a sort of miniature canyon where prickly porcupines must certainly den among the boulders. Climb out at the far end, bearing left around a low outcrop, and pass an old wood road where you level off.

There are more screened views to the right of forested ridges after leaf fall. Black birches are suddenly common as you descend into a col then amble up and cross a wood road. Bear right and descend gently to a ledge that juts

Periodic clearing by volunteers keeps the summit of Warner Hill open, making it a fine spot for a rest break.

out like a ship's prow, on the right. Wild strawberries, whose small fruits are relished by many creatures, have gained a foothold in pockets of soil atop the rock. You'll continue left, then right, and pass over a number of fallen stone walls and enter a scruffy woodland of gnarly old apple trees and viburnum shrubs. Cross an unmarked path and begin a gradual climb amid more apple trees and 6- to 8-inch-diameter shad trees.

The light green fronds of hay-scented ferns of summer wither to an amber hue after frost ends their growing season, filling the slope just below the summit of Warner Hill. A sign on a tree tells you that you've finally reached your objective—the 2,050-foot summit of Warner Hill (the AT turns right at this point and descends another mile to Blotz Road). Sprouting gray birch and highbush blueberry spring from pockets of soil amid the rust-stained summit gneiss bedrock, but this modest growth still permits a fine view north 16 miles to the Greylock Range. Periodic clearing of brush by AT volunteers keeps the view open. The rotating white blades of wind turbines are visible on ridges to the north and northwest. When ready, retrace your steps northward to your vehicle along Grange Hall Road.

DID YOU KNOW?

Kay Wood Shelter is named for Dalton resident Kay Wood (a.k.a. Grandma Kay), who hiked the entire AT from 1988 to 1990, completing it at age 71. For years, she had welcomed so many hikers into her home that it became a recognized stopover along the trail.

MORE INFORMATION

Motorized vehicles, horses, and hunting are not permitted on or along the AT. Camping is allowed in designated areas only. The AT in Massachusetts is maintained by volunteers of the Berkshire Chapter of the Appalachian Mountain Club's Appalachian Trail Management Committee (413-528-6333; amcberkshire.org/at; at@berkshire.org).

NEARBY

Mass Audubon's Canoe Meadows Wildlife Sanctuary in Pittsfield has 3.0 miles of walking trails along the Housatonic River. From the Dalton Division Road and East Street intersection, follow Dalton Division Road south 1.6 miles to Williams Street and turn right. Follow it for 2.0 miles to Holmes Road and turn left. Drive 0.3 mile to the sanctuary entrance on the left. Admission is free; donation appreciated. Open 7 A.M. to dusk, year-round except major holidays (413-637-0320; massaudubon.org/canoemeadows).

TRAIL TRIBULATIONS

The Appalachian National Scenic Trail, or simply the AT for short, is one of the most extensive continuous footpaths in North America. The first of several such continental trails, it was the brainchild of Massachusetts native Benton MacKaye. Although MacKaye conceived the idea in 1921, his dream was not fully realized until 1937. Stretching for 2,175 miles from Springer Mountain in northern Georgia to the craggy summit of 5,267-foot-high Mount Katahdin in Maine's Baxter State Park, the AT is walked by hundreds of thousands of hikers yearly. But only a few hundred hardy souls, known as thru-hikers, complete the roughly five-month journey each year. Many more set out in the attempt. And numerous others complete state segments or spend a month or more on the trail annually until they have traversed its entire length.

A significant number of the hikes described in this guidebook follow portions of this fabled footpath. Its 6-inch-high by 2-inch-wide white blazes are iconic. The trail invariably passes over some of the most scenic ridgelines in the Berkshires, from the Vermont border to the Connecticut line—some 90 miles. Today's AT is better than the original, as many segments have been relocated farther from roads and onto acquired conservation land. Changes and improvements continue.

Along the AT's 2,000-plus-mile route, a string of rough shelters provide respite for long-distance hikers. In summer, you're likely to encounter at least a few of these hardy souls on their way north. Many adopt an emblematic moniker or trail name that you'll find at the bottom of journal entries at AT trail registers. The majority set out from Georgia in March, before winter has fully retreated. Their goal is to reach Katahdin in September before winter reasserts itself. Therefore, most pass through the Berkshires in June, some pausing in the relative luxury of Bascom Lodge atop Massachusetts' tallest peak, where hot showers and warm meals are a welcome change from their daily routines. If you can get a thru-hiker to stop long enough to chat, you'll almost certainly enjoy the experience.

Although under the jurisdiction of the National Park Service, which designated the footpath as a National Scenic Trail in 1968, in Massachusetts a cadre of dedicated, hard-working volunteers of the Appalachian Mountain Club's Berkshire Chapter maintains the AT for all of us. They deserve our considerable gratitude.

TRIP 21
OLD MILL TRAIL

Location: Hinsdale and Dalton, MA
Rating: Easy
Distance: 3.0 miles
Elevation Gain: 155 feet
Estimated Time: 1.5–2.0 hours
Maps: USGS Pittsfield East; trail map available online

This out-and-back trail is steeped in the area's industrial history. It is also a fine hike to take with children.

DIRECTIONS
From the north: From the intersection of MA 8, MA 8A, and MA 9 in Dalton, drive south on MA 8, passing into the town of Hinsdale after 2.5 miles. Continue for another 0.4 mile to Old Dalton Road on the left (no sign). Follow Old Dalton Road for approximately 100 feet and turn left into the Old Mill Trail parking area with space for eight to ten vehicles.

From the south: From the intersection of MA 8 and MA 143 in Hinsdale, follow MA 8 north for 0.7 mile to Old Dalton Road on the right (no sign).

GPS coordinates: 42° 26.877′ N, 73° 07.831′ W.

TRAIL DESCRIPTION
Walk down to a map kiosk that relates the interesting industrial history of the area. The crushed stone treadway is universally accessible for almost one-half its length. The East Branch of the Housatonic River—a narrow stream here—borders the majority of the route, which is well blazed with plastic discs on trees. Stroll beneath sugar maples and white ashes—with distinctive cross-hatched bark, and past the 2-foot-tall, leafless, green stems of scouring rush. Ostrich ferns (which produce edible fiddleheads when young), also thrive in the moist soil. A couple of flowering dogwood trees—more common to our south—stand on the left just before a fiberglass and wood bridge. Cross the bridge to follow the river downstream along its opposite bank.

Water-thirsty cottonwoods line the banks like sentinels, while wild grapevines provide tasty meals for wildlife in late summer and fall. In quick succession, cross two short bridges. A dense stand of Joe-Pye weed flanks one; goldenrods and asters provide nectar and pollen for insects. After reentering

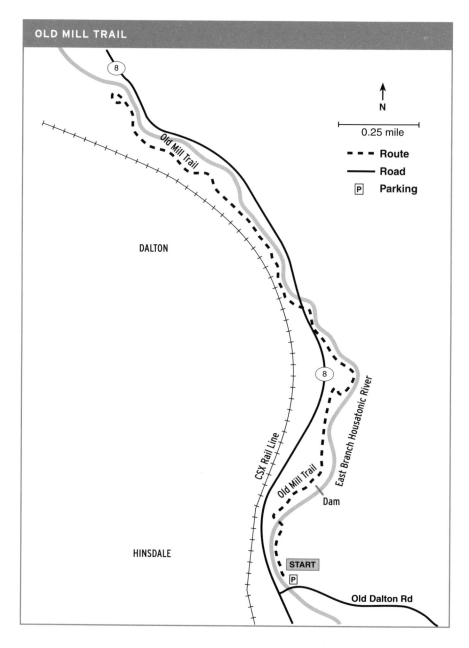

OLD MILL TRAIL

0.25 mile

- - - Route
— Road
P Parking

N

8

Old Mill Trail

DALTON

8

East Branch Housatonic River

CSX Rail Line

Old Mill Trail

Dam

HINSDALE

START

P

Old Dalton Rd

the maple woodland, you'll notice a rusting automobile just beyond a quartzite boulder on the left. Three stones mark a short side trail that leads 100 feet to the right, to the ruins of a breached dam upstream of the old Plunkett Brothers Mill, which produced textiles in the mid-nineteenth century. As you continue on the main trail, homes come into view through the maple and ash canopy.

A portion of the route follows an expertly built stone treadway along the East Branch of the Housatonic River.

For much of its route, the path follows river terraces. At times, you walk near the water's edge, and at other times, higher above the stream.

You'll enter a dense, streamside hemlock stand where a cooler microclimate is quite noticeable. It gives rise to northern hardwood species like yellow birch. The wide path follows the route of the original penstock along the stream. The penstock carried water from the dam down to the Renfrew Cotton Mill, where it powered the machinery. For a stretch, the path is tunneled into the earth, only to turn right and then down an easy hairpin turn to the river. The forest floor is almost devoid of vegetation beneath the dense evergreen shade. Red maples soon join the hemlocks and a few patches of hobblebush pop up here and there. Continue on, passing several massive glacial boulders between the river and the highway. Shining clubmoss patches poke up from the leaf litter. The accessible trail ends at a trail register affixed to a hemlock, where walkers leave comments about their trail experiences.

The path narrows and soon leads over the top of a concrete penstock that housed a large steel water pipe that you'll soon see. Tread over a small bridge and carefully cross MA 8. Pick up the trail at the far end of the guardrail, parallel the road for a bit, and then reenter forest. Follow along the base of the slope where boulders protrude. This is arguably the most picturesque portion of the hike. The treadway has been expertly fashioned from native stones into well-placed steps. However, watch your footing in icy conditions. In contrast to this tranquil scene, an active CSX railroad line runs atop the slope on your left.

The trail climbs easily and moves temporarily away from the Housatonic River, crosses through a bramble-filled power line cut, and reenters mixed forest of birch, beech, maple, and hemlock before returning to the river. In autumn, fallen leaves may obscure the trail, but watch for the plastic markers on trees. You'll cross one final bridge over a feeder stream and continue to walk above the river. In spots, Christmas fern provides welcome color year-round. The imposing black cherry tree on the right is virtually hollow at the base. Yellow birch, with fine-peeling brassy bark, becomes more numerous and some are quite large. Note also clumps of plantain-leaved sedge. Its ribbon-shaped leaves are about 1 inch wide.

You'll follow the path down to the river again and cross over quartzite boulders in the narrow floodplain. Invasive Japanese knotweed has established a foothold here. A patch of native shrubs called leatherwood is also present. Its bark is so strong that it was once used by American Indians as rope and for bow strings. Ahead in the river are spaced concrete structures that once supported the penstock, a 4-foot-diameter steel pipe encased in concrete. The trail passes between more concrete supports that lead to what remains of the exposed penstock pipe on the left. This is also where the trail ends, among large hemlocks. The land bordering is posted private, no trespassing. When ready, retrace your steps upstream 1.5 miles back to your vehicle.

DID YOU KNOW?

The East Branch of the Housatonic River originates at Muddy Pond in the towns of Washington and Hinsdale, flows through the Hinsdale Flats Wildlife Management Area, and continues through downtown Dalton to connect with the main stem in Pittsfield. It is one of three stems that join in Pittsfield to form the main stem Housatonic.

MORE INFORMATION

Open during daylight hours. Motorized vehicles, fires, camping, littering, and cutting or removing vegetation are prohibited. Hunting, fishing, and trapping are permitted in season. Trail created by the Housatonic Valley Association (HVA) on land donated by Crane and Company, Dalton. The Massachusetts

Department of Fish and Game manages the property; maintained by volunteers. HVA Berkshire County Office, P.O. Box 251, South Lee, 01260 (413-394-9796; hvatoday.org). MA Division of Fisheries and Wildlife, Western Wildlife District, 88 Old Windsor Road, Dalton, MA 01226 (413-684-1646; mass.gov/eea/agencies/dfg/dfw/).

NEARBY

Hinsdale Trading Company, located right across Old Dalton Road from the Old Mill Trail parking area, offers pizza, sandwiches, and subs. Located at 371 Old Dalton Road, Hinsdale, MA 01235 (413-655-0161).

TRIP 22
SHAKER MOUNTAIN

Location: Hancock, MA
Rating: Moderate
Distance: 6.5 miles
Elevation Gain: 790 feet
Estimated Time: 3.0–4.0 hours
Maps: USGS Pittsfield West; trail map available online

This hike leads from the beautifully maintained Hancock Shaker Village to ruins and religious sites atop the neighboring hills in what is now Pittsfield State Forest.

DIRECTIONS

Traveling north on US 7/US 20, before reaching Park Square in the center of Pittsfield, turn left onto US 20 (a.k.a. West Housatonic Street) and follow it west for 6.0 miles to the entrance road on the left for Hancock Shaker Village. Park in the large paved lot and walk eastward to the visitor center to register. *GPS coordinates*: 42° 25.808′ N, 73° 20.429′ W.

TRAIL DESCRIPTION

When you register at the contemporary visitor center (restrooms available), you will be asked for your name and contact information, and to check in upon your return. Passes for hiking are given free of charge. Consider leaving a donation to support the good work being done by this nonprofit. Pick up Boy Scout Trail interpretive material that gives a great deal of information about this Shaker community. You might want to tour the village's many historic buildings now or upon your return, but be sure to leave sufficient time to complete your hike. You may also want to consider making the hike during a weekday to avoid all-terrain vehicles (ATVs).

After registering, walk through the visitor center and out toward the famous stone round barn. Turn left just before the barn and exit through a gap in the fence by the ochre buildings. Be cautious crossing US 20 and be sure to use the painted crosswalk. On the other side, walk down a gravel farm road to the first interpretive sign on the left of the Boy Scout Trail, an interpretive trail created in 1982. Note the white circle in a green triangle that blazes the Boy Scout Trail.

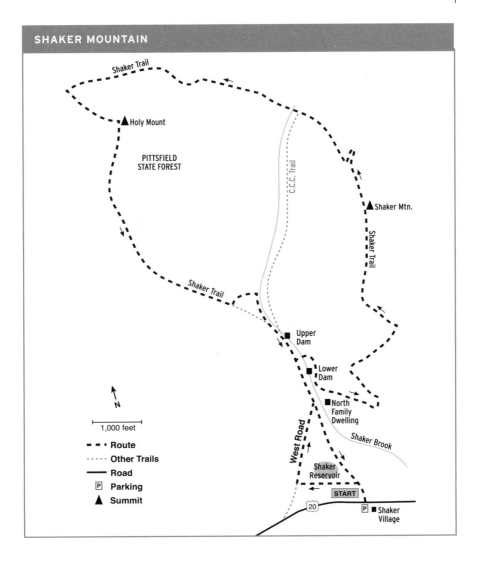

SHAKER MOUNTAIN

Shaker Trail

▲ Holy Mount

PITTSFIELD
STATE FOREST

C.C.C. Trail

▲ Shaker Mtn.

Shaker Trail

Shaker Trail

■ Upper
Dam

■ Lower
Dam

■ North
Family
Dwelling

Shaker Brook

West Road

N

1,000 feet

- - - Route
- - - - Other Trails
—— Road
Ⓟ Parking
▲ Summit

Shaker
Reservoir

START

20

Ⓟ ■ Shaker
Village

At the split, bear left and walk up along the field edge. At gravel West Road, turn right and shortly arrive at 1-acre Shaker Reservoir, constructed in 1790 and enlarged in 1800. Continue straight on the mowed path and enter deciduous woodland dominated by white ash and sugar maple. At the Y intersection, bear left and amble under a canopy of oak, maple, hickory, black cherry, and black birch along Shaker Brook. A low stone walls, the first of many, is on the left.

You'll reach bridge foundations that once led over the stream to the North Family Dwelling site. A patch of native bloodroot blooms white in early spring on this side of the brook.

Extensive stone walls enclose several fern-filled acres. One section is an impressive example of the stone wall builder's craft.

A bit farther up the roadway, you'll arrive at the Lower Dam, which supplied waterpower to the village. A slope rises up to the left, and yellow birch becomes evident as the road begins a gradual ascent. Soon you'll come to a wooden footbridge across Shaker Brook; use it to get to the eastern side. Note: Be sure to follow the trail in this counterclockwise direction rather than continuing straight, as the trail is unblazed in that direction. You'll now walk a short distance downstream on dirt East Road past Shaker mill site foundations to the North Family Dwelling Site, dating to 1821. The site is named for the geographic location of this communal dwelling, which housed 20 to 40 or more people. Past occupation is evident by the extensive carpet of shiny green periwinkle (*Vinca*) carpeting the large site. Here you'll find Shaker Mountain Trail to Mount Sinai (Shaker Mountain) on the left.

Follow the contours and switchback to ascend the moderately steep slope. You'll encounter white pines, some large, and hemlock mixed with oak and beech. In late spring, look for the yellowish pinecone-like form of squawroot—a parasite on oak roots. At a branch in the cart road, turn left. Soon you'll arrive at a four-way intersection with a steep wood road and utility line that leads up to an airplane beacon near the summit. Cross this rocky roadway and bear left; you'll arrive at a second, higher intersection with the same road. Cross it again and continue steadily up the blazed Scout Trail toward the Hancock Shaker community's Holy Ground atop Shaker Mountain, marked by an interpretive sign. In spring and fall, special religious services were held here. This brushy area has four sections of white picket fence demarcating the four corners of the site. American chestnut sprouts are numerous within, as is bracken fern.

Continue uphill on an easy grade, passing through young white pine and hemlock. The predominant trees, though, are oak, with black cherry, American beech, and white birch. You'll descend past dense hobblebush patches into hemlock woods on the contouring wood road. After a sharper descent, level out through thick hay-scented ferns and you'll reach a four-way intersection of forest roads showing heavy ATV use. Turn left and then immediately right (not straight ahead) to continue on the blazed Scout Trail toward the Shaker's Holy Mount. Bearing left leads down the ravine between the two promontories—the most direct route back to the village. Smooth gray schist bedrock protrudes from the treadway as you make your way across the head of the valley. Stately oaks rise where the stone walls on your right once bordered open pastures.

You'll reach an intermittent Shaker Brook tributary and cross it on stones; a stand of young hemlocks rises to your right. Hardwoods––white ash, sugar maple, and black cherry—thrive on the slope. After frost has killed other ferns, a luxuriant growth of spinulose wood fern has the forest floor to itself. ATV activity turns this path into a flowing brook during wet seasons as you head uphill.

At the intersection, turn left. Many of the rocks in this stone walls contain white quartz, visible through the mossy covering. Beech trees become more common now among the oaks, and below them is a miniature "forest" of clubmosses. These attractive nonflowering plants reproduce by spores as well as by runners, and are indicators of once-pastured ground. On the left, beyond the rock wall, hay-scented fern grows profusely. After you start climbing again amid lowbush blueberries, you'll turn right and pass through a stone-wall gap (wide enough to permit a team of oxen to pass) and enter a flat area of red maple, oak, cherry, and beech. This is the Lebanon, New York, Shaker Community's Holy Mount. Extensive stone wallss demarcate an enclosure of several fern-filled acres. Follow the wall to a side path on the left that leads 100 feet to the best example of the stone-wall builder's craft on this hike. Once, both these summits were denuded of timber and long views were possible.

Return to the main trail and bear left. The path, which leads downhill, is needle-cushioned beneath a stand of young, white pines. You'll encounter more stone wallss and wide gaps as you descend moderately under oaks and beech to the Sacred Gap, a natural amphitheater where the brethren gathered for prayer and reflection. A small rock dam impounded water from a spring. Turn left on the woodland path up through hardwood forest and then down, arriving at a fire road open to motorized vehicles that soon parallels Shaker Brook. Turn left and follow the rocky double track. An impressive black oak bears the long scar of a lightning strike on the right. A little farther, at the base of a white ash on the left, sharp-lobed hepatica offers delicate lilac blossoms in early spring.

At the intersection, turn left on Griffin Trail and proceed uphill. Be mindful of loose rocks underfoot. Continuing straight on the road leads to a brook crossing. A stone walls borders the path on the right. The route leads up fairly steeply for a bit and heads downward under pines and mixed hardwoods to a major intersection. Shaker Brook is just beyond. Turn right and follow the trail downstream to the site of the High Dam, where an overgrown wooden staircase leads down to the brook. Dry masonry walls are visible on the opposite bank. The flow once powered an overshot wheel built in 1810 and destroyed by flooding in 1976. A little more walking brings you back to the footbridge over Shaker Brook to close the loop. Continue straight to retrace your steps down West Road to the grassy Y intersection. Bear left to return to the village.

DID YOU KNOW?

During the early part of the nineteenth century, the celibate religious sect known as the Shakers built a thriving community of 350 people at this site in Hancock, which they called City of Peace. Residents of a nearby Shaker community in New Lebanon, New York, are said to have called to their fellow Shakers across the 1-mile-wide valley between the two religious sites you encountered.

MORE INFORMATION

Village hours are 10 A.M.–4 P.M. daily. Motorized vehicles, firearms, hunting, and fishing are not permitted. Pittsfield State Forest is open to hunting in season. Restrooms and a café are located on village grounds. Hancock Shaker Village, 34 Lebanon Mountain Road, Hancock, MA 01237; P.O. Box 927, Pittsfield, MA 01202 (413-443-0188; hancockshakervillage.org). Pittsfield State Forest, 1041 Cascade St., Pittsfield, MA 01201 (413-442-8992; mass.gov/eea/agencies/dcr/massparks/region-west/pittsfield-state-forest-generic.html).

NEARBY

For more about the Shakers, travel 4.2 miles west to the Shaker Museum and Library in New Lebanon, New York, a National Historic Landmark. The 90-acre property and ten historic buildings are open to the public via guided tours mid-June through mid-October, Friday–Monday, 11 A.M.–4 P.M. Contact 518-794-9100 or shakermuseumandlibrary.org for a schedule. The site is located off US 20 at 202 Shaker Road, New Lebanon, NY 12125.

TRIP 23
DOROTHY FRANCES RICE SANCTUARY
FOR WILDLIFE

Location: Peru, MA
Rating: Easy to Moderate
Distance: 3.8 miles
Elevation Gain: 570 feet
Estimated Time: 2.5 hours
Maps: USGS Pittsfield East

A 276-acre property laced with well-marked trails and stone walls.
Red spruce, balsam fir, and northern hardwoods clothe this home
to moose and beaver.

DIRECTIONS

From the junction of MA 8 and MA 143 in Hinsdale, drive east on MA 143
for 4.3 miles (past Ashmere Lake) into Peru to the intersection with South
Road on the right at a flashing yellow light. Follow South Road for 0.9 mile to
the parking area and entrance on the left. *GPS coordinates*: 42° 25.606′ N, 73°
02.920′ W.

TRAIL DESCRIPTION

Park clear of the locked gate on the wide gravel turnout. Trail maps may be
available at the large sign. Walk eastward down level, grassy Rice Road flanked
by large white ash trees and sugar maples. Soon reach a mowed side path on
the left that leads to a beaver dam and pond built by the masterful rodents.
Be alert for beavers and abundant bird life in the surrounding vegetation.
Continue east on the road lined with red spruce, red maple, black cherry, and
striped maple. Fern growth crowds the borders. Continue straight at an overgrown path on the left, but only for about 30 feet—Yellow Trail (note yellow
arrow on tree) enters the forest through a stone-wall gap on your right. This
intersection is easy to miss!

Some trees, such as red maple at this location, are identified with descriptive
tags. Follow the single track, blazed with yellow paint, through northerly
appearing woodland that includes fragrant young balsam firs. Goldthread,
with orange roots and glossy deep green leaves, lines the path. Cross an

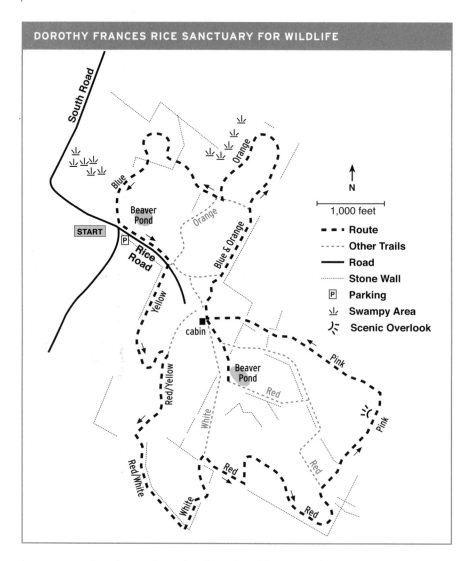

DOROTHY FRANCES RICE SANCTUARY FOR WILDLIFE

South Road

Blue

Orange

Orange

N

1,000 feet

- - - Route
- - - - Other Trails
—— Road
·········· Stone Wall
P Parking
⊻ Swampy Area
⅄ Scenic Overlook

Beaver Pond

START

P Rice Road

Blue & Orange

Yellow

cabin

Beaver Pond

Red

Pink

Red/Yellow

White

Pink

Red/White

Red

Red

White

Red

intermittent brook on a boardwalk and amble up the far bank thick with New York ferns; their fronds taper at both ends. In autumn, the red maple canopy is ablaze with color. Although somewhat overgrown late in the season with goldenrod, ferns, and raspberry canes, the path is reasonably easy to follow.

Yellow Trail parallels a stone walls on your right, then bears left and follows along the opposite side of the shrubby clearing. A thick growth of young red spruce imparts a northwoods feel. Gray birch, cherry, and red maple have colonized the clearing, providing browse for white-tailed deer (listen for their snorts) and moose.

Arrive at Red Trail and turn right (posted with red and yellow arrows), and shortly you'll come to the intersection with White Trail at a grassy woods road. Bear right and follow the red-and-white blazes gradually downhill between stone walls. Hay-scented fern fills the forest floor. At a posted T intersection, turn left on White Trail and enter a shaded forest of yellow birch and hemlock. Hemlock needles are short and flat, rather than sharp-tipped like those of red spruce. Twin-leaved, red-fruited partridgeberry and tiny prince's pine add beauty. Soon you'll cross a stream where rockwork hints at human engineering. Follow along the slope's flank.

The trail follows the sanctuary's boundaries closely here and throughout the hike. Numerous stone walls are additional demarcation. The trail ascends gradually, crosses a stone walls, and then levels out. Red oak and lowbush blueberry indicate drier, more acidic soils. An intriguing assemblage of northern species (yellow birch and red spruce) and a southern one (red oak) comingle here. At a white ash with three trunks, pass through a stone-wall gap and quickly arrive at an old logging road crossed by Red Trail. Turn right. Note the many beeches with black, disfigured bark—the work of a fungus that enters through holes made by minute sap-sucking insects. Ferns, such as hay-scented in dry glades and cinnamon and interrupted ferns in damp spots, enliven the path.

At the intersection with Pink Trail, turn right, pass through a regenerating logged clearing, and reenter the forest of red maple, red spruce, beech, and yellow birch. Bunchberry edges the trail here in late spring. What look like white petals are actually bracts. Climb more steeply to a vista complete with wooden bench. A view of distant ridges to the southwest makes this the perfect place for lunch or a snack. When ready to resume your hike, continue walking along the slope, turn left, and suddenly descend. Reenter dark woodland and pass through three more stone-wall gaps and over a brook on a wooden bridge before reaching a wide, mowed path that leads to a clearing in the center of the property. A large painted trail map, picnic table, and apple orchard are located adjacent to the Rice Cabin (not the original). Oran and Mary Rice established this sanctuary in the late 1920s in their daughter's memory. In 1974, the New England Forestry Foundation (NEFF) was entrusted with it.

At this point, you can make a short side trip via the pink/white-blazed Pond Trail for another chance at observing beavers. Stay straight as the trail splits. A bench by an angular boulder provides an idyllic spot for observation. Lush woodland bordering the ponds, and alder, birch, winterberry, maleberry, and arrowwood shrubs fringing them, make for particularly productive birding. In the water, red-spotted newts (poisonous to fish) use their vertically flattened tails to propel themselves in search of insect prey.

To continue the hike, return to the cabin and bear right. Multiple trails intersect near the shed. Follow Blue Trail (blazed orange/blue/yellow at this point) to the right, then straight ahead. Reenter mixed woods and reach an intersection with Yellow Trail. Continue on the blue/orange-blazed trail, bearing right. Note the large red spruces, one of which has fallen across a stone wall exposing its shallow root ball. At the Y intersection, follow Orange Trail to the right. Young balsam firs 6 to 10 feet high crowd each other on the forest floor. The four-veined leaves of little bunchberry plants thrive in the shade of these conifers.

Follow the treadway through mixed woodland. Eastern hemlocks sport shorter needles than balsam fir. Traverse a seepage area on a boardwalk that leads into woodland equally composed of hardwoods—maple and birches— and evergreens. Left of the intersection with Blue Trail stands an impressive yellow birch with a 2-foot-diameter trunk. Turn right and follow the now blue/ orange-blazed path. You'll reach another junction at the edge of a sapling-filled former light gap. Stay straight on Blue Trail, as Orange Trail turns left.

After the clearing, reenter older woodland of beech, black cherry (flaky black bark), and red maple. A bit farther, red spruce and balsam fir make a handsome evergreen pair again. Heart-shaped leaves of hobblebush along the footpath transform from green to maroon, yellow, and orange in autumn. Arrive at a rock-lined structure on the right—a former cistern perhaps— where the roots of a gray birch anchored itself to the rocks years ago. Shortly you'll reach South Road; turn left and walk to your vehicle some 100 feet away.

DID YOU KNOW?

In 2007, MassWildlife biologists estimated the Massachusetts moose popula-tion at 850 to 950. As moose numbers increased in northern New England due to improved logging practices and an absence of hunting, moose moved south by the early 1980s to reclaim their historic Massachusetts range. Adults weigh 500 to 1,000 pounds depending on sex and age.

MORE INFORMATION

The sanctuary is open daily for hiking and cross-country skiing year-round from dawn to dusk. Access is free. Hunting, fishing, camping, trapping, fires, and motorized vehicles are prohibited. NEFF, P.O. Box 1346, 32 Foster Street, Littleton, MA 01460 (978-952-6856; newenglandforestry.org).

The tiny dogwood bunchberry is an iconic flowering plant of the sanctuary's northern forest. What look like petals are really bracts.

NEARBY

The paper company Crane & Co. has continually supplied the U.S. Treasury since 1879. Their Crane Museum of Papermaking, a little-known Berkshire gem, relates the history of papermaking from Revolutionary times to the present. It is on the National Registry of Historic Places. Housed in the 1844 Old Stone Mill's rag room, the museum is open free of charge from Tuesday through Thursday, 1 P.M.–5 P.M. Beginning June 2 through the end of October, the museum is open Monday through Friday, 1 P.M.–5 P.M.; 40 Pioneer Street, Dalton (413-684-7780; crane.com/about-us/crane-museum-of-papermaking).

TRIP 24
PLEASANT VALLEY WILDLIFE SANCTUARY–
FIRE TOWER LOOP

Location: Lenox, MA
Rating: Strenuous
Distance: 3.0 miles
Elevation Gain: 825 feet
Estimated Time: 2.0 hours
Maps: USGS Pittsfield West; trail map available at office, and online

On this trip, you'll ascend Lenox Mountain's east-facing slope over bony ledges to its summit and then descend along gurgling brooks and tranquil hemlock ravines.

DIRECTIONS
From the south: From Exit 2 (Lee) off the Mass Pike (I-90), turn right after the tollbooths and drive north on US 20 for 6.6 miles to West Dugway Road on the left (watch for the blue tourist-oriented directional sign). Follow the road (which junctions with West Mountain Road) for 1.6 miles to the sanctuary's gravel parking area and office.

From the north: From the center of Pittsfield at Park Square, take US 7 south for 4.9 miles to West Dugway Road on the right, and then follow directions above. *GPS coordinates*: 42° 38.259′ N, 73° 29.897′ W.

TRAIL DESCRIPTION
After registering at the office (trail maps available here), cross the gravel drive and begin at the south end of Pike's Pond Trail, immediately opposite the office. Sanctuary trails are blazed blue outbound and yellow returning. Bear right and turn left immediately to traverse a boardwalk through a boggy area of ferns and alders where the liver-colored spathes of skunk cabbage push up through the cold earth as early as February and the shiny yellow petals of marsh marigolds fairly glow in May. After skirting a planted red pine stand, the path descends gradually toward namesake Pike's Pond, constructed in 1932 to increase the sanctuary's habitat diversity. Named in memory of William Pike, whose family funded construction, it is an excellent vantage point from which to observe beavers, especially at dusk.

Soon you'll reach Yokun Brook on the left, which is a beaded necklace of small beaver ponds. Emergent bur reed with spiky inflorescences populates the shallows. A bridge leads across one pond to the foot of Lenox Mountain. After treading over a tilted outcrop of schist, turn left onto Trail of the Ledges, the start of your ascent. Remnant stone walls attest to sheep grazing here as recently as 1909. Shortly, you'll arrive at the Waycross Trail intersection. But continue straight up—between here and a vista point called Farviews, at 1,850 feet elevation, you'll ascend 500 vertical feet in less than one-third of a mile. Beyond the Ravine Trail junction on the right, some slopes approach 45 degrees. As some over-rock scrambling is required, hikers are advised not to descend on this section.

A transitional forest of oak, white pine, birch, beech, and maple clothes the lower slopes of the ridge. Crow-sized pileated woodpeckers seek out mature trees infested with carpenter ants, while yellow-bellied sapsuckers (the only local woodpecker that regularly migrates long distances) dine on the sweet sap of birches and maples and the insects attracted to the flow. Mountain laurel increases as one gains elevation, and at Farviews, laurel and eastern hemlock predominate. From here you can gaze eastward all the way to October Mountain State Forest.

Although you are only about halfway to the top, you've achieved 60 percent of the total rise. The remaining section to the summit is not as steep, as the narrow trail leads to several more views to the east and north. As you continue up the slope, notice that the stature of the timber decreases as you go. Shallow soils and a harsher climate stunt their growth. As a rule of thumb, temperatures decrease 1 degree for every 400 feet one ascends. Finally, emerge into a small "grassy bald" where the former state fire tower has been refurbished with state police communications equipment. The tower, on state-owned land and surrounded by a chain-link fence, is not accessible.

The red maples aren't tall, but are high enough to block any easterly view. A nearby bench offers a nice spot from which to take in the vista. The best view from the 2,126-foot summit is westward toward the nearby Taconic Range running the length of the New York–Massachusetts border. Almost directly below is Richmond Pond. Beyond, the Taconics are among the continent's oldest mountain ranges, having been thrust up over 400 million years ago when what is now Africa rammed into what is now North America. Geologically speaking, Lenox Mountain is considered to be an outlier of the Taconics. On a clear day, the Catskills, 40 miles to the southwest, are the distant bluish ridge. Walk a few feet down the westward flank and gaze to your right (north) for a glimpse of Mount Greylock (3,491 feet; see Trips 7, 8, 9, 10, 14, 15, and 16).

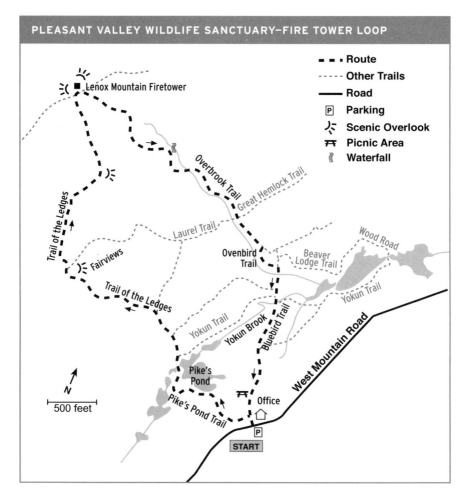

When ready to descend, follow the fence line on the south side (the side you came up on) easterly into the forest—the start of Overbrook Trail (signs on the fence point out the correct direction). After a few feet, you should see yellow blazes and a white sign on a tree indicating that this is the return path to Pleasant Valley Sanctuary. Amble through a mixed woodland and listen in summer for the ethereal song of the 7.5-inch-long hermit thrush. The initial grades are moderate with some steeper slopes to come, but none approaching the house roof–like angles of the ascent. You'll cross a shallow brook five times en route to Great Hemlock Trail intersection. Just above the first is a picturesque 12-foot-high waterfall.

A winter ascent on snowshoes via this trail can be enjoyable. Hemlocks crowd the ravines, weighed down by the accumulation of snow on their needle-dense boughs. The inner bark of hemlock was once used to tan leather, but these trees escaped harvest due to their location. It is hard to imagine now that most of the mountain was once denuded. Timber was cut for charcoal making, lumber, and firewood, and to clear land for pasture. Just above Great Hemlock Trail, you'll walk along the rim of a hemlock ravine where some of the conifers are massive.

You'll reach a four-way intersection with Laurel Trail on the right and Great Hemlock Trail on the left. Continue straight down on Overbrook along a cascading stream among stately hemlocks. The trail bears left and widens into a former wood road. Turn right briefly onto Ovenbird Trail. In late spring and summer, the loud *teacher-teacher-teacher* refrain of the ovenbird is ubiquitous. This species builds a roofed nest with a side entrance like an old-fashioned oven. The path descends steeply for a short spell to an intermittent brook at the base of the mountain at Bluebird Trail. Cross the brook on a short bridge and head toward an imposing grove of white pines. Some are 3.5 feet in diameter and tower over 100 feet tall.

Soon you'll reach Yokun Brook, the property's only year-round stream. Brook trout, two-lined salamanders, and dusky salamanders call it home. Louisiana waterthrushes are among the first warblers to return from the tropics in late April and construct their nests along its banks. The birds bob their hindquarters incessantly as they walk along. Continue over the brook and under more pines to a sloping field. Ahead on the left, clumps of common milkweed attract a myriad of butterflies in summer. From Alexander Trail, it is about 200 yards along the field edge back to the office, passing two pole-mounted solar arrays on the right that provide one-third of the sanctuary's electrical power, opposite the education center, and the sanctuary barn on the right a bit farther. Restrooms (potable water available) are attached to the near end of the barn.

DID YOU KNOW?

The Lenox Fire Tower, built in 1970, was a Berkshire landmark until it burned in March 1995. Although a popular observation tower that afforded 360-degree views, the 70-foot steel structure had not been staffed and utilized as a fire lookout since the 1988 fire season. It remained in a derelict condition until renovated to support emergency communications equipment.

MORE INFORMATION

Trails open year-round, daily, dawn to dusk, except Mondays. Open seven days, July–Columbus Day. Open Monday holidays, year-round. Office is open same days as grounds, 10 A.M.–4 P.M. Nonmember fees: $5 for adults,

In spring and fall especially, enjoy the sight and sound of a 12-foot high waterfall during your descent on the Overbrook Trail.

$3 for children (3–12) and senior citizens; Mass Audubon members, Lenox residents free. Pets, vehicles (including bicycles), horses, hunting, trapping, fishing, and collecting are not permitted. Berkshire Wildlife Sanctuaries, 472 West Mountain Road, Lenox, MA 01240 (413-637-0320; massaudubon.org/pleasantvalley).

NEARBY

Tanglewood Music Festival has been the world-renown summer home of the Boston Symphony Orchestra since 1937. Each summer, hundreds of thousands of visitors flock to the Berkshires for the Tanglewood season. The main entrance is located at 297 West Street in Lenox, only about 2 miles from the sanctuary; call 888-266-1200 for ticket information; bso.org.

BRINGING BACK THE BEAVER

You won't find the beaver on a short list of most beloved animals. In fact, for many, the mere mention of its name engenders disdain. But why? The answer seems clear enough. America's largest rodent is sometimes in direct competition with us for waterfront property. These herbivorous furbearers are adept at constructing engineering marvels that in their way rival our own, while their persistence and ingenuity are legendary.

From the time of European settlement, beavers were killed for their splendid pelts. Long, glossy guard hairs protrude above a dense, luxuriant underfur that insulates the animal against damp and cold—just the right attire for a creature that doesn't hibernate and that spends a good portion of its waking hours submerged in cold water. Beavers constituted the bread and butter of the fur trade that provided impetus for the exploration of much of North America. By the late eighteenth century, though, beavers had been eliminated from Massachusetts.

In the late 1920s and early 1930s, there were some who sought to repatriate the former native. After an absence of almost 150 years, they felt it was time to recalibrate the balance of nature. Thus in 1932, Pleasant Valley Bird and Wildflower Sanctuary warden S. Morris Pell acquired—after considerable effort—one adult female and two adult males from the Blue Mountain Lake region of New York. Pell and his helpers constructed a sturdy fenced enclosure around 1.5 acres of willows and alders bordering Yokun Brook. The trio was introduced to their new quarters at 5 P.M. on October 8; by dawn the next morning, they had constructed their first dam and pond.

Beavers build ponds to safeguard themselves from land-bound predators. Although certainly not defenseless on terra firma, in its watery realm, the pudgy beaver transforms into a study in grace. An enlarged liver enables it to remain submerged for up to 15 minutes. And just like humans, they use the water's buoyancy to float cargo, be it construction material for dams and their homes, called lodges, or food in the form of leafy twigs.

Beaver wetlands have many virtues. They absorb storm runoff like the proverbial sponge and release it slowly, minimizing flooding. Wetlands serve as nature's purification plant for runoff entering groundwater aquifers. And beaver wetlands provide homes for a litany of other creatures, from mosquito-eating dragonflies to fish and wood ducks. If frogs could vote, beavers would win the popularity contest hands down.

TRIP 25
PLEASANT VALLEY WILDLIFE SANCTUARY– $ (walking) (maps)
BEAVER PONDS LOOP

Location: Lenox, MA
Rating: Easy
Distance: 1.5 miles
Elevation Gain: 115 feet
Estimated Time: 1.0 hour
Maps: USGS Pittsfield West; trail map available at office, online

Lying in a scenic valley on the east flank of Lenox Mountain, Pleasant Valley's 1,300 acres and 7-mile trail system offer wonderful hiking and wildlife observation opportunities. An active and easily observed (at dusk) beaver colony is a highlight of this loop route.

DIRECTIONS
From the south: From Exit 2 (Lee) off the Mass Pike (I-90), turn right after the tollbooths and drive north on US 20 (which, just after Cranwell Resort, becomes US 7/US 20) for 6.6 miles to West Dugway Road on the left. Follow West Dugway Road 1.6 miles to the sanctuary's gravel parking area.

From the north: From the center of Pittsfield at Park Square, take US 7 south for 4.9 miles to West Dugway Road on the right, then follow the directions above. *GPS coordinates*: 42° 22.959′ N, 73° 17.939′ W.

TRAIL DESCRIPTION
All visitors are asked to register at the circa 1790 farmhouse that serves as the sanctuary office. Registration cards and trail maps are available inside and sometimes outside, after hours. Check the board for recent wildlife sightings and examine the nearby orientation panel that includes a large artist's rendition of the trail system.

Turn right onto the wide gravel drive and walk northward toward a bright red barn on the left where attached public restroom facilities and potable water are available year-round. A picnic area is close by. Wheelchair accessible All Person's Trail/Sensory Trail begins here and ends at nearby Pike's Pond. Continue straight, however, on Bluebird Trail past the education center and solar array. In the brushy field opposite, tree swallows and sometimes eastern bluebird nest. In July, the sweet-smelling pink flower heads of common

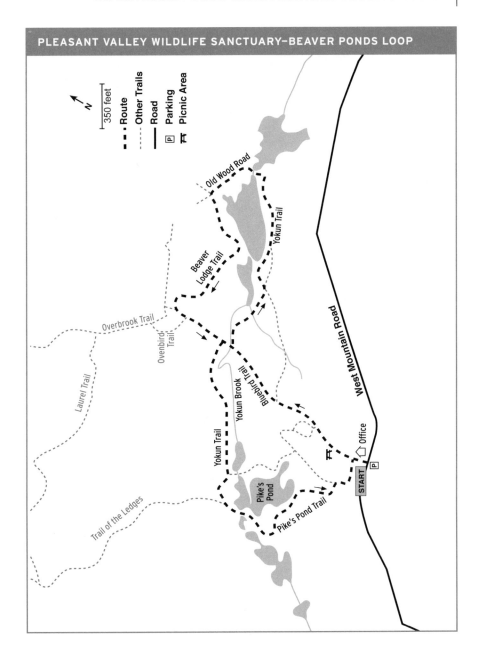

PLEASANT VALLEY WILDLIFE SANCTUARY–BEAVER PONDS LOOP

milkweed lure a myriad of butterflies including various hairstreaks, skippers, and monarchs. The looming Lenox Mountain ridge beckons.

Walk straight ahead past a formidable eastern cottonwood at the intersection of Alexander Trail, and through another field prickly with raspberry canes before entering a stand of tall white pines bordered by a remnant stone wall.

While beavers are the most visible large mammals at Pleasant Valley, lucky hikers occasionally stumble upon other mammals such as this white-tailed deer fawn.

Ahead is Yokun Brook, a tributary of the Housatonic River, and the sanctuary's only perennial stream. Rather than crossing the brook, turn right onto Yokun Trail. Both the trail and brook take their name from a notable Mahican leader of the early 18th century. The path winds through low-lying woodland of white ash, black cherry, and birch. Opposite the far end of the short Alexander Trail, turn left onto a loop spur that leads to the first of a series of beaver ponds that descend staircase fashion along 1.0 mile of Yokun Brook. Signs of the big rodent's handiwork are evident including a sizable cherry tree felled years ago. In 1932, beavers were reintroduced at this location after an absence of almost 150 years. A well-vegetated beaver dam is close to the bench. Continue on the short loop to the main trail and turn left. You'll soon pass hollows on the right where gravel was once mined. To your left is a larger beaver-engineered pond and near its far end, a conical mass of sticks and mud—a beaver lodge. Each lodge is home to one family. If you are here in early morning or at dusk, you may observe a curious beaver cruising about with only its head and a bit of its back visible above the surface.

When you reach Old Wood Road, turn left and pause on a long wooden bridge that spans a small pond between two beaver dams. The upstream dam to your left is 3 to 4 feet high, while the smaller one on the right is lower. Glance down and you'll surely see beaver scat—oval pellets of compressed "sawdust." The semi-aquatic beavers create ponds in order to protect themselves from predators. At the far end of the bridge, the closed blue-purple blossoms of bottle gentians bloom in September.

Beyond the bridge grow a few mountain laurel shrubs and some impressive white pines. There is an abundance of spiny Japanese barberry shrubs—an invasive exotic. Some have been uprooted, but many persist. At the four-way intersection, turn left onto Beaver Lodge Trail. In the vicinity of the boardwalk, be alert in summer for the sudden launch of an American woodcock—a chunky "shorebird" sporting a nearly 3-inch-long, crochet hook–like bill with a flexible tip used to adroitly pull earthworms from the moist soil.

Winterberry bushes have established themselves in a beaver-dug channel on the left beyond the winding boardwalk. The coral-red berries add a welcome splash of color to the late fall scene. During warm seasons, a multitude of ferns (mostly New York fern) carpet the sunny openings. Soon you'll pass the first beaver pond you reached, but from the opposite side. Here the path curves right onto a low mound above another small pond where the trail's namesake beaver lodge sits hidden by woody vegetation until after leaf fall. A bench near a couple white pines, some 150 years of age, serves as a nice spot for a snack.

Continue on Beaver Lodge Trail around the swamp and into a stand of pines and hemlocks where golden-crowned kinglets shelter during the cold months. At the shaded junction with Bluebird Trail, turn left and cross another boardwalk. Now at the base of Lenox Mountain, turn left to cross a short span over an intermittent brook. Ahead of you towers a stand of cathedral pines—their straight and lofty trunks soaring 100 feet above the needle-cushioned forest floor. Their girth suggests considerable age. You'll discern a definite hushed atmosphere in their shade. Back at gushing Yokun Brook, turn right onto the southern section of Yokun Trail and amble up under a pine canopy to a point above the brook where the soothing sound of flowing water is omnipresent.

The trail continues through mixed woodland that now includes red oak and yellow birch. The vernal green of pleated false hellebore leaves pushing up through the brook's moist floodplain soil is a welcome sight in April after a long and snowy winter. You'll emerge into the sunlight at another beaver pond.

At the intersection, turn right onto Pike's Pond Trail. Green frogs emit shrieks as you approach, while in the woods, eastern chipmunks utter a fluty whistle and scamper for their burrows when danger threatens. They harvest the abundant acorns, beechnuts, and beaked hazelnuts for winter dining below ground. The path is bordered in places by mountain azalea shrubs that waft intoxicating perfume from their tubular pink flowers in late May. After the path crosses a protruding schist outcrop, it bears left to a picturesque bridge. Trailing arbutus, the Massachusetts state flower, blooms here in early May.

Its sandpapery leaves and delicate pink blossoms hug the ground in sunny openings.

Although not fragrant, mountain laurel clusters of nickel-sized white and pink blossoms are a sight to see in late spring or early summer. Beyond the bridge, the trail bears left to continue around the pond—best viewed as the path climbs a few feet to higher ground at two substantial sugar maples. Saw-billed hooded mergansers nest in big wooden boxes fastened to trees for use by cavity-nesting mergansers and wood ducks.

Move away from the pond and walk beneath a stand of planted depression-era red pines where high-strung red squirrels chatter. The path curves left into a small shrub wetland traversed by a boardwalk bordered by alder, larch, and luxuriant ferns. Interrupted ferns stand shoulder high on drier ground, while royal and cinnamon ferns (the latter with cinnamon-hued fertile fronds) crowd the decking. At its far end, turn right to walk a few feet back to the office and parking area.

DID YOU KNOW?

Beavers are strict herbivores that do not hibernate through the depths of winter, but rather retrieve twigs that they have stockpiled in the pond mud near the lodge. Twigs (especially the nutritious bark) serve as their sole food until more succulent vegetation becomes available during the spring green-up.

MORE INFORMATION

Trails open year-round, daily, dawn to dusk, except Mondays. Open seven days per week, July–Columbus Day, and Monday holidays year-round. The office is open same days as the grounds, 10 A.M.–4 P.M. Nonmember fees: $5 for adults, $3 for children (3–12) and senior citizens. Mass Audubon members, Lenox residents are free. Pets, vehicles (including bicycles), horses, hunting, trapping, fishing, and collecting are not permitted. Carry in, carry out rules apply. Berkshire Wildlife Sanctuaries, 472 West Mountain Road, Lenox, MA 01240 (413-637-0320; massaudubon.org/pleasantvalley).

NEARBY

The Arcadian Shop in Lenox carries an assortment of outdoor and camping gear, shoes, clothing, guidebooks and maps, kayaks, mountains bikes, snowshoes, and other recreational equipment. Kayaks, bikes, snowshoes, cross-country skis, and paddleboards are available for rent. The shop's Trailside Café invites shoppers to stay for a bite to eat; 91 Pittsfield Road (US 7/20) (413-637-3010; store.arcadian.com).

TRIP 26
JOHN DRUMMOND KENNEDY PARK

Location: Lenox, MA
Rating: Easy to Moderate
Distance: 4.8 miles
Elevation Gain: 355 feet
Estimated Time: 2.5 to 3.0 hours
Maps: USGS Pittsfield West, USGS Stockbridge; trail map available online

This fine hiking trip for the whole family features points of historic interest including the site of the famed Aspinwall Hotel, a marble balanced rock, and long views.

DIRECTIONS

From the south: From Exit 2 (Lee) off the Mass Pike (I-90), turn right after the tollbooths and drive north on US 20 (later becoming US 7 and US 20) for 6.6 miles to West Dugway Road on the left (note sign for Pleasant Valley Wildlife Sanctuary). Drive down West Dugway Road for just over 0.1 mile to the park's gravel parking area on the left, with space for approximately fifteen vehicles.

From the north: From Pittsfield's Park Square, drive south on US 7/20 for 4.9 miles to West Dugway Road on the right. Follow West Dugway Road for just over 0.1 mile to the park's gravel parking area on the left.

GPS coordinates: 42° 22.975′ N, 73° 16.717′ W.

TRAIL DESCRIPTION

Examine the kiosk, which contains a brief history of the property and use regulations. Although almost all trail intersections are signed and posted with maps, the intricacy of the trail system requires attentiveness. Turn right and follow a sandy path over a wooden span into a forest of maple, ash, oak, birch, and cherry. Pass a side trail on the left and walk up a slight grade on Cold Spring Trail to the trail's namesake, a stone-lined, octagonal reservoir that captures and holds spring water that once supplied the luxurious Aspinwall Hotel. You can investigate a short dead-end path to the spring's source on the right, where a dense growth of hardy kiwi festoons the grotto of marble boulders, reminiscent of Mayan ruins lost to the jungle!

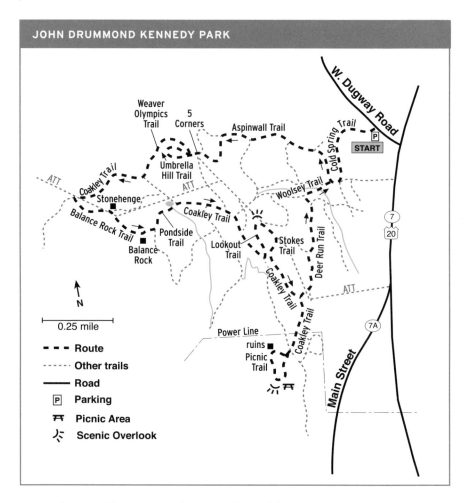

JOHN DRUMMOND KENNEDY PARK

Weaver Olympics Trail
5 Corners
Aspinwall Trail
W. Dugway Road
Cold Spring Trail
START
ATT
Coakley Trail
Umbrella Hill Trail
ATT
Woolsey Trail
Stonehenge
Balance Rock Trail
Coakley Trail
Pondside Trail
Lookout Trail
Stokes Trail
Deer Run Trail
ATT
Balance Rock
7
20
7A
Coakley Trail
N
0.25 mile
Power Line
ruins
Picnic Trail
Coakley Trail
Main Street

- - - Route
······ Other trails
——— Road
P Parking
Picnic Area
Scenic Overlook

Back on Cold Spring Trail, turn right and follow the old roadway, bearing right past kiwi-infested light gaps, which have been treated with herbicide. In late summer, ripe black cherries litter the path. You'll reach wide Woolsey Trail at a four-way intersection with a map kiosk and bench. Turn right and almost immediately right again on Aspinwall Trail, named for the former 400-room hotel that succumbed to fire in 1931.

The dirt road becomes rougher as it bears left and continues up a gentle grade. Ignore the side paths. The still numerous white and gray birches are being outcompeted by more shade-tolerant hardwoods. Rock outcrops protrude from a slope on the left, and a sizable sugar maple stands opposite at the fringe of a dark hillside grove of hemlocks and yellow birch. An easy climb soon steepens. Hemlock Trail junctions from the left, but continue straight at this intersection and then bear left on Aspinwall Trail where Nose Trail bears right. Beyond, there are boulders and gneiss ledges up to 15 feet high with white quartz bands capped by the 7-inch fronds of common polypody fern. Lowbush blueberries are scattered about this drier forest floor.

You'll arrive at a five-way intersection known as 5 Corners. Continuing straight takes you, via a short loop, to the forested top of Umbrella Hill, the park's high point at 1,634 feet. After returning to 5 Corners, turn left onto wide, level Weaver Olympics Trail, named for Lenox Nordic skier and Olympian Patrick Weaver. A plaque in his honor is affixed to a boulder on the left. In late summer, white wood asters form a decorative fringe along these paths. Pass under a young canopy of red maple and black birch, and ignoring side trails, reach a **Y** intersection. Bear right and in 75 feet join Main or T. F. Coakley Trail. Thomas Francis Coakley was a renowned local horseman who developed most of the current trails and maintained them until his death in 1952.

Turn right and you'll notice a wolf pine on the right that grew up in what was then an open field. Another tree worthy of attention farther on is a massive, deeply furrowed oak on the left. At the **Y** intersection with Balance Rock Trail, turn left and head up a wide and rough road past jumbled rock outcrops, ignoring a descending side trail on the right. Maple-leaved viburnum and sapling sugar maples pose an identification challenge; distinguish the fine-toothed leaves of the viburnum. A screened glimpse of Parson's Marsh is possible right, just before you traverse an AT&T transcontinental telephone corridor (easy to miss). A thick patch of large-leaved horse balm produces pointed airy stalks of pale yellow blossoms that appear vaguely orchidlike in late summer, but it is a mint.

At the next trail split, follow the left path to Stonehenge Trail on the left, which leads to a mound topped by twelve concrete pilings, each 4.5 feet high, and a presumably older set of lower, cement-and-stone footings. These two supports may have supported two tanks that once fed water, by gravity, to the hotel. After exploring the site, return to Balance Rock Trail; walking straight, immediately past Kirchner Trail on the left, and bearing right on the old roadway through oak woodland with a "grassy" groundcover of sedges. Note that the downslope margin of the roadway was fortified with stones. You'll pass little-used Ferncliffe Trail on the left. At the **Y**, a short side path leads right, to Balance Rock. A grayish, marble boulder rests atop a sculpted base of the same composition, creating a natural sculpture. Retrace your steps to the main trail and a big white oak at the intersection. Turn right and continue moderately downhill on Balance Rock Trail, choosing either fork where it splits to soon arrive at Pondside Trail.

Bear left onto Pondside Trail, passing through remnants of a fallen stone walls and walk down under beech, maple, and ash trees to reach a small murky pond. Follow Main/T. F. Coakley Trail right. Look for a small patch of wild ginger at the base of a mature bigtooth aspen on the right. Ginger's heart-shaped leaves obscure the ground-level maroon blossoms pollinated by beetles attracted to the fetid odor. You'll reach Under Mountain Trail on the right, but continue straight on T. F. Coakley Trail past unsigned Aspinwall Trail on the left near an exposed bedrock ledge. Soon you'll arrive at a major **Y** intersection with two benches. A sign attached to a trunk on the left reads Woolsey. Continue straight on T. F. Coakley Trail—in the direction of Church on the Hill (at least for now).

Bypass Cutoff Trail on the left by walking straight on the old roadway that contours the hillside. Just past Red Neck Trail on the right, turn hard left onto Lookout Trail, a gravel road that morphs into a twin track through dry oak woodland. Your destination is a wooden gazebo built in 1992 at a vista point for Mount Greylock, and other promontories, but views are best after leaf fall. The various summits and cardinal points are noted in the structure. Stepping out of the gazebo, turn left along the AT&T corridor. Ignore the subsequent left junction with Lookout Trail, descending easily instead to Stokes Trail on the right. Follow Stokes Trail through attractive mixed woods and soon find yourself back on T. F. Coakley Trail. Bear left and remain on the wide roadway. After leveling off, pass the Upper Deer Run Trail junction on the left.

Pass through an overhead power line cut flanked by pleasing views of farms and forested ridges. At the major four-way intersection of Main Trail and Red Neck Trail, continue straight and head uphill on a paved section for approximately 50 feet and bear right onto a narrow woodland path—Picnic Trail—past cement structures, stone ruins, cellar holes, and foundations of Aspinwall Hotel outbuildings. A short side trail labeled "Ruins" leads to foundations. Return to Picnic Trail and turn right to follow the path up a steep hemlock-shaded hillside with a precipitous drop on the right. The grassy hotel lawn, now a picnic area, and the site of the Kennedy Park Belvedere (a granite memorial to Jordan Feldman, MD) offers southerly views that include Monument Mountain (Trip 35) and Mount Everett (Trip 46). The hotel's hanging gardens once graced the slope below the low concrete wall beyond which staghorn sumac is now prolific.

Turn left and walk about 70 feet under white pines to a grassy rectangle where the posh hotel, built in 1902 and host to the rich and famous of that era, once stood. The panoramic view back across the picnic area is optimized from here. Continue across the field and onto an asphalt access road (T. F. Coakley

Spring-fed Cold Spring reservoir once supplied water to the famed Aspinwall Hotel, which burned to the ground in 1931.

Trail). Turn left and amble down to the major intersection, bear left to the **Y** and take the right fork (T. F. Coakley Trail) back to the power line cut. At Upper Deer Run Trail, turn right. Bishop's weed (a.k.a. goutweed), an invasive exotic, which has poison ivy–like leaves and flower clusters like Queen Anne's, forms a trailside monoculture. After the AT&T corridor, reach an intersection with Deer Run Trail. Bear left. A stone wall runs along below the rather inclined slope to your right. Pass the Weaver Olympics Trail on the left. The stone walls continues close now on the right.

The trail briefly passes between mossy outcrops. Ignore Greenfield Trail on the right and reach a **T** intersection with spacious Woolsey Trail. Turn right, cross a drainage, and descend easily past Wilderness and Aspinwall trails, both on the left. Back at the four-way intersection with the map kiosk, turn left onto Cold Spring Trail to return to your vehicle.

DID YOU KNOW?

Edward J. Woolsey bought the nucleus of what would become Kennedy Park beginning in 1853 with a dozen land acquisitions totaling 500 acres. Known as Aspinwall Park, the park was renamed in 1973 in honor of the longtime Lenox Planning Board member who played a key role in acquiring the property in 1956.

MORE INFORMATION

Open sunrise to sunset, daily, year-round. Dogs, horses, mountain bikes, and skiing are all allowed. Dogs must be under owner's control at all times. Motorized vehicles, alcohol, fires, tree cutting without permission, hunting, and trapping are not permitted. John Drummond Kennedy Park Restoration Committee, Town of Lenox, Lenox Town Hall, 6 Walker Street, Lenox, MA 01240 (413-637-5500; townoflenox.com/Public_Documents/LenoxMA_WebDocs/KennedyParkMap2013_web.jpg).

NEARBY

The Church Street Café, 65 Church Street in Lenox, offers a varied menu utilizing seasonal and organic products, and features outdoor patio dining (413-637-2745; churchstreetlenox.com).

ALIEN INVADERS

They're green; they've arrived from far, far away; and they are threatening to take over. Little green men from Mars? No, invasive exotic plants! Ask a land manager today what their biggest concern is regarding species diversity and it's a good bet they'll answer "Invasive species." Continent-wide, invasive exotics are second only to habitat loss on the list of threats to biological diversity.

Well-known invaders include purple loosestrife, Eurasian watermilfoil, the exotic form of common reed, Japanese barberry, oriental bittersweet, and garlic mustard. What makes a perfectly respectable plant (or animal for that matter) from one part of the globe such a menace in another? Plants translocated from their native haunts to foreign soil have no insect or mammal herbivores, fungi, or diseases to keep them in check. In their homelands, each species faces a long-evolving system of checks and balances to rampant growth. When transported (either by accident or willfully) outside its range, the possibility exists that a new arrival, sans controls, will outcompete the natives already there.

In Kennedy Park, the adjacent Pleasant Valley Wildlife Sanctuary, and a few other locations, a newly recognized threat has the potential to do serious damage to our forests. That threat is hardy kiwi (*Actenidia arguta*). If you've never heard of it, you're not alone. So recent is this realization that it has yet to be added to the official state registry of invasive exotic plants.

Hardy kiwi hails from Southeast Asia, a region from which a number of other troublesome plants, including oriental bittersweet, arrived. Both species have found our soils and climate to be welcoming because they mimic those of their homelands. Like bittersweet, hardy kiwi is a climbing vine, but one that is even more aggressive and that says a lot! Kiwi spreads mostly by runners, but it also produces tasty, grape-sized, green seed-filled fruits that are distributed by birds and mammals looking for a treat. Although it doesn't constrict the trunks of trees the way bittersweet does, it grows so prolifically as to completely engulf woody natives and rob them of sunlight. Kiwi-filled light-gaps are a frightening vision of complete alien dominance. Natives have little chance against it. Although restricted in its range currently, it is poised to become a major threat to deciduous forests in the Berkshires.

TRIP 27
LENOX MOUNTAIN–BURBANK TRAIL

Location: Richmond and Lenox, MA
Rating: Easy to Moderate
Distance: 3.2 miles
Elevation Gain: 540 feet
Estimated Time: 1.5–2.0 hours
Maps: USGS Pittsfield West; trail map available online; Yokun Ridge
Map & Guide

**This enjoyable loop takes you through diverse woodland to a
pleasing lookout on the southern slope of Lenox Mountain.
A historic homesite and an estate's reservoir add interest.**

DIRECTIONS
From Exit 2 (Lee) off I-90 (Mass Pike), turn right and follow US 20 for 4.1
miles (joining US 7 just after Cranwell Resort; it then becomes combined MA
7 and MA 20) to MA 183 South (Walker St.) on the left at a traffic light. Drive
for 1.1 miles to the center of Lenox (at the monument) and continue straight
on MA 183 South for another 1.5 miles (past the entrance to Tanglewood
Music Center) to where Richmond-Lenox Road bears away from MA 183 to
the right. Follow it uphill for 1.4 miles to a circular gravel parking area on the
left (sign marks Olivia's Overlook). The lot is bounded on the left by a stone
walls. *GPS coordinates*: 42° 21.109′ N, 73° 20.259′ W.

TRAIL DESCRIPTION
The best view of this excursion is from the parking area and takes in
Stockbridge Bowl (a.k.a. Lake Mahkeenac) and the verdant ridges beyond.
This parking area is named for Olivia Stokes Hatch, whose family donated the
land to the Berkshire County Land Trust and Conservation Fund. A plaque
atop an elegant stone walls explains that Tennessee Gas Pipeline Company
constructed the parking area in 1992.

To reach the trailhead, however, you must cross Lenox Road; use caution!
A kiosk complete with large trail map (and often a supply of hardcopy maps)
is situated about 50 feet into the forest. Walk up into diverse woodland of
eastern hemlock, oak, ash, and red maple. Note the gray schist outcrops veined

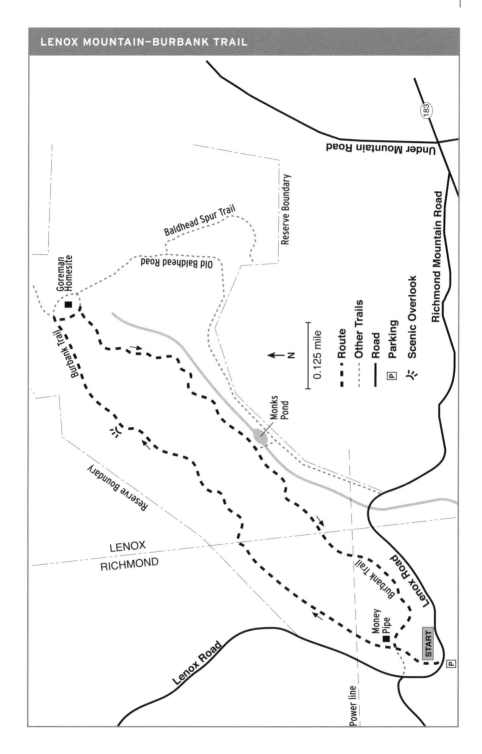

LENOX MOUNTAIN–BURBANK TRAIL

with milky quartz. This erosion-resistant rock type forms the spine of the Lenox–Stockbridge Mountain ridge. Soon you'll enter a darker forest in which hemlock predominates. Yellow, black, and gray birches and shade-tolerant American beech and sun-loving oak join in. In spring, a wet depression to the right is filled with a profusion of purple violets.

Follow the fine red-blazed path and arrive at a signed, four-way intersection and money pipe. (Note: trail blazing is slated to change to blue by 2016.) Continue straight ahead on Burbank Trail. Begin a moderate climb past schist outcrops and emerge into sunlight as you reach a power line cut. Wintergreen on the left bears coral-red fruits in late summer and fall. This sunny, dry, linear landscape also provides suitable growing conditions for pale corydalis with tubular pink and yellow flowers in May. Eastern towhees are among the species that nest in such artificial shrublands. Listen for their *chewink* calls and *drink-your-tea* songs.

Back in the moister forest, the trail undulates under oaks, hemlocks, and mountain laurel shrubs. Woodland wildflowers here include *Clintonia* (a.k.a. bluebead lily), Indian cucumber-root, and sessile-leaved bellwort (a.k.a. wild oats), which all produce yellow flowers. In time, the pathway climbs, gently at first and then more steeply, paved in spots with bedrock. Witch hazel is the spreading shrub that blooms in autumn while striped maple is the small tree with greenish bark. Even its flowers, produced in May, are green.

After a few more undulations through oaks and hophornbeam, you'll arrive at a short side trail that leads left to a vista point. The view to the northwest through a gap in the forest is limited, but very nice. A plaque behind you indicates that the trail was named for Kelton (Kim) Burbank, a local attorney and conservationist. Lowbush blueberries thrive in the acidic soils beneath the pines and oaks. Return to the main trail and turn left. Striped maple, red maple, and witch hazel are numerous beneath the oaks. Gaudy scarlet tanager males sing their burry refrains from high in the oaks in late spring and early summer. In contrast, their yellow-green mates blend in with the foliage. When you reach a signed path, turn right toward Old Baldhead Road.

The treadway descends through a forest of white ash, bigtooth aspen, black and gray birches, red maple, and red oak. On the left rests a cellar hole—all that remains of the Gorman homesite, occupied by that family from 1852 to 1892, although dates on a cement marker indicate occupation from 1838 to 1898. The Gormans farmed this 44-acre hardscrabble lot until they sold it to Wall Street financier Anson Phelps Stokes to become part of his Shadowbrook estate. Philanthropist Andrew Carnegie later owned it.

Burbank Trail joins Old Baldhead Road and bears right. Shortly reach an intersection and turn right to remain on Burbank Trail. Morrow's honeysuckle, an introduced, exotic ornamental, outcompetes native shrubs here.

After treading across a series of bog bridges, bear left to continue a gradual descent to a stone walls composed of small pieces of schist. Sheep fences are seldom built of such small material. Reach a hemlock stand and drop into a shallow gorge through which a small brook spills. Some towering specimens of the evergreen border the stream. Gray birches, which preceded the conifers, have succumbed to the hemlock's shade, but yellow birches thrive in the cool shadows. The wide path makes its way past a sofa-sized boulder on the right.

Turn right at a log bench by the brook and amble under hemlock and hardwoods. You'll traverse a bridge and bear left. The path changes to a wider old cart road. It leads downslope to an opalescent pond in a serene setting on the left. This was the estate's reservoir. During the twentieth century, it took on the name Monks Pond. A Jesuit order owned the property at the time. The Kripalu Center for Yoga and Health, below Olivia's Overlook, now occupies the former monastery. Reach a signed intersection at the far right end of the reservoir and bear right to remain on Burbank Trail. Follow the path past the earthen dam's concrete spillway. Burbank Trail follows high above the flow, and ledge outcrops make the scene picturesque. Listen for the calls of the 21-inch-tall barred owl—*who cooks for you, who cooks for you all*. The path rises moderately along this steep hillside; the downslope was reinforced with rock during construction, making for excellent footing. Cross the power line again, where tall mountain laurel shrubs bloom profusely in late June.

The treadway undulates easily under hemlocks and then through deciduous woodland of birch, beech, maple, and oak before reentering evergreens. Before long you are back at the first intersection and money pipe. Turn left and cautiously retrace your steps across Lenox Road to your vehicle.

DID YOU KNOW?

During the eighteenth century, virtually the entire ridge was denuded of timber. Much of it was reduced to charcoal to feed local iron furnaces—a thriving early Berkshire industry—until almost all the nearby timber had been harvested. As a result, coal became a cheaper source of fuel for the furnaces.

MORE INFORMATION

Open during daylight hours, year-round. Hiking, mountain biking, horseback riding, and hunting in season are permitted. Motorized vehicles, fires, camping, littering, and cutting or removing trees or plants is prohibited. Berkshire Natural Resources Council, 20 Bank Row, Pittsfield, MA 01201 (413-499-0596; bnrc.net).

NEARBY

Chill out at Stockbridge's Kripalu Center for Yoga and Health, visible below Olivia's Overlook. The center offers presentations, trainings, and workshops in yoga and healthy living. From the intersection of MA 183 and Richmond Mountain Road, follow MA 183 west 1.6 miles to the entrance on the right (866-200-5203; kripalu.org).

TRIP 28
WEST STOCKBRIDGE MOUNTAIN–
CHARCOAL, WALSH, AND RIDGE TRAILS

Location: Stockbridge, West Stockbridge, and Richmond, MA
Rating: Moderate
Distance: 2.2 miles
Elevation Gain: 530 feet
Estimated Time: 1.0–1.5 hours
Maps: USGS Stockbridge; trail map available online

West Stockbridge Mountain comprises the southern portion of Yokun Ridge Reserve. This enjoyable loop leads through mature woodlands and features a couple of pleasing vista points.

DIRECTIONS
From the center of Lenox at the intersection of Walker Street, MA 183, and US 7A (Main Street), follow MA 183 (West Street) for just over 1.5 miles to Richmond Mountain Road on the right. Bear right and drive 0.4 mile to a gravel parking area on the left at Olivia's Overlook. Note this is the same parking area as for the Burbank Trail (Trip 27). *GPS coordinates*: 42° 21.109′ N, 73° 20.259′ W.

TRAIL DESCRIPTION
The trail begins from the west end of the parking area at a white quartzite boulder inscribed with the name of Michael Walsh. You'll walk across a Tennessee gas pipeline corridor flush with grasses, goldenrod, catchfly, and other forbs in summer. You'll cross a short wooden span to a map kiosk at the edge of a shady forest. Turn left onto Charcoal Trail and follow blue triangular blazes along an old roadway under hemlocks and oaks. The wide treadway descends gently along a ravine for the first portion of the route.

White oak, whose leaves have rounded lobes, joins the deciduous woodland mix, while witch hazel and American chestnut sprouts form a trailside understory. You'll stride across stretches of schist bedrock as you continue an easy descent through abundant mountain laurel that blooms in mid-June to early July. You'll pass the signed intersection for Brothers Trail on the left— it leads to Baldhead and Monks Pond, but you'll continue straight. At the reservation boundary, Charcoal Trail turns right. Listen for the deeply resonant

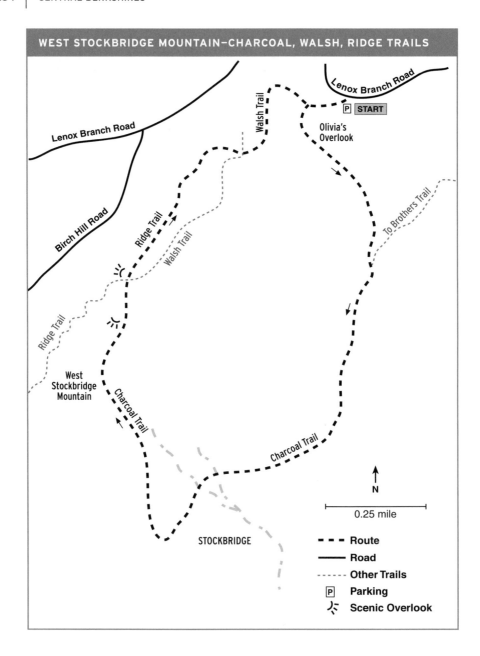

WEST STOCKBRIDGE MOUNTAIN–CHARCOAL, WALSH, RIDGE TRAILS

Lenox Branch Road

Walsh Trail

P START

Olivia's Overlook

Lenox Branch Road

Birch Hill Road

Ridge Trail

Walsh Trail

To Brothers Trail

Ridge Trail

West Stockbridge Mountain

Charcoal Trail

Charcoal Trail

N

0.25 mile

STOCKBRIDGE

- - - Route
——— Road
········· Other Trails
P Parking
⅄⅂ Scenic Overlook

drumming or maniacal call of the big pileated woodpecker and the mellow tremolo of the wood thrush. Shade-tolerant black birches become common, while evergreen Christmas fern enlivens the woodland year-round.

You'll begin an easy climb through mixed deciduous/coniferous woods— a variety of oaks, black birch, and hemlock. The deep shade and acidic soil prohibit the growth of virtually any other plant life. The slopes are dissected by drainage streams that have carved small ravines of varying depths. You'll cross several on well-placed rockwork. White ash and sugar maple here are impressively tall and straight. The mature oaks are of noteworthy proportions also. Stride up a stone staircase amid fallen hemlocks and reach an angular boulder where the path levels out briefly and then climbs easily. You'll cross a trickling drainage and remnant stone walls to your right. A few massive white pines escaped the lumberman's ax here. Wend along the base of an outcrop studded with mosses and ferns including hay-scented, spinulose woodfern, and rock-loving common polypody.

Higher up the slope, the trees—American beech and red maple—are of much smaller stature due to the thin soil. Stone steps lead to a fern glade near the height of land, and lowbush blueberries and Canada mayflower grace the forest floor. The hoarse, singsong voice of the male scarlet tanager fills the late spring and early summer air, but it is seldom seen. After about 1.5 miles, you'll reach a rocky bald where a split-log bench offers a view south to Monument Mountain and Butternut ski area beyond. Note that the schist bedrock is tilted vertically. The best view is yet to come. Continue straight on what is now Walsh Trail (don't turn left on the red-blazed trail), and reenter acidic oak woods.

Shortly arrive at a **T** intersection under hemlocks and turn left to Vista Point, only a few feet away. You can take in the gorgeous view west from this rocky perch. A few small sassafras saplings, with mitten-shaped leaves, are found here. When ready, return to the main trail, but turn left on red-blazed Ridge Trail and walk north. You'll descend through oak, hemlock, and laurel. Blueberries and Canada mayflower thrive in the acid soil, while common polypody fern caps some boulders. At times, the downward angle increases. At a **Y** split you can choose either path as they join up again a little later. *Clintonia*, a native lily, and bush honeysuckle bloom yellow, while the small shrub maple-leaved viburnum adds its umbels of whitish-pink blossoms in late spring.

Before long, come to a four-way intersection; you'll continue straight toward Olivia's Overlook. Drop down easily and pass more angular outcrops on the left under an oak canopy. A few additional trail twists and turns lead you back to the map kiosk.

DID YOU KNOW?

Michael H. Walsh was Chairman and CEO of Tenneco, Inc., of Houston. Walsh died of cancer in 1994 at the age of 51. Tenneco funded the construction of

A split log bench resting on vertically tilted schist offers a view south to Monument Mountain and Butternut Basin ski area beyond.

Olivia's Overlook—named for Olivia Stokes Hatch, who, with her husband John D. Hatch, Jr., and her brothers Anson Phelps Stokes, Jr., and Isaac N.P. Stokes, donated the land.

MORE INFORMATION

The reserve is owned and managed by the Berkshire Natural Resources Council (BNRC), a regional land trust founded in 1967 that protects 18,000 acres of conservation land in the Berkshires; 20 Bank Row, Pittsfield, MA 01201 (413-499-0596; bnrc.net).

NEARBY

The Mount is the former home and 113-acre estate of Pulitzer Prize–winning novelist and short story writer Edith Wharton (1862–1937), best known for her ghostly tales. Purchased in 1902, the home, its public gardens, and the Terrace Café are open to the public daily, May through October, 10 A.M.–5 P.M. There is an admission fee. The property closes early some days, so call ahead (413-551-5111), or email info@edithwharton.org; 2 Plunkett Street, Lenox, MA 01240.

TRIP 29
SCHERMERHORN GORGE TRAIL

Location: Lenox, Lee, and Washington, MA
Rating: Moderate to Strenuous
Distance: 3.7 miles
Elevation Gain: 620 feet
Estimated Time: 2.0–2.5 hours
Maps: USGS East Lee; trail map available online

From the still waters of wildlife-rich Woods Pond to the cascading flow of Schermerhorn Brook, flanked by massive trees, this hike provides dramatic contrasts.

DIRECTIONS

From Exit 2 (Lee) off I-90 (Mass Pike), turn right and follow US 20 through Lee (later joining US 7) for 4.6 miles to Housatonic Street in Lenox. Turn right onto Housatonic Street and drive 1.3 miles to where the pavement makes a sharp turn to the right. Leave the pavement by continuing straight ahead on gravel, parking on the right between the railroad tracks and the pedestrian bridge. Be sure not to block the driveway to the private residence on the left. Also, be careful not to obstruct access to the canoe landing on the pond edge to the right. There is space here for approximately four vehicles. One may also park outside the tracks, on the right. Be aware that this is an active rail line. *GPS coordinates*: 42° 20.985′ N, 73° 14.638′ W.

TRAIL DESCRIPTION

Cross the arched steel-and-wood pedestrian bridge over a constriction at the south end of Woods Pond and admire the sight of October Mountain. The reflection off the pond is especially eye-catching during fall foliage season in early to mid-October. The Housatonic River plunges over Woods Pond Dam—which backs up the river's flow to create the 100-acre pond—about 200 yards to the right (south). Exotic Morrow's honeysuckle lines the gravel roadway beyond the bridge.

Bear left upon reaching a gravel road and pass under high transmission lines. If you visit from May to early July, you'll be impressed by the exuberance of bird life. Yellow warblers and myriad other avian life forms abound in and around the pond, including belted kingfisher, Canada goose, wood duck, mallard, and warbling vireo to name a few.

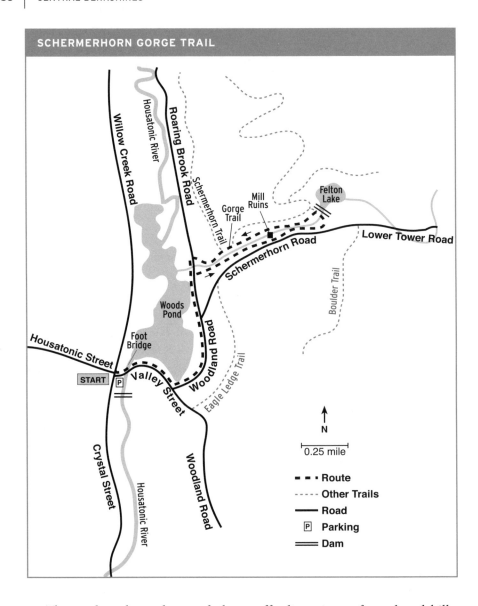

SCHERMERHORN GORGE TRAIL

The roadway hugs the pond shore, affording views of pond and hills. The bucolic scene belies the fact that Woods Pond holds the highest concentrations of carcinogenic polychlorinated biphenyls (PCBs) in this river system. Bear left at another gravel road to continue around the pond. Primarily young woodland of white ash, black birch, sugar maple, and gray and yellow birches stand above the water body. A few massive white pines tower in stark contrast to the young deciduous growth—the body of one multitrunked giant lies where it crashed to Earth. Walk past a huge red oak on the right and then encounter more impressive trees along the roadway.

Pass two wood roads on the right separated by a modest high-gradient stream flowing down the hillside into the pond. Reach the state forest boundary to your right not long before the intersection with paved Schermerhorn Road on the right. Continue straight, paralleling on the left the boundary of the George L. Darey Wildlife Management Area along the Housatonic. These giant oak trees escaped the ax long ago.

The sound of Schermerhorn Brook heralds your arrival at the trailhead. Note the small wooden sign on a tree that reads "Gorge Trail," and enter the forest to the right on a signed and blue-blazed footpath to begin a moderate climb under sugar maples, ashes, and oaks. The brook to your left gushes over and around boulders of gneiss and quartzite. The low evergreen shrub—American yew—thrives in the shade near the cascade.

The trail turns right, continues to climb, and then bears left to ascend above the flow, but watch your footing. A two-step waterfall is soon visible below. The rugged slopes of the gorge hold some impressive oaks and hemlocks. One hemlock trunk is 3 feet across. The trail moves farther from the stream as the incline eases. Eventually, you'll level out and rejoin the brook, perhaps 30 feet above it. Mountain maple, a small understory tree similar in size to striped maple but with brown bark and smaller, toothier leaves, grows in the gorge along the flowage.

Tread up stone steps and past a jumble of big gneiss boulders as the streambed continues to be very rocky. Note the characteristic alternating dark and light bands of the gneiss. In spring and early summer, the loud, ringing notes of the bobbing, striped, Louisiana waterthrush can be heard even above the roar of the water; these warblers winter in the tropics and nest along fast-flowing upland streams. On the right, a hemlock is growing from a rock crevice, inexorably splitting the rock apart. The brook soon splits in two, forming a narrow floodplain. After a bit, reach the partial stone foundation of what was probably a millhouse long ago.

Emerge briefly into a brighter patch of young maples; Schermerhorn Road is very near. After reentering shady hemlock forest, you'll pass a 100-year-old fallen tree cut years ago to accommodate the trail. White pines and a mammoth oak stand on the left a few feet farther. The steep aspect of these slopes made timber harvesting here less economical, resulting in some truly impressive specimen trees today. The deep, reverberating drumming of the crow-sized pileated woodpecker is an increasingly common percussion in such mature Berkshire woodlands. Even if you don't hear or see one of these memorable birds, you will happen across their deep, rectangular excavations. These aren't nest cavities, but rather spots where dead tissue was removed by the bird so as to reach carpenter ant colonies.

The gorge deepens again, and soon the path approaches the brook closely. After the brook negotiates a 90-degree bend to the left, the well-blazed trail follows it up to a gravel roadway. A keystone arch bridge built of native stone lies ahead, beneath which flows Schermerhorn Brook, the outlet stream from Felton Lake. Turn left to cross the bridge. An earthen dam to your right impounds the water body. You will return along the opposite side of the gorge. Three-inch-long bullfrog tadpoles sometimes swim about in the concrete spillway.

The blue-blazed return trail begins just beyond the far end of the bridge, under planted Norway spruces, and is marked by a sign. The path follows the stream and passes a small derelict shack some 100 feet to your right. The gorge seems deeper from this side and the descent is moderately steep. Light gaps are filled with hobblebush, maple-leaved viburnum, and bush honeysuckle. There are patches of young American beech as the path closely approaches the brook. The ruins of the mill are more easily observed from this side now. You are walking under a mixed canopy of hemlocks, oaks, and northern hardwoods just before you cross an intermittent tributary stream on large, flat stones and continue downward along Schermerhorn Brook.

Hobblebush shrubs bloom here in early May. The woodland is more predominately deciduous in this area—especially rich in oaks. Both Solomon's seal with greenish flowers hanging down from each leaf node, and false Solomon's seal, with white blossoms at the tip of the stalk, thrive on the forest floor. This trail appears less traveled than the other. The brook tumbles over moss-cushioned boulders. The roaring of the brook intensifies with the gradient. A few stone steps take you down to brook level again.

The yellow trumpets of bush honeysuckle are numerous. Blue cohosh, which has oddly purple-green leaves, blooms in spring in a sunny canopy gap. Your descent steepens as the gorge narrows markedly and the brook drops precipitously. The trail is characterized by steeper sections, and the cascades become more dramatic as you proceed downward. One four-step cascade is particularly picturesque. Finally, bear right away from the brook, amble down more excellent stone steps, and then negotiate a series of short switchbacks down the slope. You'll reach the brook again, pass a huge oak on the right, and arrive back at Woodland Road. Turn left and retrace your steps to Woods Pond (bearing right at the intersections), the pedestrian bridge, and your vehicle.

DID YOU KNOW?

The George L. Darey Housatonic River Wildlife Management Area and the adjoining western slopes of October Mountain State Forest constitute

A handsome keystone arch spans Schermerhorn Brook soon after it leaves October Mountain State's Forest Felton Lake.

a significant portion of the 12,280-acre Upper Housatonic Area of Critical Environmental Concern designated by the Commonwealth in 2009. It is home to 32 state-listed species and dozens of vernal pools.

MORE INFORMATION

Open sunrise to 30 minutes after sunset year-round. Access is free. Alcoholic beverages are prohibited. Pets are permitted but must be on a 10-foot-maximum leash and attended at all times. Proof of rabies vaccination required. Motorized vehicles are not permitted on the Schermerhorn Gorge Trail. October Mountain State Forest, 317 Woodland Road, Lee, MA (413-243-1778; mass.gov/eea/agencies/dcr/massparks/region-west/october-mountain-state-forest-generic.html).

NEARBY

Railroad buffs will enjoy visiting Berkshire Scenic Railway Museum located at 10 Willow Creek Road, within view of where you parked. Cross the tracks and almost immediately turn right onto Willow Creek Road, travel 100 yards to the museum on the right. The restored 1903 Lenox Station once welcomed Gilded Age "cottagers" to their Berkshire summer homes. Open weekends and federal holidays 9 A.M.–4 P.M., Memorial Day weekend to late October (413-637-2210; berkshirescenicrailroad.org).

TRIP 30
STEVENS GLEN

Location: West Stockbridge and Richmond, MA
Rating: Easy to Moderate
Distance: 1.4 miles
Elevation Gain: 320 feet
Estimated Time: 1.0–1.5 hours
Maps: USGS Stockbridge; trail map available online

Towering trees and cascading Lenox Mountain Brook make Stevens Glen one of the area's most refreshing walking destinations on a warm summer day.

DIRECTIONS

From the center of Lenox, at the intersection of MA 183, US 7A (Main Street), and Walker Street, travel southwest on MA 183 for 1.5 miles to Richmond Mountain Road on the right (where MA 183 curves left). Follow Richmond Mountain Road for 1.6 miles, past Olivia's Overlook on left, to Lenox Branch Road on the left. Turn left and drive for 0.6 mile to a signed pull-off on the right with parking for five or six cars. Additional parking is available about 100 yards farther on the right, opposite Deer Hill Road. *GPS coordinates*: 42° 21.026′ N, 73° 20.895′ W.

TRAIL DESCRIPTION

Stride down wooden steps under the shade of a yellow birch to a map kiosk where trail maps are often available. The trail, blazed with rectangular red blazes, leads right, through a balsam fir plantation. (Note: Trail blazing is slated to change to blue by 2016.) The trees are tall and straight, their bark marked with resin "blisters." A geranium relative, Herb Robert, with pink blossoms, blankets the forest floor in early summer. The dirt path leads easily down, past invasive garlic mustard as well. You'll reach a money pipe at a Y intersection. Turn right and continue to follow the red blazes. Both directions lead to the Glen; you'll be returning along the other pathway.

Little sunlight penetrates the fir boughs, and as a result, little grows beneath them. Pockets of spinulose wood fern do add splashes of color year-round. You'll cross a damp spot on bog bridges, and begin an easy descent

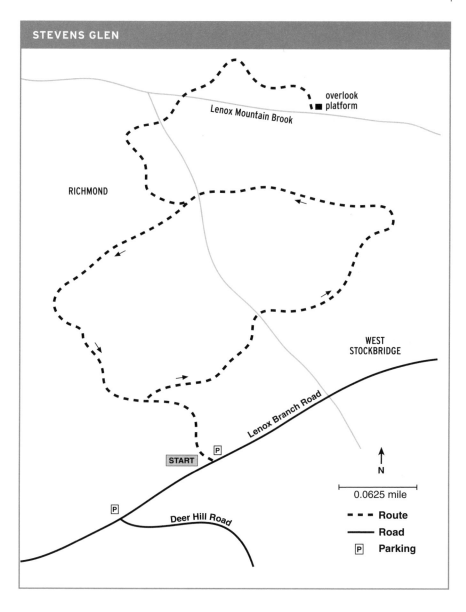

STEVENS GLEN

overlook
■ platform

Lenox Mountain Brook

RICHMOND

WEST
STOCKBRIDGE

Lenox Branch Road

P

START

P

Deer Hill Road

N

0.0625 mile

- - - Route
—— Road
P Parking

under a deciduous canopy of white ash, basswood, bigtooth aspen, and eastern hemlock. You'll turn right to cross a tributary stream via the first of four recycled plastic lumber bridges along the route. Moss coats the span's handrails. Dark green, paired leaves of partridgeberry form a creeping groundcover beneath the hemlocks; black, yellow, and white birches; impressive ashes; and sugar maples. In early summer, partridgeberry produces twin, fuzzy white star flowers, which are replaced by bright red berries.

There are sizable white pines here—trees that pioneered this ground when it was open and sunlit. You'll bear left at a log bench (the first of many) and just before entering a power line cut, be alert for poison ivy on the right. A mowed path leads through the shrub-filled linear clearing decorated with showy red-flowering raspberry in early summer. Back in the forest, note the hemlock scarred by a lightning strike. By the time you reach another log bench, the sound of flowing water becomes evident as you tread along the slope. Descend and bear left over a longer bridge. Some big boulders in the streambed are moss covered. Wild ginger tops one on the left.

Before long, you'll arrive at the signed intersection with a side trail to the Glen. Bear right and pass a sizable sugar maple and a multitrunked oak on the left. The trees are impressively tall and straight in this mature woodland. Reach the high-gradient stream that you first crossed up above and traverse this unnamed Lenox Mountain Brook tributary via a short bridge. It joins the larger stream a short distance below. Turn left and really feel nature's air-conditioning kick in. A cascade is visible to the right as you cross a longer span. A massive hemlock stump and trunk lie just beyond it to the left.

More picturesque cascades appear as you proceed. Watch for several species of spring wildflowers here including shinleaf, Canada mayflower, foamflower, and maidenhair fern. You'll encounter the first real ascent of the outing as you stride up over two series of schist steps, but you'll level out before too long. After a few more rock steps, you'll climb down a sturdy metal stairway to the well-situated platform overlook. A brass plaque on the outcrop relates the property's acquisition. From the platform, enjoy a fabulous sight—as Lenox Mountain Brook careens steeply down a fissure barely a couple of feet wide in places. The almost deafening roar is a major part of the ambience.

When you are ready, retrace your steps—uphill this time—back to the signed junction. Turn right and follow the slope contour past a mossy, striated boulder that resembles a ship's hull. This side of the loop is blazed with red triangles. Christmas ferns become numerous just before you enter the power line cut again. Soon you're back at the **Y** intersection with the money pipe, at which point you turn right, back to your vehicle.

DID YOU KNOW?

In the nineteenth century, farmer Romanza Stevens, whose family had owned the Glen since 1760, built a series of bridges to enable guests to access its wonders and charged 25 cents for the privilege. Stevens Glen was a major tourist attraction then for wealthy Berkshire residents and summer visitors. The site eventually lost popularity and faded into obscurity until Claire and Millard

Pryor and Zora and Frederick Pryor donated the land and a conservation restriction in 1995.

MORE INFORMATION

Open sunrise to sunset, year-round. Stay on existing trails. Mountain biking and horseback riding is allowed. Dogs must be kept leashed. Hunting is allowed in season. Motorized vehicles, fires, camping, littering, and cutting or removing trees or plants prohibited. Berkshire Natural Resources Council, 20 Bank Row, Pittsfield, MA (413-499-0596; bnrc.net).

NEARBY

For an eclectic mix of coffee shop, café, bakery, art gallery, store, and event space in an old train station, try Six Depot Roastery & Café, 6 Depot Street, West Stockbridge; breakfast and lunch served; open daily 8 A.M.–4 P.M., except Tuesday (413-232-0205; sixdepot.com).

TRIP 31
OCTOBER MOUNTAIN STATE FOREST– FINERTY POND

Location: Becket and Washington, MA
Rating: Moderate
Distance: 6.0 miles
Elevation Gain: 870 feet
Estimated Time: 3.5 hours
Maps: USGS East Lee

From a busy highway, the route follows the Appalachian Trail over a couple of wooded promontories to a serene pond ringed by mountain laurel in Massachusetts' most expansive state forest.

DIRECTIONS

From the west: Take Exit 2 (Lee) off I-90 (Mass Pike), turn left after the toll-booths and follow US 20 (Jacob's Ladder Scenic Byway) east for 4.2 miles to a paved pullout on the right and the Appalachian Trail (AT) parking area at the Lee/Becket border. The gravel lot accommodates seven cars.

From the east: From MA 8 North/US 20 in Becket, follow US 20 west for 7.8 miles to the paved pullout and AT parking area on the left.

GPS coordinates: 42° 17.577′ N, 73° 09.684′ W.

TRAIL DESCRIPTION

This is the same parking area and trailhead as the Upper Goose Pond hike (Trip 33). From the kiosk, complete with display maps of the AT route, walk east, past the kiosk to the pedestrian crossing sign on the left. Do not walk along US 20 as this is very hazardous—no shoulder in spots. Use caution crossing the highway. A narrow blue-blazed access trail leads into a forest of American beech, eastern hemlock, and white pine. Tiny and fuzzy, the paired white blossoms of partridgeberry bloom in ground-hugging mats here in early summer.

The path parallels US 20 for about 100 yards. Bits of rusted barbed wire are embedded in tree trunks on the left—evidence of former livestock pasturing. You'll soon reach the AT at a **Y** intersection. Turn left and follow the white-blazed AT uphill under red and sugar maples, bearing left at an especially large sugar maple. Cross a damp area filled with light green sensitive fern, a species

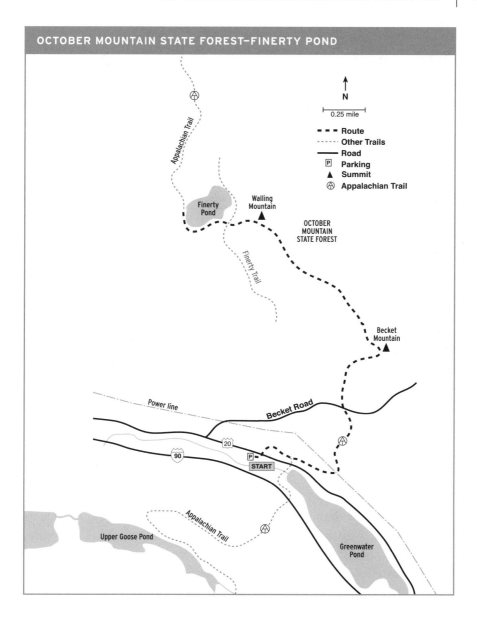

OCTOBER MOUNTAIN STATE FOREST—FINERTY POND

used to delineate wetlands. A sign attached to a tree gives distances to various landmarks along the route. A probable vernal pool lies in a depression a bit farther on the right. Turn and climb stone, then log, steps up a slope of maple, hemlock, birch, and oak. A mammoth twin white pine commands attention on the left. Canada mayflowers bloom in spring beneath the pines. Abundant beech saplings, often sprouting in clones from the same rootstock, populate the understory.

A short side trail leads to a pond access point where in late June and early July mountain laurel puts on a fine show.

Cross the first of several boulder fields. The hard gneiss rocks are alternately banded light and dark. A moderate climb brings you to a level woods road where the trail turns right. The sound of flowing water should be evident as you cross two wide snowmobile trails in rapid succession near their junction. Continue to follow the white blazes as the AT skirts a dark hemlock ravine cut by a brook. The trail soon bears left away from the wood road and enters a power line right-of-way. Various ferns and yellow loosestrife flourish in the sunny depression. Rejoin the brook under a canopy of hemlocks and cross it on moss-covered stones. The soothing sound of running water replaces the mechanized din of the highway and turnpike.

The trail climbs gradually through mixed rock-strewn woodland. Inter-mixed with the dominant beeches are multitrunked oak trees that indicate that the species may have been selectively logged here a century ago, since multiple stems sprout from cut stumps. Cross a shallow brook on stones and follow the level path up to paved Becket (Tyne) Road. You could start your hike here by parking on the wide gravel shoulder (space for just a few cars), cutting off 0.7 mile each way. Cross the pavement and climb easily under hardwoods and edging a boulder field on the slope to your right.

For a bit you'll parallel an old skid road over which logs were once hauled out. A gray gneiss boulder on the left has weathered into tiers. It lies next to a dead beech. The vast majority of the American beech trees in this forest unfortunately are diseased and dying. Minute scale insects make tiny incisions to get at the tree's sap. *Nectria* fungus invades the tree through the hole and wreaks havoc on the tree's circulatory system. An outward symptom is rough, broken black bark all over instead of smooth, gray bark. Bear right and pass over a knoll with some big nonnative Norway spruces. The narrow trail traverses striated bedrock in spots through young beech woods and ferns. Many of the beech trunks have been snapped by high winds.

A short climb takes you to the top of Becket Mountain at 2,178 feet, where you level out in a hay-scented fern glade. Concrete footings are all that remain of a tower that stood here when the summit was open. A trail register hangs from a tree. Turn left and pass a cluster of gneiss boulders to begin an easy descent through a beech, birch, and maple woodland. A rectangular flat-topped boulder on the right is capped by wild oats (a lily, not a grass) that flowers pale yellow in spring.

Begin an easy climb and cross another jumble of rocks. In early summer, red-berried elder shrubs sport crimson fruits. You'll zigzag up another slope and amble through a hay-scented fern glade under broad-leaved trees. Begin another easy descent and level out among hobblebushes in rocky woods. The large, heart-shaped leaves of hobblebush shade black-throated blue warbler nests. Soon the character of the forest changes markedly. Scattered maple trees on this flat ridgeline permit enough light to reach the forest floor for a dense layer of raspberry, ferns, elderberry, and climbing false buckwheat to thrive. The area was probably logged.

Climb again and level out on top of Walling Mountain. It might be difficult to tell that you're at 2,200 feet above sea level given the minor elevation change since the last bump along the ridge. Pass car-sized hunks of gneiss and woodland wildflowers *Clintonia* and Indian cucumber-root. The latter has modest but beautiful flowers with recurved yellow petals hanging from a second tier of whorled leaves. The descent gets a bit rougher. Patches of shining clubmoss, a nonflowering fern relative, look like a carpet of green bottlebrushes. Wood frogs and red efts wander the forest searching for invertebrate prey as the path switchbacks down.

You'll reach Finerty Trail, a wood road used by all-terrain vehicles, and cross it. Finerty Pond is visible through the trees ahead. A now wider AT leads down to a 10-foot-high laurel bush on the right and turns left to follow near the shore. If you pass this way in late June into early July, you'll be treated to a fantastic laurel flower show. About 100 feet past the laurel is a short side trail that leads to the best shoreline access point. Beavers have felled a couple of hardwoods here and a lodge is visible on the far shore.

In summer, bullfrogs bellow and green frogs announce your arrival with a little "eek" as they flee. An impressive old yellow birch stands on the left just before you tread on a cushioned path astride an angular boulder beneath hemlocks to a contemplative spot near the water's edge bordered by abundant laurel shrubs. Listen for the dry rattle of the belted kingfisher (about a foot long, with a shaggy crest) from somewhere across the pond.

Here the AT swings away from the shore. You may choose to linger and enjoy the serenity. When ready, retrace your steps some 3 miles to the parking area. Near the end of the hike, be sure to continue straight, rather than turning left to follow the AT down across US 20. It's much safer to walk back above US 20 than along the pavement.

DID YOU KNOW?

October Mountain State Forest, at 16,500 acres, is the largest state forest in Massachusetts. Writer Herman Melville, whose home "Arrowhead" in Pittsfield afforded a fine view of it, is reputed to have coined the name. Once the private reserve of William C. Whitney, President Grover Cleveland's Secretary of the Navy, the Commonwealth purchased the initial 11,000 acres from the Whitney estate in 1915.

MORE INFORMATION

Carry out all litter. No motorized vehicles, mountain bikes, horses, tree cutting, or fires permitted. Camping allowed in designated areas only. The Appalachian Trail Management Committee is responsible for maintenance, management, and protection of the nearly 90 miles of the AT in Massachusetts; volunteers do this work, with assistance from the Massachusetts Department of Conservation and Recreation. Massachusetts AT Committee, Berkshire Chapter AMC, P.O. Box 2281, Pittsfield, MA 01201 (413-528-8003; at@ amcberkshire.org; amcberkshire.org/at).

NEARBY

Jacob's Pillow Dance Festival, situated on a 220-acre former farm in Becket, is internationally renowned as a focal point for contemporary dance. A National Historic Landmark and National Medal of Arts recipient, Jacob's Pillow is home to America's longest running dance festival, founded in 1933 by Ted Shawn. The summer season extends from mid-June to late August. Located at 358 Carter Road, Becket (413-243-0745, box office; jacobspillow.org).

TRIP 32
BASIN POND

Location: Lee, MA
Rating: Easy
Distance: 3.1 miles
Elevation Gain: 290 feet
Estimated Time: 1.5–2.0 hours
Maps: USGS East Lee; trail map available online

A walk through magical mixed broadleaf and evergreen woodland, this partial loop trail is as yet a mostly undiscovered Berkshire gem and a wonderful walk to take with small children.

DIRECTIONS

From Exit 2 off I-90 (Mass Pike) in Lee, follow US 20 east (turn left after leaving the toll booths) for 4.0 miles to its intersection with Becket Road in Lee. Turn left (north) onto Becket Road and follow it uphill for 0.3 mile to a small gravel parking area (with space for about six vehicles) on the left. Watch for the sign. *GPS coordinates*: 42° 17.751′ N, 73° 09.676′ W.

TRAIL DESCRIPTION

An angular gneiss boulder at the edge of the parking area serves as a rocky portal and a portent of things to come. A few feet beyond, a map kiosk relates the fascinating and tragic history of Basin Pond. Twice—first in 1886 and again in 1968—the failure of flawed earthen dams led to multiple loss of life downstream. In 1975, the Clark-Aiken company sold the property to conservationist N. Robert Thieriot. Following his death in 1998, his estate bequeathed the land to the Berkshire Natural Resources Council in 2001.

Follow red blazes north under a closed canopy of sugar maple, red oak, American beech, black birch, and eastern hemlock. (Note: Trail blazing is slated to change to blue by 2016.) Soon you cross the first of numerous rocky brook beds filled with a jumble of gray boulders. Below the deciduous trees grow striped maple, hobblebush shrubs, and ferns, and below them, 6-inch-tall clubmosses. In contrast, in the deep shade of the hemlocks, virtually nothing grows. The path undulates through scenic woodland, making for easy walking for the first 0.5 mile.

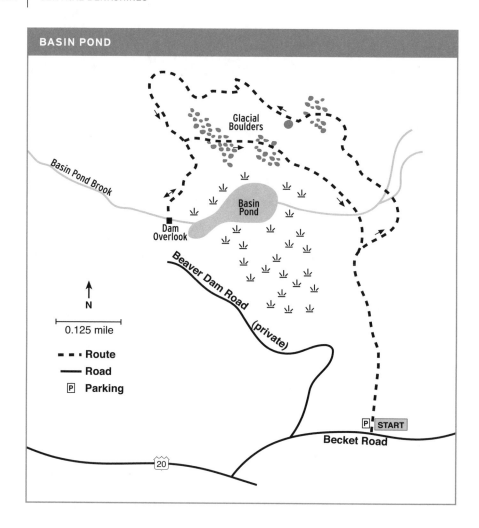

At a signed trail split, continue straight and follow the now red-triangle-blazed Upper Route easily through predominantly young beech forest. Odd flowering plants called beechdrops are parasitic on the tree's roots. They lack green chlorophyll. When seen close-up, the brownish-purple trumpet like blossoms are quite attractive, however. Yellow birch, black cherry, and white ash now appear along with the oaks. You will cross an intermittent brook bed on a large, flat capstone bridge built by master trail builder Peter Jensen and his crew. It is evident that they expended great effort throughout this trail network.

The sloping terrain is laced with rocky stream channels, most dry in late summer, and collections of angular boulders jut out everywhere from the forest floor. These are referred to as talus slopes on the map kiosk. They were certainly dropped by a retreating glacier. The hard gneiss rocks are characteristically banded dark and light.

Follow the contours of the slope roughly westward. An eye-catching red oak on the left, 4 feet in diameter, splits into twin trunks some 20 feet above the ground. Many oaks are multitrunked due to selective logging decades ago. This sun-dappled woodland, owing to the lack of major soil disturbance, is virtually free of the invasive, exotic plant species found in so many other forests of the Northeast.

Reach another signed trail split with both paths marked by painted red rectangles. Turn right onto Dam Spur Trail beneath an increasing number of red maples, to follow the quarter-mile spur trail downhill to the earthen dam and a fine view of Basin Pond. An opening filled with bracken fern and goldenrod marks the location of the dam. Crest the low rise for scenic views of wetlands and ridge, and beaver-dammed Basin Brook—a viewing platform with bench is a sunny spot for lunch or a snack. Beaver handiwork is visible in the form of lodges along the pond shore. Their U-shaped mud-and-stick dam is hidden behind hemlocks just below the deck.

Retrace your steps to the Y fork and turn right to continue. Sapling-sized mountain maples sprout up through the rocks, some topped by leathery fronds of evergreen woodfern. Farther on, the path wends between two monumental opposing glacial relics.

Soon the trail morphs into an old roadway, and along it, deep green Christmas fern flourishes. The woodland is now mostly maple and ash, at least for a while. After you reenter beech and hemlock woods, cross a brook bed where in spring water cascades over a moss-covered ledge. Bog bridges keep your feet dry as you negotiate a seepage area among yellow birches a bit farther on. Soon reach the initial intersection to close the loop. Turn right and follow the needle-cushioned treadway back to your vehicle.

DID YOU KNOW?

An eyewitness to the flood of 1886, Alvin White, age 15, recounted that floodwaters carried him out of the second story of his home and 0.25 mile downstream into the branches of a tree. His parents and two sisters perished. He described the floodwaters as "a drove of hogs tumbling down the mountain."

MORE INFORMATION

Open during daylight hours. Motorized vehicles, fires, camping, littering, and cutting or removing trees or plants are prohibited. Hunting is permitted

Mammoth glacial boulders are a highlight along the expertly constructed paths of this relatively unknown site.

in season. Berkshire Natural Resources Council is a private, nonprofit land conservation organization that protects 18,000 acres in order to preserve the rural character of the Berkshire landscape. Berkshire Natural Resources Council, 20 Bank Row, Pittsfield, MA 01201 (413-499-0596; bnrc.net).

NEARBY

Buckley Dunton Lake is the largest water body in October Mountain State Forest and a wonderful place to kayak, canoe, or fish. To find it, after leaving the Basin Pond parking area, follow Becket Road (later called Yokum Pond Road) uphill for 2.2 miles and turn left at the brown forest maintenance building. The short road ends at the dam and boat launch.

TRIP 33
UPPER GOOSE POND

Location: Becket, Lee, and Tyringham, MA
Rating: Moderate
Distance: 3.7 miles (4.7 miles with round-trip to AT cabin)
Elevation Gain: 385 feet
Estimated Time: 2.5 hours
Maps: USGS East Lee

This out-and-back hike on the Appalachian Trail reaches one of the Berkshires' most scenic ponds in a serene location reminiscent of northern New England.

DIRECTIONS

From the west: Take Exit 2 (Lee) off I-90 (Mass Pike), turn left after the tollbooths and follow US 20 east for 4.2 miles to the Appalachian Trail (AT) parking area on the right at the Lee/Becket border. The gravel lot accommodates some seven cars.

From the east: From MA 8 North/US 20 in Becket, follow US 20 west for 7.9 miles to the AT parking area on the left. *GPS coordinates*: 42° 17.577′ N, 73° 09.684′ W.

TRAIL DESCRIPTION

From the kiosk with a display map, walk east a short distance to the pedestrian crossing sign at US 20. Do not walk along US 20 as this is very hazardous—no shoulder in spots. Use caution crossing the highway! A narrow, blue-blazed access trail on the north side of the highway leads through a forest of American beech, eastern hemlock, and white pine. Paralleling US 20 for about 100 yards, it soon joins the AT. Turn right and follow the white-blazed path down to the highway.

Cross US 20 again, pass through a gap in the guardrail, and proceed down wooden steps. Old orchard trees litter the ground with apples in fall. A brown AT directional sign indicates that the side trail to Goose Pond Cabin is 1.6 miles away. Soon cross Greenwater Brook on a wooden bridge at a former mill site and arrive at the earthen dam that holds back the waters of Greenwater Pond. Turn right toward the Mass Pike; bear left under the bridge and circle up and around to cross over the westbound lanes of I-90. Cross a second

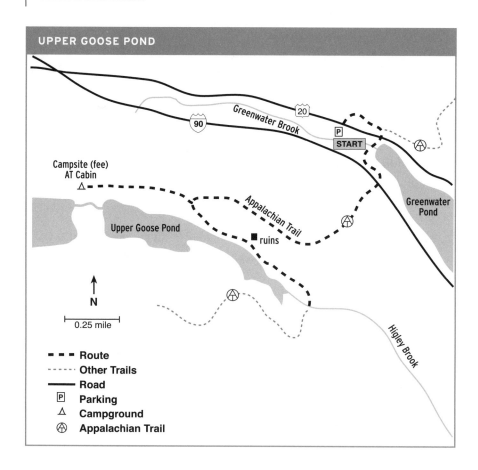

concrete span over the eastbound lanes. The October Mountain plateau looms behind you.

Reenter woodland and reach a trail split. Continue to follow the white-blazed trail, left at the fork (the other is a snowmobile corridor) and ascend fairly steeply under a canopy of sugar and red maples, white ash, yellow birch, and red oak. A metamorphic rock ledge (gneiss) pops up on the left. Bear left around the ledge and up over stone steps and past more outcrops amid the steady roar from the interstate. Ferns and green-trunked striped maple saplings, hobblebush shrubs, and beech sprouts shade evergreen clubmosses. Higher up, red oak becomes more common. After you level out briefly, watch for an impressive white ash more than 2.5 feet in diameter on the left bearing an AT blaze. Ashes provide the sturdy lumber required for ax handles and baseball bats.

As you begin climbing once again, young, shade-tolerant beech trees cover the north-facing slope along with birches, maples, and oaks. At the boundary of the Upper Goose Pond Natural Area, on the height of land, find an

So close to the Mass Turnpike, yet appearing to belong in northern New England, Upper Goose Pond is a gem.

AT trail register. You may want to peruse the register for interesting insight into the exploits of AT thru-hikers and other trail users. From here, descend gradually through small patches of hobblebush identifiable by its big, paired, heart-shaped leaves and clusters of small white flowers in spring, red fruits in summer, multihued foliage in autumn, and large, straw-colored buds in winter. The din of the highway has faded away and you're now in a different world.

An impressive gray ledge—uptilted at 30 degrees—juts out to your right as you bear in that direction. This woodland now includes mountain laurel stands and its tiny relative wintergreen. This south-facing slope encourages a dominance of oaks, through which a screened view of a ridgeline is possible. Follow the slope contour, then descend more steeply and follow an impressive gneiss ledge exposed for more than 250 feet. Brown and black rock tripe lichens cling to its vertical face, turning green only after absorbing moisture. Descend again and soon reach a signed junction indicating that Upper Goose Pond Cabin is 0.5 mile down the blue-blazed side trail. If you have the time, it's worth a visit. The cabin, which offers overnight accommodation for hikers, is situated on a laurel-studded slope above the lake. Privies are available at the cabin and at the designated camping area.

Back on the AT, continue straight on what is now an old wood road through beech, oak, black birch, and mountain laurel. Turn right, off the road, where white blazes lead down toward the lake. Reach Upper Goose Pond and turn left to follow the shoreline toward Higley Brook at the pond's eastern end. Stunning views of the 45-acre pond (elevation 1,465 feet) abound through gaps in the vegetation. You'll soon reach the site of a former sportsman's lodge—Mohhekennuck—constructed in the first decade of the twentieth century. A fallen chimney and a few foundation stones are all that remains. A short path leads to a tiny gravel beach popular as a canoe landing. Continue on the southbound AT along the shoreline through mountain laurel that blossoms pinkish-white in late June.

A thick growth of shining clubmoss carpets the forest floor at one spot on the right. White Indian pipes—parasitic on oak roots—bloom here in summer. The hardwood forest is also home in summer to many species of colorful wood warblers, camouflaged vireos, and musical thrushes. The pathway moves away from the water prior to arriving at little Higley Brook spanned by a modest wooden bridge. Golden Canada lilies bloom along this permanent water source for the pond in early July. Goose Pond Road is 1.9 miles farther, but this is the end point for our hike. Retrace your steps approximately 0.5 mile to the lodge ruins and 100 yards beyond to where the AT bears right, up the slope. Be alert, as this intersection can be easily missed.

DID YOU KNOW?

The Mohhekennuck Club, a gathering of sportsmen, was incorporated in 1909 and operated for 72 years. In 1981, the club conveyed its lands along Upper Goose Pond to the National Park Service to become part of the Appalachian Trail Corridor and serve as a wilderness preserve in perpetuity.

MORE INFORMATION

No fires permitted. Goose Pond Cabin for use by AT thru-hikers only; other camping not permitted. The Appalachian Trail Management Committee is responsible for maintenance, management, and protection of the nearly 90 miles of the AT in Massachusetts; volunteers do this work, with assistance from the Massachusetts Department of Conservation and Recreation. Massachusetts AT Committee, Berkshire Chapter AMC, P.O. Box 2281, Pittsfield, MA 01202 (413-528-6333; at@amcberkshire.org; amcberkshire.org/at).

NEARBY

Camping is available from mid-May to mid-October at nearby October Mountain State Forest in Lee. This primitive camping area has 47 nonelectric tent and RV/trailer sites on three levels including three yurts. Reservations suggested; fees apply. Located at 317 Woodland Road, Lee (413-243-1778; mass.gov/eea/agencies/dcr/massparks/region-west/october-mountain-state-forest-generic.html).

3

SOUTHERN BERKSHIRES

THE SOUTHERN BERKSHIRES REMAIN the most agricultural part of the Berkshires. Hayfields and dairy barns dot the landscape of the broad Housatonic River valley, while the valley's marble bedrock fosters lime-loving plants. The Southern Berkshires combine quaint towns and villages, pastures dotted with cattle, forests in which mountain laurel puts on a dazzling show, and summits and ridgelines that offer endless views. Some consider this section to be the most scenic in the region.

The seventeen excursions of this section include strenuous summit climbs, easy strolls in pastoral settings, spectacular waterfalls, and even some old-growth giants. For instance, magical Ice Glen (Trip 34) is a cool respite from summer heat, Guilder Pond and Mount Everett (Trip 46) offer a laurel bloom second to none, and the section's highest summit, Alander Mountain (Trip 47), boasts one of the most expansive vistas in the Berkshires, while the quartzite peak of Monument Mountain (Trip 35) is a beloved destination for many. Southern Berkshire waterfalls are justly popular with many hikers as well. Bash Bish Falls (Trip 44) is the Commonwealth's most spectacular, but Upper Race Brook Falls (Trip 45) and Sages Ravine (Trip 50) are evocative in their own right. For an easier stroll, try lovely Lime Kiln Farm (Trip 48) or the botanically renowned Bartholomew's Cobble Reservation (Trip 49). No matter what your preference of scene or level of difficulty, this section has it all.

TRIP 34
ICE GLEN AND LAURA'S TOWER

Location: Stockbridge, MA
Rating: Moderate
Distance: 1.9 miles
Elevation Gain: 580 feet (610 feet if climbing tower)
Estimated Time: 1.5 hours
Maps: USGS Stockbridge

This primordial rocky cleft, studded with mammoth hemlocks and pines, holds pockets of ice into summer. An intersecting trail leads to a summit topped by Laura's Tower with pleasing views.

DIRECTIONS

From Exit 2 (Lee) off the Mass Pike (I-90), turn left after the tollbooths and almost immediately right onto MA 102. Follow it for 4.6 miles to the Red Lion Inn in Stockbridge (merging with US 7 in Stockbridge). Turn left at the Red Lion Inn to follow US 7 south and drive approximately 0.4 mile to Ice Glen Road on the left (immediately after crossing the Housatonic River). Drive up Ice Glen Road for 0.5 mile to a small pull-off parking area on the left adjacent to a gravel driveway marked by a small sign on a wooden post for Ice Glen. Be sure not the block this private driveway! Parking is limited here to at most three vehicles. Alternate parking available at the end of Park Street (take the first left following the left turn at the Red Lion Inn). *GPS coordinates*: 42° 16.255′ N, 73° 18.674′ W.

TRAIL DESCRIPTION

Walk about 250 yards up the private gravel driveway lined by white pines; the driveway soon turns to asphalt as the grade increases. Bear left on a woodland path toward the mouth of Ice Glen, where the asphalt turns right. If you visit in summer, you'll notice a refreshing drop in temperature as you reach the trail. You are greeted by a jumble of large boulders and the twin pillars of a white pine on the left and an eastern hemlock on the right that serve as a kind of portal to the glen. The oldest hemlocks here are more than 300 years old. Truck- and cabin-sized boulders are green with moss and topped by ferns. Mosquitoes are often plentiful in this area, so be prepared.

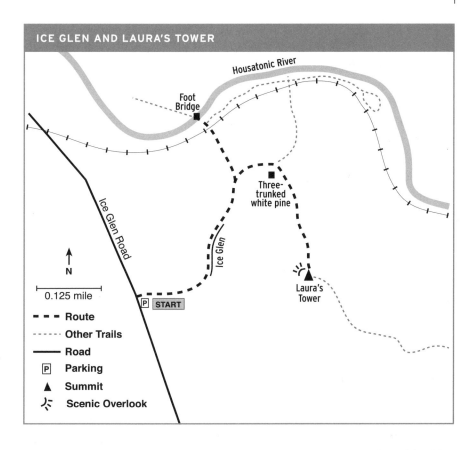

Native stone steps, artfully placed by nationally renowned trail builder Peter Jensen, lead into the defile as the slopes that create the glen rise abruptly on both sides. Ice Glen inspires a sense of awe. Occasional blue blazes on trunks and rocks help guide the way, but the best way to stay on route is to follow the numerous stone steps so expertly arranged that their placement might seem totally natural. The cool microclimate in this north-south-trending cleft, shaded by towering evergreens and insulated by massive quartzite boulders, is quite amazing. On a sultry summer afternoon, I measured the air temperature in two of the glen's cold pockets to be 22 to 25 degrees Fahrenheit cooler than where I had parked my car in the shade. If you gaze down into the crevices between the boulders, don't be surprised to see remnant ice here, even in summer. In fact, it is so cool that atmospheric moisture condenses to form an eerie ground fog.

Although the Glen is less than 0.25 mile long, there is no need to rush through this haven of tranquility. There are some narrow crevices, as well as twists and turns. Watch your footing—the rocks often are wet and a bit slippery in spots. Still, this is not a dangerous place to walk if you have the proper footwear and use caution.

According to geologists, the final act of the Glen's creation began some 15,000 years ago during the last ice age. The meltwaters from a receding glacier just north of here, as well as the effects of freezing and thawing over a multitude of years, loosened chunks of quartzite from the opposing hillsides that subsequently tumbled down into the cleft between them.

Listen to the vocalizations of hermit and wood thrushes (characterized by flutelike phrases), the trill of dark-eyed juncos, the effervescent tune of the tiny winter wren, and a multitude of other songs from warblers and vireos. Birdsong adds to the atmosphere here in late spring and early summer, as do the massive, straight trunks that reach for the sky. Four of the state's tallest white pines are located in Ice Glen—one of them is 151 feet high! The oldest are between 170 and 200 years of age.

Some trunks of fallen trees, covered in moss, serve as nursery trees for tree seedlings that have taken root in their decaying wood. Low spots collect pools of tannin-stained water. You'll shoulder past one massive boulder on the left that is decorated with rock tripe lichen. It's leafy and green when wet, but platy and brown when dry.

The trail levels out and emerges into a bowl. Some 30 feet to the left of the path is an inscription on the moss-covered rock face that commemorates donation of the property to Stockbridge in 1891 by David Dudley Field. Birches, maples, and ashes (some massive) merge with the evergreens here. Begin a gradual descent and soon arrive at an intersection with unmarked Laura's Tower Trail at a massive, triple-stemmed white pine. Turn right onto it. Going straight takes you down to the Housatonic River, which you will do upon your return from the summit.

Years ago, a violent windstorm snapped off a number of mature pines as evidenced by dead snags. Young deciduous trees compete for light under the pines. At the signed Y intersection, turn right toward Laura's Tower and begin a gradual ascent. Large maples and ashes and a few oaks thrive here too. The trail turns, and the grade increases and reaches cabin-sized boulders. The straight, furrowed trunks of bigtooth aspens are members of this woodland that also includes red oak, birches, red maple, beech, and far more undergrowth (mostly mountain laurel and sapling striped maple) than beneath the shade of pines and hemlocks. Climb the slope by way of a few moderate switchbacks.

You'll reach a sturdy 30-foot-high tower, its base 1,465 feet above sea level, and climb the steel staircase to a viewing platform just about level with a low canopy of oak, red maple, cherry, birch, and ash. While once a 360-degree panorama was possible, young tree growth has obscured much of the view to the south. A horizontally mounted brass locator disc is inscribed with the names of promontories, their elevations, and the airline distances to them. It was installed in 1931 and still serves the hiker well today. The most prominent feature to the northwest is West Stockbridge Mountain (Trip 28), 4.5 miles away. Mount Greylock lies 25.5 miles to the north, but is only visible after leaf fall. The namesake of the tower, Laura, was David Dudley Field's daughter-in-law.

A yellow-blazed trail opposite the path you ascended on leads to Beartown State Forest, several miles distant, but retrace your steps to the intersection with Glen Trail at the three-trunked white pine. Turn left at the intersection, toward the Glen for now. Then before long, turn right for a brief excursion to the Housatonic River and cross a footbridge into a totally different environment. Descend easily through a stand of monolithic white pines and listen for the high-pitched, cheerful whistle of brown creepers, which nest behind slabs of loose bark. Road noise becomes more evident as you reach a power line right-of-way filled with raspberry bushes.

Cross the active Housatonic Railroad line (use caution!) to a stone arch and steel suspension bridge built in 1936 by local engineer Joseph Franz. Tread across the wooden decking to obtain a fine view of the Housatonic River. A brass plaque announces that it replaced the original bridge given to Stockbridge in 1895 by Mary Hopkins Goodrich, the founder of the Laurel Hill Society. A trail sign is located on the far side of the river at an accessible trailhead where Park Street terminates. There is space for six to eight vehicles.

A 1.2-mile-long (roundtrip, out and back) wheelchair-accessible path—the Mary V. Flynn Trail—was created along the river in 2003. If you are inclined to add mileage to your route, follow it between the railroad tracks and the Housatonic. Benches are located along the route and a stand of maidenhair fern delights the eye near the looped end.

When ready, retrace your steps to return to your vehicle. Be sure to bear right at the Y intersection shortly after entering the forest.

DID YOU KNOW?

The Laurel Hill Association, the oldest village beautification society in America, was founded in 1853 by Mary Hopkins Goodrich, the great-granddaughter of Stockbridge missionary founder John Sargeant. The Association, which has acquired well over 400 acres in town over the years, seeks to improve the quality of life and the environment in Stockbridge.

Pockets of ice often persist into June within the crevices formed by the massive boulders of Ice Glen.

MORE INFORMATION

Trails open sunrise to sunset, daily, year-round. Access is free. There are no restroom facilities at the trailheads. Vehicles, horses, camping, and fires are prohibited. The trail is maintained by the Laurel Hill Association. Ice Glen is owned by town of Stockbridge; Stockbridge Town Hall (413-298-4714). Laura's Tower Trail is owned by Laurel Hill Association, P.O. Box 24, Stockbridge, MA 01262.

NEARBY

The Red Lion Inn, an iconic Berkshire landmark, is one of only a few continually operating inns from the eighteenth century. Established in 1773, the Inn was rebuilt in 1897 and has 125 guestrooms, and offers formal and informal dining and live entertainment. Located at 30 Main Street, Stockbridge (413-298-5545; redlioninn.com).

TRIP 35
MONUMENT MOUNTAIN RESERVATION

Location: Great Barrington, MA
Rating: Moderate
Distance: 2.7 miles
Elevation Gain: 765 feet
Estimated Time: 2.0 hours
Maps: USGS Great Barrington, USGS Stockbridge; trail map available online

It would be daunting to name another hike as steeped in history as Monument Mountain. Some 20,000 hikers annually enjoy a pilgrimage to its fabulously picturesque summit of jagged quartzite boulders capped by pitch pine. This is one of my favorite hikes.

DIRECTIONS

From the east: Take Exit 2 (Lee) off the Mass Pike (I-90), turn left after leaving the tollbooths, and almost immediately bear right onto MA 102. Follow MA 102 for 4.6 miles to its intersection with US 7 at the Red Lion Inn in Stockbridge. Drive south on US 7 for 3.0 miles to the reservation entrance on the right. The large gravel parking area has room for many vehicles.

From the south: At the junction of US 7 and MA 23 in Great Barrington, take US 7 north for 5.9 miles to the reservation on the left. *GPS coordinates*: 42° 14.598′ N, 73° 20.121′ W.

TRAIL DESCRIPTION

Begin at the map kiosk shaded by Depression-era red pines, where trail maps are sometimes available. Visitors are encouraged to support the nonprofit The Trustees of Reservations with a donation. From the kiosk, turn right and head north on blue-blazed Hickey Trail. White pines, black cherries, red maples, red oaks, and white ashes tower above sapling American beech, witch hazel, and striped maples that have smooth greenish trunks. Given that Monument Mountain Reservation was established in 1899, the forest here has had more than 100 years to regenerate. As a result, many white pines and oaks are of impressive proportions. Note the shade-intolerant pioneering gray birches that are dying out. Initially paralleling the slope contour, the well-trodden trail

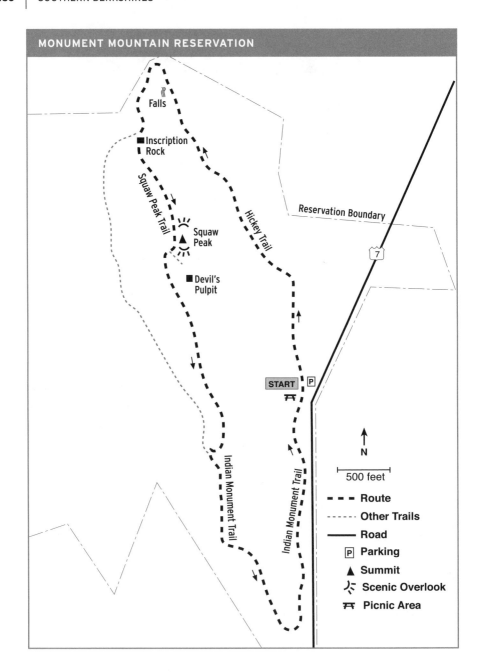

MONUMENT MOUNTAIN RESERVATION

Falls

Inscription
Rock

Squaw Peak Trail

Hickey Trail

Reservation Boundary

7

Squaw
Peak

Devil's
Pulpit

START

P

N

500 feet

Indian Monument Trail

Indian Monument Trail

Route
Other Trails
Road
P **Parking**
▲ **Summit**
⅄ **Scenic Overlook**
☰ **Picnic Area**

passes a twin white oak adjacent to a quartzite boulder. White oaks produce sweet acorns relished by wild turkey and deer.

After about 5 minutes of steady walking, the path bears left to begin a moderately steep climb. A white-blazed trail turns right and descends, but continue uphill. Note the massive red oak, fully 3 feet in diameter (whose acorns in contrast to white oaks are bitter with tannic acid) on your right. Soon you'll enter the year-round shade cast by eastern hemlocks at the junction with a wider wood road; bear right. The grade for the time being becomes gentler. Gray, angular quartzite boulders become more numerous. A talus slope, created by repeated freezing and thawing over eons, is visible after leaf fall to the left and then a formidable cabin-sized boulder hems in the trail. Crusty lichens and little polypody ferns have colonized its tough, erosion-resistant surface.

To your left, a jumble of massive quartzite boulders reposes at the foot of the mountain. Talus (meaning "toe" in Greek) slopes like this are rare in the region. The hard gray rock is actually 600-million-year-old beach sand compacted under tremendous heat and pressure deep underground. A verdant mat of ferns caps some slabs.

Bear right, then left under columnar hemlocks and pines, to continue the moderate climb. A mature white pine produces thousands of winged seeds relished by birds and small mammals. At a point where the path turns left and ascends more steeply, an attractive hemlock ravine has been carved by flowing water. Level out at the top of the ravine and traverse a log bridge over the crystal-clear brook. Soon you'll arrive at a short spur trail on the left that leads to a close-up view of a modest waterfall. Mammoth icicles in frozen flow drape the outcrop in winter. The tall and straight tree reaching skyward to the right is a tulip tree, a southern species near its northern range limit here.

Return to the main trail and walk up more steeply now. Hemlocks, red maples, and oaks mix as you push up the ravine. The path narrows and ascends in steps to the reservation's northern boundary marked by red blazes on the right. Turn left at the big outcrop and level out among mountain laurel shrubs. After negotiating another log bridge, you'll be heading up through boulders decorated with flaky rock tripe; this lichen greens up after rains.

You'll reach the signed intersection with Indian Monument Trail on the right, but continue straight on what is now Squaw Peak Trail. To the right rests Inscription Rock, whose chiseled prose relates the story of the property's donation in October 1899 by Virginia Butler in memory of her elder sister, Rosalie. From here the path winds up and over quartzite staircases and among boulders to the summit at 1,642 feet. Gnarly pitch pines, so prominent on Cape Cod, white pines, and mountain laurel dominate these craggy heights.

Watch your footing as you wend your way among the quartzite blocks. Conditions may be hazardous in winter. A number of excellent vantage points invite one to relax and enjoy the view. To the north is the bluish double

Hikers gaze down on Devil's Pulpit, a columnar formation which is a favorite perch of turkey vultures.

hump of Mount Greylock, almost 30 miles distant. Much closer, at the foot of Monument Mountain, sprawls the vegetated waters of Agawam Marsh. To the south, the Housatonic valley, lined with erodible marble, is spread out below, and Mount Everett looms to the southwest. Not all these landmarks are visible from the same perch, so move about carefully to get the full effect. When you reach a well-signed intersection with a blue-blazed spur trail on the left leading to a viewpoint for Devil's Pulpit, tread up another rock staircase and soon gaze down upon this columnar formation, a favorite haunt of turkey vultures. The summit can be a fine place from which to witness the spring hawk migration up the valley in late April.

When ready to resume walking, continue on Squaw Peak Trail as it descends moderately, cutting across contour lines and over rocks on the west flank of the mountain. In early summer, listen for the sweet trill of yellow and olive pine warblers that nest among the pine boughs. The male's song is reminiscent of the dark-eyed junco, another breeder here. You'll level out as you reach signed Indian Monument Trail. Turn left under towering white pines, hemlocks, large oaks, red maples, beech, and black birch. This old wood road has a gentle grade, and many walkers use this longer route in reverse to reach Inscription Rock and on to the summit.

The trail turns left to parallel the highway. Under hemlocks, the path undulates over rocks as it follows along the foot of the mountain's eastern talus slopes. A triple-trunked chestnut oak stands on the left. Recognize the species by its rough, platy bark and wavy-edged leaves. Evergreen woodfern and the smaller polypody thrive among the boulders. Some slabs have impressive dimensions and rusty faces where oxidation has revealed the iron content of the rock.

Momentarily, you'll arrive back at the picnic area under the red pines where you began. Note the pileated woodpecker excavations (foraging holes) on a young pine left of the path.

DID YOU KNOW?

On August 5, 1850, writers Nathaniel Hawthorne and Herman Melville made a now storied picnic excursion on the mountain. A thunderstorm forced them to take shelter in a boulder cave. It is said that Melville's conversations that day with his friend Hawthorne inspired his seafaring tale *Moby Dick*.

MORE INFORMATION

Open daily, year-round, sunrise to sunset. Admission is free; on-site donation from nonmembers welcomed. Picnic tables available, no restroom facilities on-site. Dogs must be leashed at all times. Motorized vehicles, mountain bikes, rock climbing, and fires are prohibited. Hunting is allowed in season. The Trustees of Reservations, Western Regional Office, P.O. Box 792, Stockbridge, MA 01262 (413-298-3239; thetrustees.org).

NEARBY

Taft Farms, specializing in pesticide-free, sustainable agriculture since 1961, has a produce retail store, greenhouse sales, and deli. Heirloom varieties, ethnic varieties, and GMO-free varieties are their specialties. Located at 119 Park Street North in Great Barrington. Taft Farms is open daily, 8 A.M.–6 P.M. (413-528-1515; taftfarms.com).

WRITTEN IN STONE

The great natural beauty of the Berkshires has for centuries drawn creative minds to these hills and valleys. Look no further than the Tanglewood Music Festival as proof. Whether in music, art, or literature, "the purple hills," as Roderick Peattie called them, have inspired many a poet and novelist. Best known among them is a triumvirate of contemporary nineteenth-century authors—Hawthorne, Melville, and Thoreau.

No doubt the single most chronicled meeting of literary minds ever to occur in the Berkshires took place on August 5, 1850, when Nathaniel Hawthorne and Herman Melville hiked Monument Mountain. There, it is said, they became fast friends. As the story goes, Hawthorne, who had a home in Lenox, gave Melville contemplative material for his most famous work, *Moby Dick*, while they huddled together in a cave during an electrical storm. Perhaps the bedrock ledge, over which a falls drops during the wet months, was the "cave" in question.

Melville wrote his masterpiece while residing at Arrowhead (which now houses the Berkshire Historical Society), his home on Holmes Road in Pittsfield. Literary lore has it that the sight of Mount Greylock, or Saddleback Mountain as it was known then, dusted with snow, inspired the character of the great white sperm whale. Each year on the anniversary of their outing, a group of aficionados re-creates the hike of these literary giants.

Other influential nature writers have tromped Berkshire paths, Henry David Thoreau foremost among them. Thoreau hiked to Greylock's summit via the still extant Bellows Pipe Trail (Trip 10) and wrote about it in *A Week on the Concord and Merrimack Rivers*. William Cullen Bryant, who spent ten years in Great Barrington, wrote about Monument Mountain in his poem by the same name in 1824. He penned many other works with natural-history themes at his home in nearby Cummington. Closer to our own time, nature writer Hal Borland, a longtime resident of Connecticut's Litchfield Hills, wrote evocatively about the bucolic landscape he so loved. A trail at Bartholomew's Cobble Reservation (Trip 49) is named in memory of the writer who passed away in 1978.

A quote from Thoreau seems like a fitting motto for the hiker: "An early morning walk is a blessing for the whole day." Perhaps hiking the Berkshires will inspire you as well.

TRIP 36
TYRINGHAM COBBLE RESERVATION

Location: Tyringham, MA
Rating: Easy to Moderate
Distance: 2.0 miles
Elevation Gain: 380 feet
Estimated Time: 1.5 hours
Map: USGS Otis

This wonderful loop trail takes you through bucolic pastures to a pair of ancient resistant bedrock promontories, known as cobbles, with splendid views of Tyringham Valley.

DIRECTIONS

From Exit 2 (Lee) off the Mass Pike (I-90), turn left after the tollbooths and then immediately right onto MA 102. After only 0.1 mile, turn left onto Tyringham Road (Main Street in Tyringham) and follow it through the valley for 4.2 miles into the village of Tyringham. Turn right onto Jerusalem Road and drive 0.2 mile to the gravel parking lot on the right with space for about fifteen vehicles. *GPS coordinates*: 42° 14.589′ N, 73° 12.332′ W.

TRAIL DESCRIPTION

After reviewing the information posted on the map kiosk, walk through a wooden gate to your right toward a small red cattle barn and turn left to follow along the edge of an expansive hayfield, where eastern bluebirds raise their young in nest boxes provided for them. After passing through another gate at the foot of the cobble, turn right and follow along a row of venerable sugar maples. Cobble Loop Trail is marked with circular blue-paint blazes on wooden posts, although the mowed trail is easy to follow.

The lower slopes of Cobble Hill, first cleared for pasturage by colonial farmers in the late eighteenth century, are now clothed in grasses, goldenrods, asters, crab apple trees, and white pine seedlings. Upon reaching a signed fork, turn left to walk uphill on the Cobble Loop Trail (continuing straight leads to a metal footbridge over tumbling Hop Brook and Main Road). One hundred yards beyond, bear left and push steeply upward. Swing right and enter a white pine stand at a barbed-wire fence. Pass through a wooden gate, turn left, and

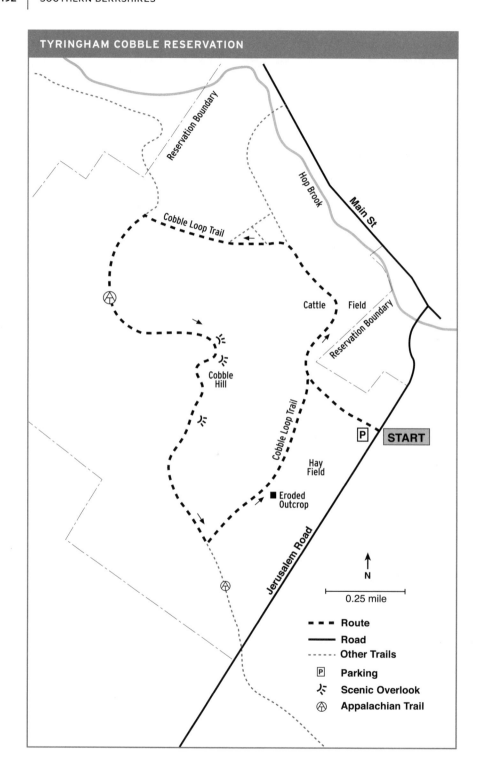

TYRINGHAM COBBLE RESERVATION

Reservation Boundary

Hop Brook

Main St

Cobble Loop Trail

Cattle   Field

Reservation Boundary

Cobble
Hill

Cobble Loop Trail

P | START

Hay
Field

■ Eroded
Outcrop

Jerusalem Road

N

0.25 mile

- - - **Route**
—— **Road**
····· **Other Trails**
P **Parking**
⅄ **Scenic Overlook**
Ⓐ **Appalachian Trail**

walk uphill following blue blazes on trees that include white ash, sugar maple, and black birch. Beware of poison ivy lining the path here.

You'll level out after a short climb, on a wide treadway among an all-too-thick growth of winged euonymus, also known as burning bush (another invasive exotic shrub), and the aforementioned barberry. Several species of woodpeckers frequent these woods, including hairy, red-bellied, and yellow-bellied sapsucker. Sapsuckers forsake the north in autumn. Omnivorous red squirrels collect and store pine seeds, gather mushrooms, and relish the occasional meal of bird's eggs or nestlings. The trail climbs easily under good-sized white ash trees. Walk through a stone-wall gap. Pass an eroded and closed trail on the left under a canopy of sugar maple, black cherry, birches, and hemlocks.

Soon reach a junction with the Appalachian Trail (AT) and bear left among white pines, cherries, white ashes, and fern growth. Green-barked striped maple and sapling American beech populate an understory layer as this easy climb continues. The route then leads through a disturbed woodland characterized by invasive shrubs and vines—winged euonymous, buckthorn, Japanese barberry, and Oriental bittersweet. The trail steepens and enters a shady hemlock stand. Amble past a magnificent oak left of the path, which switchbacks up the slope. Turn left at a gneiss boulder and follow along a stone walls built of flat chunks of the same material. More sizable oaks appear, and one on the right—over 3 feet in girth—still has rusty barbed wire embedded in it.

Reach an intersection (the other end of the discontinued trail), turn right, and pass through a wooden gate into a small meadow at the crest of the first cobble. From this grassy summit, you can see fine views of the valley, nearly 500 feet below. Continue over the top, negotiate another wooden gate, and enter a shallow wooded saddle between the two cobbles. A layered gneiss ledge on the left may catch your eye before you climb amid hemlocks. Turn left to continue along the second hill's contours. The gneiss rock's stubborn resistance to erosion created these cobbles. Note the large hophornbeam with a dead limb that juts into the path. At over 20 inches in diameter, this is a giant of the species.

The path now crosses ledges that sport a growth of ferns called common polypody—a species almost always anchored to rock. The scant soils atop this second, slightly higher cobble (elevation 1,340 feet) restrict the growth of trees making for low stature, windswept woodland of oak, hemlock, and a prickly field form of juniper. Excellent views of the valley are visible from atop the ledge via a short side trail on the left.

The combined AT/Cobble Loop Trail begins to descend, reaching a brushy field at a low bedrock outcrop littered with mica crystals. Idyllic views of the valley may convince you to linger for a bit. Follow the path through the field where buckthorn thrives. Bear left, heading gently downhill past fuzzy stems of staghorn sumac, juniper, crab apple, raspberry, and goldenrod.

Bear left again, following the margin of the shrubby field being invaded by trees until you reach a signed intersection where the AT and Cobble Loop Trails part ways. Turn left on the blue-blazed Cobble Loop and cross the field that holds apple and crab apple trees to reenter the woodland. Pass through another swinging wooden gate, turn right, and amble downhill. A sandstone outcrop is just ahead. Over eons, the forces of wind and water have pockmarked the soft stone of Rabbit Rock. As in *Alice's Adventures in Wonderland*, this rabbit seems oddly out of place.

Follow the base of Cobble Hill and soon reach an unmarked junction. Turn left, climb briefly, then drop back down, and bear left. The parking area comes into view as you reach a fence line and parallel the upper edge of the hayfield. More barberry indicates human disturbance as you pass through a wooden gate at a barbed-wire fence. You'll continue down a short distance to close the loop. Turn right and retrace your steps back to your vehicle.

DID YOU KNOW?

Tyringham Cobble has a very intriguing upside-down sort of geology. It turns out that the rock atop the formation is 500 million years old, older than the layers beneath it! Geologist Daniel Clark made that discovery in 1895, surmising that a chunk of another mountain had broken off and flipped upside down.

MORE INFORMATION

Owned and managed by The Trustees of Reservations. Open year-round, daily, sunrise to sunset. Free admission; an on-site donation from nonmembers is welcome. Dogs must be kept on a leash at all times; mountain biking is not permitted. Seasonal hunting is permitted. (413-298-3239; westregion@ttor.org; thetrustees.org).

NEARBY

The best-known structure in Tyringham is Santarella, or the gingerbread house. It was the home of English sculptor Sir Henry Hudson Kitson

A pock-marked block of stone–disconnected from the underlying bedrock–has been weathered into a fantastic form.

(1865–1947), who lived and worked in the United States, sculpting many representations of American military heroes, including the famous Minuteman statue in Lexington, Massachusetts. The structure once housed an art gallery, but is currently not open to the public. It is available for rental. This cottage is located at 75 Main Street.

TRIP 37
BECKET LAND TRUST HISTORIC QUARRY AND FOREST

Location: Becket, MA
Rating: Easy to Moderate
Distance: 3.0 miles
Elevation Gain: 400 feet
Estimated Time: 1.5–2.0 hours
Maps: USGS Otis, East Lee; trail map available online at becketlandtrust.org/quarry/quarry_forest_trail-map.htm

The Becket Quarry is a place frozen in time. This hike takes you past rusting vehicles, sheds, and other abandoned artifacts of the granite industry. A well-marked trail network winds through northern hardwood forest, among granite boulders, over a small brook, and to a panoramic vista.

DIRECTIONS

From the west: From Exit 2 (Lee) off the Mass Pike (I-90), turn left after the tollbooths onto US 20 and follow it for 12.1 miles to Bonnie Rigg Hill Road on the right. Follow it uphill for 1.3 miles to an intersection with Quarry and Algerie Roads. Turn left onto Quarry Road and drive 0.9 mile to the gravel parking area on the right.

From the east: From Exit 3 off the Mass Pike (I-90) in Westfield, turn right after the tollbooths onto US 20 and follow it west for 12.2 miles through Westfield, Russell, Huntington, and Chester, and into Becket to the intersection of Bonnie Rigg Hill Road on the left. From this point, see directions above. *GPS coordinates*: 42° 15.082′ N, 73° 01.216′ W.

TRAIL DESCRIPTION

A kiosk with trail map and trail register is situated at the far end of the circular gravel parking area. Visitors are asked to sign in and out. Your education begins at interpretive panel #1 on the parking lot island, where a Sullivan drill rests. The device was used to drill the holes into which explosive charges were placed. This is where granite blocks were loaded for final processing in the neighboring town of Chester.

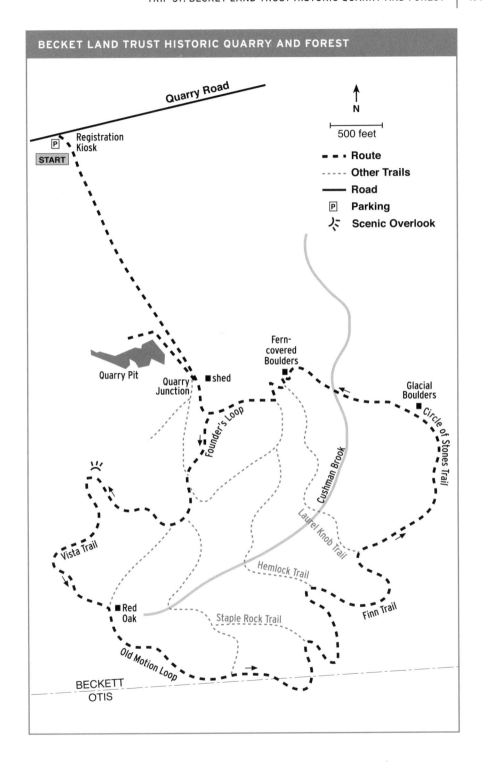

BECKET LAND TRUST HISTORIC QUARRY AND FOREST

Quarry Road

P Registration
Kiosk
START

N

500 feet

- - - Route
- - - - Other Trails
—— Road
P Parking
Scenic Overlook

Quarry Pit

Quarry ■ shed
Junction

Founder's Loop

Fern-
covered
Boulders

Glacial
Boulders ■

Circle of Stones Trail

Cushman Brook

Laurel Knob Trail

Vista Trail

Hemlock Trail

Finn Trail

■ Red
Oak

Staple Rock Trail

Old Motion Loop

BECKETT
OTIS

To begin, walk past the cable and up the old roadway beneath a canopy of oaks, maples, American beech, yellow birch, and eastern hemlock. In spring, a stunning wildflower display includes trout lily and red trillium. You'll soon reach the grout pile, a tall heap of granite chunks, on the right—the waste material resulting from decades of quarrying. Do not climb the pile. In summer, when warm moist air comes in contact with the cold air flowing from the bottom of the pile, it condenses to form fog. A bit farther, on the left, is a small grout pile. You'll soon reach Quarry Junction.

Several old roadways radiate from here. The skeleton of an electrical generator shed and the rusting hulks of two trucks, one used to haul the granite to Chester for processing, and the other a large tank that held compressed air that powered the drills, are visible (see panels 5 and 7). When you return here later, you'll have the opportunity to gaze upon the impressive water-filled quarry pit, a short distance to the right. Follow the leftmost road past the shed, and immediately reach an intersection at the stiff-leg derrick site. Opposite the derrick, on the right, is the rail grade to motion—a small quarrying site where granite blocks were cut. Stay left to proceed past rusting artifacts of a bygone era; the quarry operated for about 100 years until 1950.

Turn right onto Founder's Loop, blazed with blue diamonds, and head gently uphill among granite boulders. Rocks seem more abundant than trees here! You'll reach a junction with the old roadway again at a wall of massive granite blocks; turn left. The rock is the same hue as the beech trunks. On the right is a rusty section of rail. Soon you'll reach a Y intersection where Founder's Circle Trail bears left. Continue straight on red-diamond-blazed Old Motion Loop Trail. Unfortunately, after leaf fall, the din of the Mass Pike is audible. At another fork in the trail, follow the right path gently uphill approximately 100 feet to green-diamond-blazed Vista Trail. Turn onto Vista Trail.

The hillside is clothed in oak and beech. A fungal disease that blackens the bark of beech trees disfigures many of them here. Although mostly young, one larger specimen displays the scars left by a black bear that climbed this tree for its tasty nuts. You'll arrive at the vista point and granite bench—a nice spot to linger. Tree clearing has opened up a fine view to the east, of Round Top Hill.

Bear left around the bench. A few young red maples show scars where a moose tore strips of bark off with its incisors to get at the nutritious inner bark. The fact that the bark was torn off to a height of 7 feet is a telltale sign. A gentle descent leads past a gray granite outcrop on the right. A few red spruce and hemlock appear, but American beech still rules this woodland. Beech sprouts prolifically from cut stumps and by means of runners. Rejoin Old Motion Loop (blazed with red diamonds in both directions). Across from

Porcupines dine on leafy greens in summer and den in rocky crevices.

you, perhaps 50 feet away, stands a massive, leaning red oak. The giant—more than 4.5 feet in diameter—is pocked with den cavities where branches have rotted out.

Turn right on Old Motion Loop and you'll soon pass a large, multitrunked white pine on the left that is more than 3.5 feet in diameter. Amble along easily through beech and hemlock woodland. Granite was quarried at what is now a depression on the right where big angular blocks are piled. Sullivan drill marks are evident on some. The depression, rimmed by winterberry shrubs, fills with water and may well serve mating salamanders as a vernal pool in spring.

You'll reach an intersection on the right with Staple Rock Trail, which is blazed with purple and yellow diamonds; follow it. Descend gradually. At a hemlock-shaded junction with Finn Trail, blazed with pink diamonds, turn right. Walk down on the wide old road past pockets of hay-scented fern that yellows and dies after frost. Descend briefly and turn left onto a single track. Note the hobblebush shrubs. Shining clubmoss and ferns carpet the ground. Follow along the rocky contour of the hill and reach an intersection with Hemlock Trail, blazed with both white and light green diamonds, at a small boulder field. Turn right to continue on Finn Trail. A slope drops off on the left to a flat terrace. Large rotting stumps are testimony to logging decades ago. Young beech trees and red maples are now dominant.

You'll soon pass the first of several recently logged areas. The cutting is being done in collaboration with the Massachusetts Division of Fisheries & Wildlife and the Natural Resources Conservation Service to create 40 acres of shrubland habitat that is attractive to the endangered New England cottontail.

After an old roadway joins your path on the left, you'll reach a three-way intersection with yellow-blazed Laurel Knob Trail on the left and Circle of Stones Trail on the right. Turn right onto Circle of Stones Trail, blazed with orange diamonds. You'll soon cross a small brook on short wooden bridge sections. You may opt to cross on stones as the wooden spans are in disrepair. The shady woodland is home to singing hermit thrushes from spring through fall and tiny spring peepers year-round. These little tree frogs blend in marvelously with the leaf litter. Bear right to briefly walk along the edge of a logged area filled with beech sprouts, then reenter woodland.

Descend through more hemlocks and then cross a tote road. A cabin-sized glacial boulder protrudes from the forest floor at the edge of a small clearing and the tall common reed stalks hint at a wetland off to the right. You'll reach flowing Cushman Brook and cross it on flagstones. Hemlock and red maple thrive in the boggy soil.

The path then leads up through granite boulders—most capped by a luxuriant growth of polypody fern, spinulose woodfern, and clubmoss. This spot has the feel of a temperate rainforest. Porcupines may well den in the rock crevices. Now walk more steeply uphill and reach a wider roadway without signage. The trail bears left and then away from the faint road, widens again, and reaches an intersection with Laurel Knob Trail. Continue to the right and head uphill on Circle of Stones Trail. Soon you'll reach a more obvious and signed intersection with Founder's Loop. Turn right and follow the blue-diamond markers to the plaque erected to recognize the donors who made acquisition of this land possible. Turn right to retrace your steps to Quarry Junction.

Just past the generator shed turn left and walk past the guy derrick site (panel #6) gently up to the edge of a quarry pit with 65-foot-high granite walls. Watch your footing and stay back from the edge. Granite steps lead up to a terrace where you'll see granite blocks into which quarry workers cut their initials and the years 1868 and 1894. When ready, retrace your steps back to the parking area.

DID YOU KNOW?

When the Labrie Stone Products Company announced plans in 1999 to obtain the land and restart large-scale quarrying operations, hundreds of local concerned citizens donated the funds that enabled the Becket Land Trust to purchase the 300-acre property.

MORE INFORMATION

Owned and maintained by the Becket Land Trust, which invites public participation and support. Open year-round during daylight hours. Visitors enter at their own risk. Pets must be kept under control. Hunting is permitted in season. Collecting and motorized vehicles are prohibited. Becket Land Trust, Inc., P.O. Box 44, Becket, MA 01223 (landtrust@becketlandtrust.org; becketlandtrust.org).

NEARBY

The Becket Arts Center of the Hilltowns is a multidisciplinary community arts center located in historic Seminary Hall, Becket's first consolidated school built in 1855. The center offers events, workshops, and exhibitions; 7 Brooker Hill Road (at the intersection of MA 8 and Main Street). Open weekends mid-May through October. Contact 413-623-6635 or becketartscenter.org for hours of operation.

TRIP 38
MCLENNAN RESERVATION

Location: Tyringham and Otis, MA
Rating: Easy to Moderate
Distance: 2.5 miles
Elevation Gain: 448 feet
Estimated Time: 1.5–2.0 hours
Maps: USGS Otis; downloadable map currently not available

Though but a short distance from a paved road, this nearly 600-acre property feels remote. It is an enchanting walk through tranquil woodland, beside a cascading brook, that takes you to a picturesque beaver pond.

DIRECTIONS

From US 20 and MA 102 in Lee, adjacent to Exit 2 (Lee) off the Mass Pike (I-90), turn onto MA 102. After only 0.1 mile, turn left onto Tyringham Road (Main Street in Tyringham) and follow it south through Tyringham Valley for 4.2 miles to Tyringham village at Jerusalem Road on the right. Continue on Tyringham Road for another 2.0 miles, passing an Appalachian Trail (AT) parking area on the right after 0.9 mile, to Fenn Road on the left. Park on the right along Main Street, off the pavement. There is room for several vehicles. *GPS coordinates*: 42° 13.331′ N, 73° 10.998′ W. Hikers may also drive down Fenn Road and park at the reservation sign; note that the road is not plowed in winter.

TRAIL DESCRIPTION

Carefully cross Main Street onto gravel Fenn Road. Follow the bucolic lane across Camp Brook and enter a hardwood forest. The roadway is lined by majestic sugar maples, which may be outfitted with plastic tubing for sugaring season. Eastern hemlocks soon create a dense shade as you curve right and walk steadily uphill. A slope rises rather steeply to the left. Barbed wire engulfed by expanding tree trunks and a stone walls—built of tough quartzite and gneiss rocks—confirm an agricultural past and the former presence of livestock—most likely sheep. The road splits as you attain its high point; bear right on the wide lane. Be sure to remain on the road as it is bounded on both sides by posted private property.

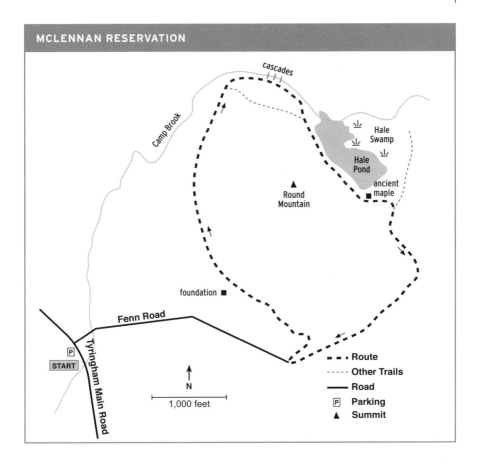

MCLENNAN RESERVATION

cascades

Camp Brook

Hale
Swamp

Hale
Pond

▲ Round
Mountain

ancient
■ maple

foundation ■

Fenn Road

Tyringham Main Road

P
START

N
1,000 feet

- - ■ Route
- - - - - Other Trails
——— Road
P Parking
▲ Summit

Except for the venerable sugar maples, the forest is uniformly quite young. In addition to maple, black cherry, white ash, American beech, and bitternut hickory form the canopy. An enormous white ash on the right is noteworthy. As the roadway begins to bear left and split, reach the signed trailhead on the left, where regulations are posted. There is no map kiosk. Tread uphill on a yellow-blazed path under hardwoods including oaks, and scattered hemlocks. Climb moderately at first. Then, advance more steeply for a bit, following a low stone walls to its terminus at which point the pathway turns left. The trail, bordered by ferns and prince's pine clubmoss, is shaded in summer by black birch, beech, maple, and oak. Ledge outcrops of quartzite and a few chunks of milky quartz add variety to the landscape. Above them hang the thick ropelike vines of wild grape. Sugar maples predominate.

Stride through a gap cut through a fallen oak and soon arrive at a mammoth specimen on the right fully 4 feet in diameter. The angular mound of Round Mountain is rock strewn—a talus slope, as viewed from the level path (some

High gradient Camp Brook cascades over bedrock slabs and into a series of small, dark pools.

older blazes along the route are white). Proceed past the end of a rock wall to the large fieldstone foundation of a former farm building on the left. Some blocks are massive and must have presented quite a challenge to the hardy farmers moving them into place. Lengths of rusty pipe protrude from the earth here and there. Beyond the foundation, young deciduous forest contrasts with the shaded hemlock woods along the mountain slope. Continue a gradual climb on the old roadway, still bounded by remnant barbed wire and enter a darker forest of hemlock and shade-tolerant black birch. You're skirting the base of Round Mountain.

Before long, the pleasing murmur of flowing water is audible from the left. Catch glimpses of high-gradient Camp Brook through the foliage as you climb and bear right. Creeping partridgeberry sports coral-red fruits in late summer. Reach a Y fork, bear left, and amble down to the stream. The brook cascades over bedrock and into small, dark pools. Continue up, along the bank, on a needle-cushioned treadway past a quartzite staircase over which the stream flows to pleasing effect. The brook and trail soon turn sharply left and make their way to Hale Pond, an on-again, off-again beaver pond.

Emerge from the shadows to the bright light of the shrub-filled pond at a beaver dam. A lodge—home to the big rodents—is situated just upstream of the dam. The rounded form of Long Mountain rests beyond. Fiery red maples add vibrant color in autumn along the pond shore, making for a picturesque setting. The route resumes through forest briefly before exiting left through a stone-wall gap and following a narrow path amid young growth along the pond margin. Watch for mammal droppings or scat, including those of river otter, on the footpath. Soon reenter woodland on a level trail, leaving the pond behind. The forest morphs to northern hardwoods as you reach a huge sugar maple at the end of a stone walls on the left, its massive arms seemingly reaching out to embrace the visitor.

Bear left around the behemoth, following the wall and fern-lined path to a signed T intersection with a wood road (an extension of Fenn Road). Turn right and walk downhill beneath abundant hardwoods. The road becomes rocky where it drops more steeply and bears right. At the bottom of the hill to your right, you can glimpse the stone and cement walls of an abandoned spring house surrounded by wire fence. Some pipe sections are visible in the road. Pass through a small goldenrod-filled light gap to a split and bear right to continue on the more traveled route past more hanging grape vines and bear right. Several immense boulders repose on the hillside above you on the right. Stay straight at the blazed split, and in 150 feet arrive back at improved Fenn Road and the signed trailhead. Follow the level roadway right, 0.5 mile back to your vehicle along Main Street.

DID YOU KNOW?

According to author Charles W. G. Smith, Camp Brook is named for the fact that Mahican Indians once established their maple sugaring camp along the brook each March. They tapped the trees, collecting the sap in birch bark buckets. After transferring the sap to larger containers, they used hot stones to boil off the excess water.

MORE INFORMATION

Open year-round, daily, sunrise to sunset. Free admission; donations from nonmembers are welcome. Dogs must be kept on a leash at all times; mountain biking not allowed. Seasonal hunting is permitted. Owned and managed by The Trustees of Reservations (TTOR) (413-298-3239; thetrustees.org/places-to-visit/berkshires/mclennan-reservation.html).

NEARBY

Ashintully Gardens, another TTOR property, is located off Sodem Road in Tyringham. Ashintully Gardens (the name in Gaelic means "brow of the hill") is a 120-acre property that boasts award-winning plantings by composer John McLennan. Open Wednesdays and Saturdays from the first Wednesday in June to the second Saturday in October; admission free to individuals (413-298-3239; thetrustees.org/places-to-visit/berkshires/ashintully-gardens.html).

POOL PARTY

In many ways, vernal pools are oddities. They're called pools, but they usually dry up by midsummer. They're referred to as "vernal" because the breeding frenzy they host happens in early spring, sometimes while snow still coats the ground. As ephemeral as they are, vernal pools are absolutely essential to a group of creatures able to reproduce nowhere else. These creatures are mole salamanders, wood frogs, and fairy shrimp. None can exist without these fleeting woodland water bodies.

Mole salamanders are a group of species that spend the bulk of their lives beneath the leaf litter. When they do emerge during the first early spring rains, when temperatures are about 40 degrees (late March or early April in the Berkshires), they head cross-country, straight for depressions flush with snowmelt and vernal moisture. The pools must contain leaves, sticks, and other woodland detritus that forms the basic energy source for the minute creatures that provide food for the salamander and wood frog larvae.

The mating ritual of spotted and Jefferson salamanders is really something to behold as the animals writhe and twirl in love's embrace. The males drop packets of sperm that females pick up with their cloacas. She will lay a fist-sized mass of gelatinous eggs that are attached to twigs beneath the surface. The eggs hatch into gilled salamander larvae and must reach sufficient size to survive on dry land before the pool disappears under the blazing summer sun.

But why rely on such undependable water sources? Well, because vernal pools by definition don't contain fish. Fish eat salamander (and wood frog) eggs and larvae. Only the toxic red-spotted newt of local beaver ponds is able to coexist with the finned tribe. Other salamander species breed in brooks, bogs, or other locations out of the reach of fish. So it is only the large yellow-polka-dotted spotted salamander and the less common blue-flecked Jefferson salamander that put all their eggs in one basket, so to speak.

If you have the opportunity to get out during what biologists call the "big night," when the bulk of salamander movement to vernal pools occurs, wear your rain slicker, take a flashlight, and prepare to be amazed by the spectacle of dozens of mole salamanders and wood frogs, driven by age-old instincts, crossing highways and country lanes en route to breeding pools they may have visited each spring for ten or fifteen years. It's a sight you won't soon forget.

TRIP 39
BENEDICT POND LOOP AND LEDGES

Location: Great Barrington and Monterey, MA
Rating: Easy to Moderate
Distance: 3.0 miles
Elevation Gain: 240 feet
Estimated Time: 1.5–2.0 hours
Maps: USGS Great Barrington; trail maps available online at the trailhead and at park headquarters

This loop includes circumambulation of one of the Berkshires' most scenic ponds, spiced up with a fine laurel bloom in late June, and a splendid viewpoint from The Ledges.

DIRECTIONS

From the intersection of US 7 and Monument Valley Road (near Monument Mountain High School) in Great Barrington, turn onto Monument Valley Road. Drive for 2.0 miles to Stoney Brook Road on the left. Turn onto Stoney Brook Road and follow it 2.7 miles to Benedict Pond Road on the left. It is 0.5 mile to the day-use area on the right. The first and larger lot is at the boat ramp, the second at the beach. *GPS coordinates:* 42° 12.226′ N, 73° 17.403′ W.

TRAIL DESCRIPTION

From the small gravel parking area adjacent to the beach, head left past a kiosk with trail maps and along a wooden fence and concrete retaining wall at the pond shore to an observation deck spanning the dam's spillway. Interpretive leaflets may be available (the interpretive trail actually begins at the boat launch parking lot and ends here). Soon you'll turn left onto blue-blazed Pond Loop Trail. Descend a few wooden steps, and then turn right under a canopy of mixed hardwoods—especially oaks. Witch hazel, scattered mountain laurel, and striped maple dot the rocky woodland beneath the canopy, while ground-hugging wintergreen is abundant. At informal trail splits, remain on the blue-blazed trail as it generally follows the pond shore past tenting sites with picnic tables.

You'll cross a graveled road (a snowmobile trail in winter). Although predominately oak, the forest now includes red maple, black birch, and a few hop hornbeams. At the junction with Mount Wilcox Trail, stay straight on the blue-blazed path and enjoy glimpses of 35-acre Benedict Pond through

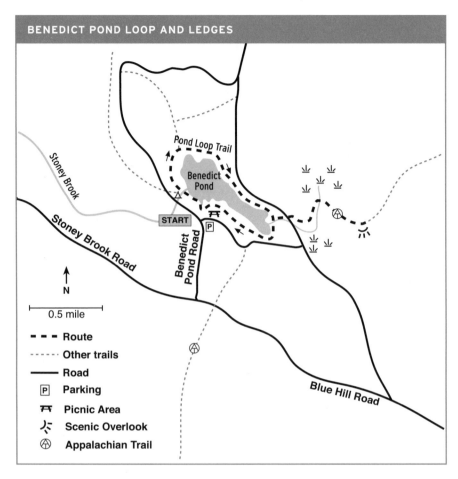

BENEDICT POND LOOP AND LEDGES

Pond Loop Trail

Benedict Pond

Stoney Brook

Stoney Brook Road

Benedict Pond Road

START

N

0.5 mile

- - - **Route**

---- **Other trails**

—— **Road**

P **Parking**

⛺ **Picnic Area**

🏃 **Scenic Overlook**

Ⓐ **Appalachian Trail**

Blue Hill Road

gaps. You'll pass through a couple of low, wet areas marked by cinnamon and sensitive ferns—wetland indicators. Sensitive fern has persistent brown bead-like spore capsules. Pointed stumps, cut by beaver, are also in evidence. Witch hazel and mountain laurel border the treadway. Ten-foot-high arrowwood shrubs, with arrow-straight branches and blue berries, line the path as you traverse bog bridges and a small wooden span through damp ground vegetated with tall reed canary grass.

As you round the northwest end of the pond, red maples become common. Pass by some white pines and a patch of trailing arbutus on the left—the state flower—that blooms delicate pink in May, hence its other moniker: mayflower. A wooden bench at the water's edge invites a pause. In winter, ice anglers seeking pickerel, largemouth bass, yellow perch, and bluegill dot the otherwise featureless white expanse. Tilted gray gneiss bedrock outcrops pop into view on the left. Towering straight white pines grew up in woodland crowded by others of their kind. White ash, black cherry, yellow and gray birches, and beech join the mix, although massive oaks still rule. Camouflaged brown creepers hitch their way up the furrowed pine trunks looking for insect eggs and larvae hidden in bark crevices.

Cross another small wooden span and continue under pines and oaks. Patches of delicate maidenhair fern soon appear. An 18-foot-high gneiss outcrop juts up 50 feet to the left. After another dampish area with a few small spruces, hobblebush, and beaked hazelnut shrubs lead to a second wooden bench under pines and a fine view. Note the Pond Loop Note Box affixed to a tree. A modest clump of low-growing sheep laurel shrubs are easy to overlook just left of the bench, while highbush blueberries hug the shore. Watch for a beaver lodge. The trail undulates past taller mountain laurels and enters a dense hemlock stand. Common polypody fern is anchored to a picturesque ledge. Water dripping from and through crevices in the rock creates a fantastic icicle display in winter. Watch your footing, as this section can be very icy!

Continue to a broad roadway that accommodates snow machines. Bear right to follow it gently downhill. To your left is another tilted gneiss spine. A few white paper birches are to be admired on the left. Black birches meanwhile populate the rising slope beyond. After passing a stand of spruces on the right, arrive at the AT intersection. Turn left to follow the white-blazed AT north toward The Ledges, about 0.75 mile, or 15 minutes distant. Walk uphill easily at first, under oak, maple, and birch. Level off and observe more ledges—some dotted with leafy brown rock tripe, a lichen that turns green after a rain.

Bear left and ascend rocky steps tight along a rock face for the hike's first real elevation gain. The path wends its way through oaks and laurel above the left slope of a rocky ravine. At the head of the ravine, turn right to cross a wooden bridge over an outflow stream that originates a few feet upstream at a sizable beaver swamp. You can view the swamp by detouring straight a short distance first. Clamber over bedrock, bearing right, and walk along the opposite side of the 40-foot-deep defile near the verge, amid oaks and pines. After leaf fall, distant blue ridgelines become evident. Lowbush blueberry and tiny, shiny-leaved wintergreen thrive in the acidic soil beneath the trees—of shorter stature here on the bony ridge top.

Watch for more trailing arbutus just before the vista point. When you reach a benchlike outcrop at a gap in the woody vegetation, you have arrived at The Ledges. A more convenient spot for a relaxing snack with splendid views would be tough to find! Mount Everett, at 2,624 feet high, is visible as the high point along the third ridgeline to the southwest. In winter, two downhill ski runs are also apparent.

When ready, retrace your steps to the wide roadway, turn left, cross the brook over a wooden bridge set on handsome mortared stone abutments, and turn right to follow the blue-and-white-blazed trail around the southeast end of the pond. After a small spruce stand and a large yellow birch, negotiate the soggy ground safely via a series of bog bridges. Northern white cedar trees, or arborvitae, between the treadway and the pond are unusual for this area. These flat-needled evergreens are generally bog denizens. After a minor brook, the trail bears right to hug the shore. But shortly the AT veers left and up to the wood road; walk straight ahead to continue on Pond Loop Trail. The Benedict Pond shoreline is here bordered by a dense growth of evergreen mountain laurel that blooms luxuriantly in late June.

Although not as showy as laurel, hobblebush shrubs have conspicuous ocher buds in winter and white flower doilies in spring. The flower heads include both tiny fertile flowers and larger infertile ones that attract the attention of pollinators. Pass through a hemlock grove and by picnic tables—a sure sign that you are back at the boat ramp. A kiosk is also situated at this end of the loop (trail maps and interpretive leaflets may be available here). At the paved road, turn right toward the beach parking area and your vehicle.

DID YOU KNOW?

Benedict Pond was built by the Civilian Conservation Corps (CCC) in 1934 and is named for Fred Benedict, a local dairy farmer who owned the surrounding land. In 1921, the Commonwealth acquired the property from lumber dealer Warren H. Davis, who had cleared off much of the timber, and the former estate of Fred Pearson.

MORE INFORMATION

Open daily, year-round, sunrise to sunset. A small per-vehicle charge applies Memorial Day weekend through Labor Day weekend. Restrooms and drinking water—at day-use area—available seasonally. A composting toilet is available year-round at the campground. Pets must be on 10-foot-maximum leash at all times, and owners must have proof of current rabies vaccination. Camping available in designated area year-round; reservation required mid-May through mid-October. Off-season camping, mid-October through April, is on a first come, first served basis. All-terrain vehicles are permitted on designated trails May through November only. Snowmobiles permitted with 4 inches minimum of hard-packed snowbase. Alcoholic beverages are prohibited.

Enjoy splendid views of the rounded form of Mount Everett from the bench-like outcrop known as The Ledges.

Open to hunting in season; 69 Blue Hill Road, P.O. Box 97 Monterey, MA 01245 (413-528-0904; mass.gov/eea/agencies/dcr/massparks/region-west/beartown-state-forest.html)

NEARBY

For breakfast and lunch options, and well-regarded baked goods, try Monterey General Store, perched on a bank of the Konkapot River. The store is housed in a post-and-beam structure dating back to 1780. Open daily. Located at 448 Main Road (413-528-5900; monterey-general-store.com).

TRIP 40
EAST MOUNTAIN AND ICE GULCH

Location: Sheffield and Great Barrington, MA
Rating: Moderate
Distance: 7.2 miles
Elevation Gain: 680 feet
Estimated Time: 4.0–4.5 hours
Maps: USGS Great Barrington; ATC Map of AT in MA and CT;
MA sections 7–9

This out-and-back hike on the Appalachian Trail (AT) combines splendid views of the Housatonic Valley and Taconic Range with the cooling breezes emanating from the rocky cleft known as Ice Gulch. The return offers a second opportunity to take in the stunning vistas.

DIRECTIONS
From the traffic signal in downtown Great Barrington at Castle Street and US 7, drive south 1.25 miles to Brookside Road on the left (Brookside later becomes Brush Hill Road and then Homes Road in Sheffield). Take it for 2.0 miles to the AT crossing. Parking is available off pavement on the left. *GPS coordinates*: 42° 09.286′ N, 73° 20.469′ W.

TRAIL DESCRIPTION
Follow the AT eastward, gently up into woods of sugar maple, hickory, black birch, and massive white pines. Canada mayflower (wild lily of the valley) graces the forest floor. Note the spreading, dead wolf pine on the left that matured in what was once an open field. A residence is visible off to the right, but the trail soon veers left, away from it. Chunks of quartzite dot the ground as witch hazel and striped maple comprise the understory. The path meanders through this woodland, but soon begins climbing more steeply.

You'll arrive at gneiss boulders and a ledge outcrop covered with flaky brown rock tripe lichen. The route leads up a stone staircase, the first of several you'll encounter. The soils and hence the vegetation change dramatically. Soils in pine/oak woodlands like this are drier and more acidic. Chestnut oak and root sprouts of American chestnut, as well as lowbush blueberry, live in this sandy soil. A sharp turn to the right is indicated by a log across the trail ahead

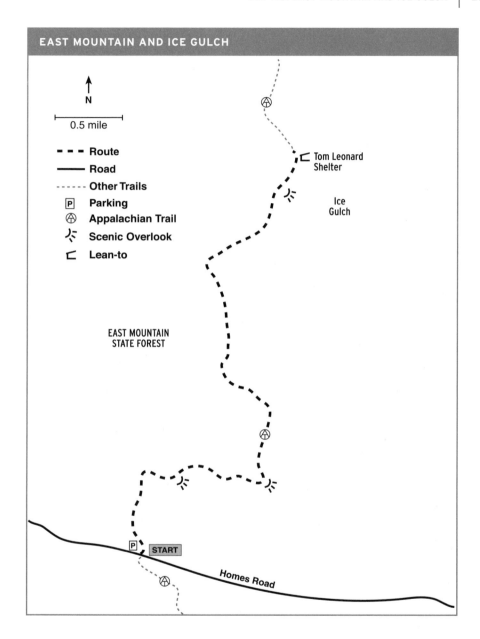

EAST MOUNTAIN AND ICE GULCH

N

0.5 mile

- - - Route
——— Road
- - - - - Other Trails
Ⓟ Parking
Ⓐ Appalachian Trail
⋏ Scenic Overlook
⊏ Lean-to

Tom Leonard
Shelter

Ice
Gulch

EAST MOUNTAIN
STATE FOREST

Ⓟ START

Homes Road

painted with the word "Stop." You'll climb along a ledge outcrop and turn right to amble over it. Listen for the *drink-your-tea* song of the eastern towhee.

Next, stride up a steep, sloping gneiss outcrop and glance back for screened views of the Taconics and Mount Everett. But better views await you. Huckleberry shrubs border the rock. Distinguish this blueberry relative by its resinous, sticky leaves, and pinkish, rather than white, flowers. Huckleberry soon becomes ubiquitous. In late May or early June, you'll detect the sweet smell of mountain azaleas and their pink blossoms. Another pink flower to watch for this time of year is the pink ladyslipper orchid.

The trail undulates under oaks and reaches a split boulder. Cross the springfed flow through it on a short wooden span. This forest of oaks and red maple has a shorter stature; leathery bracken ferns line the treadway. But you'll soon pass through taller woodland with witch hazel in the understory. Winterberry, a native groundcover with shiny leaves and bright red fruits, is loaded with fragrant oil of wintergreen. Listen for the slow *beer-beer-bee* refrain of breeding black-throated blue warblers in late spring and early summer. They're partial to mountain laurel for nest sites.

Chestnut oaks dominate again atop the rocky spine of East Mountain. At a trail junction, bear left, walk up, and then drop easily via a switchback to a low gneiss ledge. Take in the fabulous views from atop it, but be mindful of the sharp drop-off. The expansive scene across the Housatonic Valley to Mount Everett is exhilarating. You'll continue to follow the undulating AT north, past another split boulder; descend into a gully watered by a spring, and climb out. You'll arrive at another open vista atop an exposed ledge shared by two pitch pines. On a clear day, the views southwestward to New York's Catskills are striking.

Pass another exposed boulder-top viewpoint at 1,790 feet elevation (not as stunning as the previous two), briefly scramble over another outcrop and you'll reach a narrow wood road. Walk right 40 feet, then left. Wild sarsaparilla blooms here in late spring. Cross a moss-lined flow under an oak canopy and continue on the undulating path. White oaks briefly mix with other oaks. Stride around a big, slanting boulder to screened views of the Taconics, and listen for the ethereal flutelike song of the hermit thrush. Drop into a damp spot where the rich, black soil beneath oaks nourishes wild geranium and interrupted fern. Soon, the closed canopy includes the northern hardwood yellow birch. Oaks dominate and some, among a jumble of big boulders, are of an impressive size. After gaining ground, mountain laurel and huckleberry proliferate. The first hemlocks make an appearance in a shallow cleft, while a bit farther, cinnamon fern fills a swale on the left. You'll negotiate more rocks, stride along a jutting ledge, and then walk through a seepage area. A blue-blazed side trail leads down to the Tom Leonard Shelter.

Follow the AT left for another 0.1 mile, across a brook, up and through a tight squeeze in the ledge, and along a sheer cliff face. The path bears right to an evocative view of Ice Gulch, but be careful of the drop-off! The boulder-filled ravine is shaded by hemlocks. Climbing into the gulch is unsafe and not

Cool air and a peaceful atmosphere emanates from the boulder-filled ravine known as Ice Gulch.

recommended. Do enjoy the cool air and peaceful atmosphere. This is the turnaround point for the hike. When ready to start back, retrace your steps along the well-blazed AT to Homes Road and your vehicle, 3.6 miles distant.

DID YOU KNOW?
The lean-to shelter is named for Tom Leonard, an AT ridge runner who passed away suddenly in 1985 at a young age. The shelter was built in 1988 by volunteers of the Appalachian Trail Committee of the AMC with materials flown to the site via helicopter by the Air National Guard.

MORE INFORMATION
The Appalachian National Scenic Trail is managed by the National Park Service and maintained by volunteers of the Appalachian Mountain Club's Berkshire Chapter; amcberkshire.org; Jim Pelletier, Chair, AT Committee; at@amcberkshire.org. East Mountain State Forest is managed by Massachusetts Division of Conservation and Recreation, Regional Office, P.O. Box 1433 (740 South Street), Pittsfield, MA 01202 (413-442-8928).

NEARBY

For a picnic meal after your hike, give the Bistro Box a try. It's a little roadside stand with tasty treats including fresh milkshakes made with local ice cream. After returning to US 7, turn left and drive south a short distance to 937 Main Street (US 7), Great Barrington (413-717-5958). Open Mondays, Tuesdays, and Thursdays–Saturdays, 11 A.M.–7 P.M., Sundays, 11 A.M.–5 P.M. Closed Wednesdays, except in summer.

TRIP 41
JUG END STATE RESERVATION & WILDLIFE MANAGEMENT AREA

Location: Egremont, MA
Rating: Easy
Distance: 2.9 miles
Elevation Gain: 365 feet
Estimated Time: 1.5 hours
Maps: USGS Great Barrington; trail map available online and may also be available at parking area

Bucolic meadows with a stunning backdrop of ridges clothed in mixed woodlands beckon hikers to enjoy a landscape reverting to a time before commercial development. This is a great hike to take with young children, and a fine place to bird watch or cross-country ski.

DIRECTIONS
From the intersection of US 7, and MA 23/MA 41 in Great Barrington, turn onto MA 23/MA 41 and drive south for 4.0 miles. Turn left onto MA 41 south (at Mill Pond) and in 0.1 mile turn right onto Mount Washington Road. Follow it for 1.7 miles to Jug End Road on the left. Stay on Jug End Road for 0.5 mile and turn right into the large gravel parking area. *GPS coordinates*: 42° 08.904′ N, 73° 26.995′ W.

TRAIL DESCRIPTION
The Jug End Loop Trail begins at the far (south) end of the parking area near the concrete footing of the former barn's silo. The massive deluxe cattle barn that once stood here was turned into a hotel in 1935. A brief climb in two steps leads to an old wood road where you turn right to follow blue blazes. Sugar maple, white ash, and black cherry form a canopy over the path. Signs of former habitation include daffodil and yew plantings and lengths of rusty barbed wire. A substantial stone walls dissects the meadow below to your right. Up the slope to your left is an old apple orchard.

On the right, columnar bigtooth aspens rise before an easy rolling descent, and a sizable sugar maple stands on the same side. Reach a field on the left bordered by apple trees. You'll walk easily along its right perimeter, passing

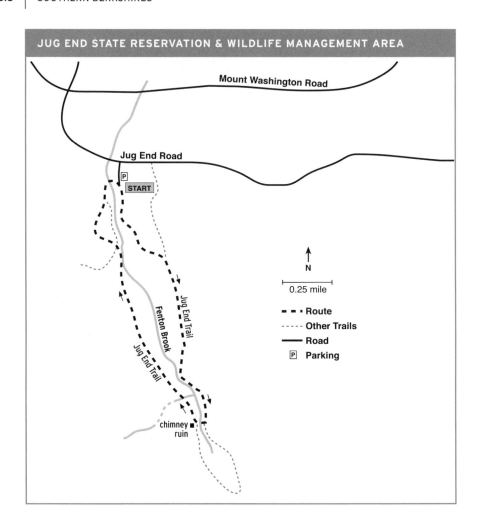

JUG END STATE RESERVATION & WILDLIFE MANAGEMENT AREA

Mount Washington Road

Jug End Road

P

START

N

0.25 mile

▪ ▪ ▪ Route
------- Other Trails
▬▬▬ Road
P Parking

Jug End Trail

Fenton Brook

Jug End Trail

chimney ▪
ruin

---

trees heavy with pinkish-white blossoms in early May. The flowering apples attract buzzing pollinators and birds that feed on insects.

Reenter deciduous woods of maple, cherry, ash, and birch that shade the tall shrub witch hazel. You'll cross two small streams and soon arrive at a dark wall of planted Norway spruces. The path skirts the spruce plantation. On your left is a brushy tangle of raspberry canes, cherry, Japanese barberry, and multiflora rose. Chestnut-sided warblers prefer early successional habitats like this. Listen for the *pleased, pleased, pleased to meetcha* refrain heard in the late spring and early summer. No plant life exists in the total shade of the spruces in contrast to the shrubs thriving in the forest opening. Native grape and exotic, invasive oriental bittersweet vines crowd the trail. The grape vines cause no harm to the supporting trees.

You'll soon find yourself surrounded by deciduous woodland of aspen, maple, ash, and a few white pines. At a more open mowed field, the path hugs the woodland edge where oaks, maples, and white birches—the latter in a row—flourish. You are walking in a bowl bordered by ridges. The fine view from your right (west) to left includes Mount Whitbeck, Mount Sterling, and, beyond the radio towers, Mount Darby. A number of ski runs once cut the slopes of Sterling (elevation 1,980 feet). Bear left, reenter broadleaf woodland with some pine, and curve right onto an old wood road. More old barbed wire remains here.

When you are back in the forest, you'll notice the copious sugar maple seedlings as you make your way along a sometimes wet road cut deeply into the earth from years of former use. Reach a mowed hillside meadow. Some New England farmers joke that their cows have longer legs on one side of their bodies in order to graze such hillsides. Shad (juneberry) trees show white-petaled blossoms before they produce leaves in late April along the field margins. Pass a marble boulder near a big spreading sugar maple and continue past the end of a treeline separating this meadow from another beyond it. The path continues to follow the upper field edge. The sound of flowing water in the valley soon fills the air.

Head back into the forest and over a series of bog bridges through soggy ground. Here you may find American woodcocks, which are chunky "shorebirds" that have long bills perfectly suited to extract earthworms from moist soil. Below to the right is a shaded hemlock gorge from which the sound of flowing water is now unmistakable. As you walk among the hemlocks in summer, the cooler microclimate results from their deep shade. Hard, gray schist litters the road. Red trillium blooms in spring around an old cellar hole that rests on the right just before the brook comes into view.

At the fork in the road, bear right following blue blazes and stones to cross Fenton Brook. You'll probably be surprised to come upon a stone fireplace and chimney ruin in the midst of a hemlock forest where the trail turns right. This was once a cabin of the Jug End Resort. Follow the old roadway under hemlock, ash, black birch, yellow birch, red maple, and oak to where mountain laurel appears.

Descend easily on the old road to cross a rocky feeder stream on stones. One chunk of milky white marble has been elegantly polished by the flow. This open forest of maturing hemlocks—some tall and straight—is evocative. But soon the woodland is once again dominated by sugar maple and white ash. Cross a handful of minor feeder streams during your gradual downhill ramble. Violets—yellow, white, and purple—adorn the woods, and jack-in-the-pulpit

Jug End Loop Trail skirts a large, sloping meadow, beyond which rises a ridgeline clothed in mixed hardwoods.

holds forth under his canopy of maroon and green. Likewise, nonflowering plants such as Christmas, sensitive, and lacy maidenhair ferns grace the forest floor.

A rock wall on the left once kept in sheep. You'll approach Fenton Brook and bear left, then right at another old roadway. Reach a brushy field, and at a **Y** intersection, turn right. A view of the ridge again appears as the path continues to follow the brook downstream. You'll cross a tiny flow on a short wooden span to a **T** intersection. Little yellow warblers and Baltimore orioles pour out their songs from perches in late spring and early summer.

Instead of following the blazed trail to the right, turn left and follow the field edge, bearing right to reach a grassy track. I must admit to a bias in favor of fields and other open areas where views are likely and wildlife may be more plentiful along the interface between field and forest. And besides, this is a just a short detour. Bear right at the grassy track, then reach another **Y** intersection and turn right again. You'll soon join the path you shunned earlier and follow it left, downstream, along the brook past ancient Norway spruces as well as other ornamentals—forsythia, arborvitae, and rhododendron. Turn right to cross the sturdy wooden bridge and amble back to your vehicle.

DID YOU KNOW?

The somewhat odd name Jug End is actually derived from the German word Jugend, meaning "youth." For 40 years, beginning in the 1930s, the property was a booming year-round resort and ski area known as Jug End Barn. Many young people enjoyed family visits to the Jug End Resort.

MORE INFORMATION

Open sunrise to sunset, year-round. Access is free. Day-use only parking permitted. Pets must be on 10-foot-maximum leash, attended at all times; owners must have proof of current rabies vaccination. Carry in, carry out trash policy. Motorized vehicles and alcohol beverages prohibited. Hunting permitted in season. Mount Washington State Forest, RD 3, East Street, Mount Washington, MA 01258 (413-528-0330; mass.gov/eea/agencies/dcr/massparks/region-west/jug-end-state-reservation-and-wildlife-management-area.html).

NEARBY

Mill Pond, at the intersection of MA 23 and Mount Washington Road, is a favorite locale of area bird watchers because it attracts an interesting variety of waterfowl and other birds that prefer wet habitats. Common gallinule, a rare breeder in Massachusetts related to the American coot, has nested in the area. Pull off the pavement onto the wide gravel shoulder, as there is no formal parking area. Viewing is best done from your vehicle with binoculars.

TRIP 42
QUESTING RESERVATION

Location: New Marlborough, MA
Rating: Easy
Distance: 2.3 miles
Elevation Gain: 300 feet
Estimated Time: 1.5 hours
Maps: USGS Tolland Center, USGS Ashley Falls, USGS Great
Barrington; trail map available online

**This loop trail showcases a forgotten history of early colonial
settlement. Towering hardwoods and conifers now shade traces
of Leffingwell, but a sense of former human presence is almost
palpable.**

DIRECTIONS
From the intersection of MA 57/MA 183 and MA 23 in Monterey, take MA
57/MA 183 south and east for 2.3 miles to the village of Hartsville; continue
on MA 57/MA 183 for another 2.6 miles to New Marlborough Hill Road
on the right. Follow New Marlborough Hill Road for 0.6 mile to a hillside
gravel parking lot on the left with room for 8–10 vehicles. *GPS coordinates*: 42°
07.749′ N, 73° 15.020′ W.

TRAIL DESCRIPTION
Pass by a metal gate and map kiosk, heading gradually and steadily uphill on a
wide gravel roadway. An intermittent brook has carved a shallow ravine to the
right. In fall, the predominant sugar maples produce a shower of orange and
yellow leaves. Quartzite boulders and a variety of ferns including interrupted,
sensitive, Christmas, bracken, long beech, and the delicate maidenhair variety
border the roadway.

Beneath a canopy of white ash and red maple, the spindly, spreading form
of witch hazel puts forth modest yellow flowers in autumn, when you would
least expect it. Indian cucumber root and false Solomon's seal bloom here in
early summer. After the road levels off, a layer-cake schist outcrop juts out
from the forest floor on the left. Another ledge shows off a 6- to 10-inch-thick
milky-white quartz vein. Pass an intersection with a single-track road on
the left and continue on the wide roadway to emerge into a wildflower filled
meadow after 10 to 15 minutes of walking.

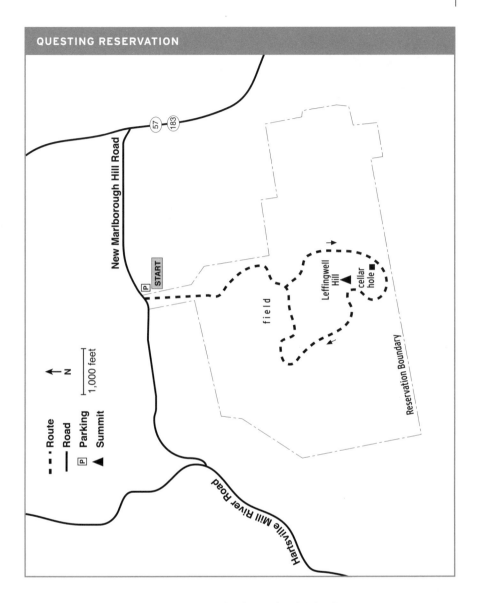

QUESTING RESERVATION

Follow the wide-mown path left along the field edge; in summer enjoy watching colorful butterflies in this 17-acre meadow including monarch, tiger swallowtail, red admiral, and pearl crescent. Showy New England asters and goldenrods refuel southbound migrant monarchs in late summer with fat-rich nectar, while fuzzy bumblebees heavy with pollen clamber over flowers. Reach a fork in the trail. Bear left and enter woodland of red maple, white ash, black cherry, and scattered large white pines. Hay scented and New York ferns carpet the forest floor. The yellow-blazed path soon turns sharply right and passes through a stone wall gap—the first of many. Raspberry canes abound.

A 17-acre flower-filled meadow is alive with butterflies, buzzing bees and other insects in summer.

A few spicebush shrubs thrive in the moist rich soil and offer bright red berries to migrant thrushes in late summer. Where the trail turns left, a massive multi-trunked red oak more than four feet in diameter rears up behind a stone walls composed of relatively small schist rocks. The well-built wall stands 4.5 feet high in places. More woodland lies beyond the wall on the gentle slope of Leffingwell Hill.

Follow along the wall through dense shrubs under a canopy of red maple, black cherry—the one with the flaky black bark and white pine. After a jog through a stone walls gap, the forest shows signs of disturbance—relatively young woodland and the presence of invasive exotic oriental bittersweet vines. A few gnarled apple trees also attest to former human presence. In late summer tall white-blooming snakeroot hems in the path.

Turn right onto another former roadway bordered on the right by an impressive stone walls. Here the forest has an open appearance. A bit farther stone foundations appear on the left. Japanese barberry—also an invasive exotic—is another sign of disturbed soil. This woodland has an "unruly" look, unlike the forest you passed through earlier. Soon bear right at another chained gateway along a posted private property line. Pass by a rock pile on the right. Settlers piled stones too small for stone walls construction in field corners. The county's first non-Native American children were born in Leffingwell; the settlement was abandoned in the late 1800s.

White pine (note the five slender needles) becomes predominant. Winged seeds of this species require bright sunlight to germinate, indicating that this pine woodland was once a field. Light green hay scented or boulder fern, as it is sometimes called, is abundant here. Lowbush blueberry and huckleberry are also present in these drier woods. Enter a hemlock grove within which stands a magnificent red oak of greater diameter (well over 4 feet) than I have seen almost anywhere in Berkshire County. It sprouted from an acorn near the inception of the Leffingwell settlement. Far smaller and younger red maple, gray birch, white ash, and black cherry are more numerous.

After entering more shady hemlock woodland (some of the trees here are moderately large), amble down slope under white pines and mixed hardwoods. As you continue down, white ash with tight crosshatched bark becomes the most common tree. Soon reach the southeast corner of the meadow that you happened upon earlier. Follow the wide-mown path to the right along the woodland edge. Young white, black, and gray birches line the path and a wooden bench invites a pause. One late summer day a ruffed grouse flushed before me, while a regal red-tailed hawk soared above. Close the loop at the trail intersection, turn left, and then right to retrace your steps 0.5 mile back to the parking area.

DID YOU KNOW?

The property's name—Questing—comes from a mythical beast called "The Questing Beast" or "Barking Beast" from King Arthur's Court. It is said to have had the head and neck of a snake and the body of a leopard.

MORE INFORMATION

The reservation is owned and managed by The Trustees of Reservations, a private-non-profit conservation organization. Open daily, sunrise to sunset. Admission is free. Open to hunting in season by written permission. Visitors are strongly encouraged to wear signal orange clothing during hunting seasons. Dogs must be leashed at all times. Mountain biking is not permitted; 413-298-3239; thetrustees.org.

NEARBY

The Southfield Store, 163 Main Street, Southfield, MA 01259, operates as a coffee shop and café (takeout lunches available) year-round and offers casual late-week dinners mid-May until November 1 (413-229-5050, store.oldinn.com). Famous for its Sunday brunch, it's just down the road from the renowned Old Inn on the Green, built as an historic stagecoach relay station in 1760.

TRIP 43
TOLLAND STATE FOREST– GILMORE TRAIL

Location: Otis and Tolland, MA
Rating: Easy
Distance: 3.5 miles
Elevation Gain: 75 feet
Estimated Time: 2.0–2.5 hours
Maps: USGS Otis; trail map available online

Otis Reservoir, one of the largest water bodies in western Massachusetts, is the focal point for numerous anglers, hunters, campers, and off-road vehicle enthusiasts. The seldom-used trail system maintains its wilderness feel.

DIRECTIONS

From Exit 2 (Lee) off the Mass Pike (I-90), take US 20 east for 6.8 miles to MA 8 South on the right. Follow MA 8 for 8.4 miles to Reservoir Road in Otis. Turn left onto Reservoir Road and drive 1.6 miles to Tolland Road on the right. Follow Tolland Road south; stay right where Kibbe Road goes left. After crossing the dam, Tolland Road turns left, but continue straight for 1.5 miles and turn left on East Otis Road and follow it to the contact station and parking area. *GPS coordinates*: 42° 08.645′ N, 73° 02.659′ W.

TRAIL DESCRIPTION

After paying the day-use fee at the contact station, walk south to the far end of the parking lot. Pass the signed Gilmore Trail entrance (this will be your return point as this trail description follows the trail in reverse) to reach the outbound trailhead just 25 feet beyond; turn left onto the trail. Follow the chipped path a short distance and turn right at the first junction, where signs identify Long Loop (your route) and Short Loop (straight). The trail is marked by blue blazes.

Climb easily over a fallen stone walls and breathe in the earthy fragrances of this moist forest of American beech, eastern hemlock, and yellow and white birches, black cherry, and red maple. The understory contains mountain laurel and princess pine (also known as tree clubmoss), ground cedar, and shining clubmoss, New York and hay-scented ferns, ground-hugging Canada

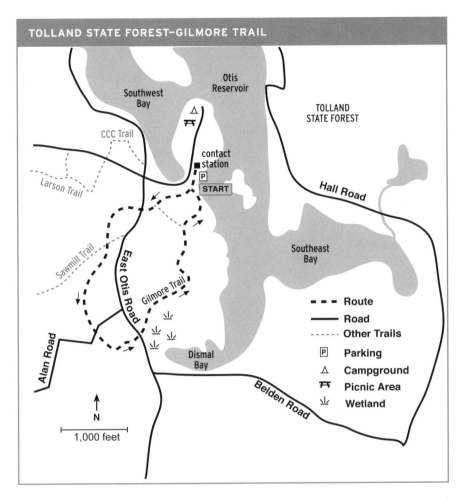

TOLLAND STATE FOREST–GILMORE TRAIL

Otis Reservoir

Southwest Bay

TOLLAND STATE FOREST

CCC Trail

Larson Trail

contact station

P

START

Hall Road

East Otis Road

Gilmore Trail

Sawmill Trail

Southeast Bay

Dismal Bay

Alan Road

Belden Road

- - - Route
─── Road
- - - - Other Trails
P Parking
△ Campground
🛆 Picnic Area
⚇ Wetland

N

1,000 feet

mayflower, and shiny-leaved goldthread. The trail climbs modestly and enters a white pine stand of medium age. Eastern white pine is a colonizer of abandoned farmland—forming thick, rather even-aged stands.

After passing through a sugar maple stand, you'll cross narrow, dirt East Otis Road. Descend ever so slightly on an old wood road and come to the border of a mowed field—perhaps two acres—on your right. Northern flickers frequent open habitats and search for ants by probing their long, stout bills into ant nests in the ground. In early fall, watch for hawks, migrating monarch butterflies, and other airborne creatures.

The trail soon turns sharp left. An angular, gneiss boulder on the right has a white quartz vein bisecting it. Shade-tolerant hemlocks—from whose reddish inner bark tannin (used in the leather tanning process) originates— become numerous on the slope that drops off to the right.

Near the end of the hike the path parallels the shore where gaps in the beech and hemlock woodland offer up views of Otis Reservoir.

Before long, you'll reach a spring. Water flows from an iron tube encased in red clay pipe. It is recommended that you not drink untreated water such as this. Large yellow birches provide blue-headed vireos with nest sites and nesting material. Listen for their deliberate, melodic phrasing in late spring and early summer. The trail skirts the top of a fairly old beech/hemlock stand with scant vegetation beneath and ascends gradually to some rather large black birches. Their sap contains fragrant oil of wintergreen.

Just before you reach Sawmill Trail (a woodland track used by off-road motorcycles), encounter a small fern glade and the remnants of an old stone walls. Hay-scented fern is partial to rocky pastures—as this once was. You'll pick up Gilmore Trail again after crossing Sawmill Trail. Stride across an intermittent streambed. After crossing a woodland track heavily used by off-road motorcycles, enter an attractive forest of birches, red maple, hemlock, and beech. Middle-aged red oaks become much more common. Oaks are among the latest trees to change color in fall—turning yellowish and coppery hues. Gneiss boulders protrude from the forest floor. A damp spot hosts chest-high cinnamon and interrupted ferns. You'll stroll through young woodland regenerating to birch, beech, and red maple.

Striped maples increase in abundance below the beech canopy. Most of the beeches show signs of fungal disease that cause rough, bumpy lesions in the bark. Pass under mixed hemlock, white pine, and hardwoods before the trail crosses gravel Alan Road and continues in a southeasterly direction. Gilmore Trail is indicated by signs in both directions.

The trail, blazed blue and red for a distance, leads across damp, spongy ground. After passing through a boggy glade flush with ferns and sedges, the trail winds amid mixed woodland, including tall white pines. Woodpeckers flake off the bark of dead trees to expose fat, juicy beetle grubs, and red-breasted nuthatches creep along, surveying bark crevices for spiders and insects. You'll find white ashes and white pines growing in the next damp area. White ashes produce winged seeds resembling canoe paddles.

After crossing a stone walls, you'll pass through open forest and along a planted Norway spruce stand bordered by raspberry canes, to reach gravel East Otis Road again. On the east side of the road, the trail—blocked by boulders to discourage motorized vehicles—descends gradually and heads northerly through beech, birch, and maple woodland. Their usual associate—eastern hemlock—frequents shaded, moist spots. Watch for the big tracks of resident moose.

You'll cross two small streams, the first on bog bridges, which flow through the stand. The wetland to the right is an extension of Dismal Bay at the extreme southern end of the reservoir. A native holly, winterberry, grows along this wetland edge. Gilmore Trail climbs gradually away from the wetland under a canopy of hemlock and beech, then sugar maples, and again more hemlock. Here the trail makes a sharp left turn. You'll follow the trail down through a forest of young beech, sugar maple, and hemlock. You may hear the roar of motorboats before you glimpse the lake through the trees.

At the **T** intersection, turn right toward the lake. The trail leads under hemlocks, and an abundance of goldthread borders the treadway. You'll continue downhill. Otis Reservoir soon comes into view. The path leads to the shore and then parallels it. Heart-leaved hobblebush grows thickly near the shore, where gaps in the woody growth offer up views of the lake. After swinging briefly away from the shore, the trail returns to it amid a forest of beech and hemlock, below which the groundcovers wintergreen and partridgeberry flourish. You'll emerge from the woods at the parking area where you started.

DID YOU KNOW?

Otis Reservoir, covering 1,065 acres, was constructed in 1865 as a water-power supply when the Fall River, a tributary of the Farmington River, was dammed; the dam was reinforced with granite blocks in 1888. Tolland State Forest was established in 1925. During the 1930s, the Civilian Conservation Corps (CCC) constructed many of the property's facilities.

MORE INFORMATION

Hours are sunrise to sunset, year-round. There is a small day-use/parking fee. A chemical toilet is located past the contact station at the public boat ramp. Camping available—reservations can be made. Open to hunting in season. Tolland State Forest, 410 Tolland Road, P.O. Box 342, East Otis, MA 01029 (413-269-6002; mass.gov/eea/agencies/dcr/massparks/region-west/tolland-state-forest-generic.html).

NEARBY

The photogenic, red Tannery Bridge over the west branch of the Farmington River—although not an authentic covered bridge due to the fact that it has no arch or truss system—is worth a look. It was built in 1981 and was covered in 1998. To reach it, you'll travel south on MA 8 for approximately 4.4 miles to the bridge on the left. Parking is limited. Be sure to park off the highway.

TRIP 44
BASH BISH FALLS

Location: Mount Washington, MA; Copake Falls, NY
Rating: Easy to Moderate or Moderate to Strenuous,
depending on route
Distance: 2.0 or 2.6 miles
Elevation Gain: 470 or 900 feet
Estimated Time: 1.5 or 2.5 hours
Maps: AMC Massachusetts Trail Map #2: C1; USGS Copake Falls,
Bash Bish Falls

**A tale of two trails: Choose either an easy stroll to Massachusetts'
most spectacular waterfall, and a short, steep climb for a fine view
of Bash Bish Gorge, New York's Harlem Valley, and the distant
Catskill Mountains; or a strenuous loop hike made challenging by
a stream ford and a steep ascent of Bash Bish Mountain. Both pay
ample dividends.**

DIRECTIONS

From the junction of US 7, MA 23, and MA 41 in Great Barrington, take
the combined MA 23 and MA 41 west for 3.9 miles to Egremont, where MA
41 splits off to the left (MA 23 continues straight). Follow the shore of Mill
Pond briefly, bearing right onto Mount Washington Road (called East Street
in Mount Washington). Drive for an additional 7.6 miles, following signs, to
the signed intersection with Cross Road. Turn right (Church of Christ chapel
is located on opposite corner). Cross Road intersects West Street. Bear right on
West Street, which becomes fairly steep and winding. At the bottom of the hill,
bear left to cross Wright Brook and turn left immediately onto Bash Bish Falls
Road. Follow it for 2.4 miles into New York State, where it becomes NY 344
(passing the upper parking area in Massachusetts along the way) to the large,
paved lower parking area of Taconic State Park on the left. *GPS coordinates:* 42°
07.020′ N, 73° 30.460′ W.

TRAIL DESCRIPTION

Check the kiosk, which displays a detailed area map, at the far end of the lot
edged by tall Norway spruces and eastern hemlocks. You can learn about
the locale's fascinating tourism and iron industry history at the other kiosk.

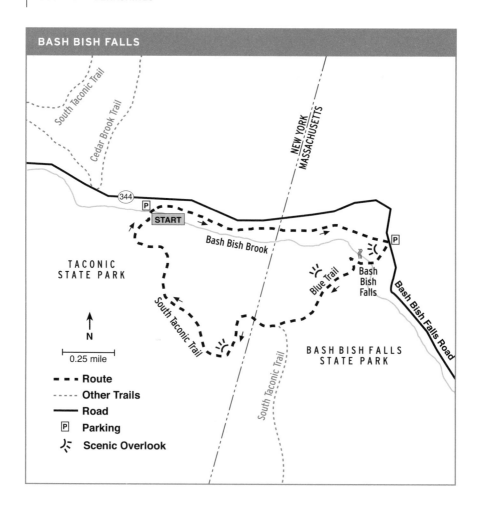

BASH BISH FALLS

South Taconic Trail

Cedar Brook Trail

344

START

Bash Bish Brook

NEW YORK
MASSACHUSETTS

TACONIC
STATE PARK

South Taconic Trail

Blue Trail

Bash
Bish
Falls

Bash Bish Falls Road

N

0.25 mile

BASH BISH FALLS
STATE PARK

South Taconic Trail

- - - Route
- - - - - Other Trails
──── Road
P Parking
爻 Scenic Overlook

Walk down the gravel roadway bordered by more hemlocks and sugar maples. Tall autumn blooming witch hazel shrubs line both sides of the road as you follow Bash Bish Brook closely upstream. The frothy green water flows with a thunderous roar after rains or snowmelt. Shiny, platy schist protrudes from the roadway and lines the stream as you amble gently down to brook level for a closer look. Large red and black oaks and white ash dot the hillside on your left, while the north-facing slope is shaded by hemlocks.

Just after a bench, a jutting schist boulder on the left offers Eastern phoebes small shelflike platforms upon which to build their moss-covered nests. But the brook's roar makes it almost impossible to discern birdsong. As you begin climbing gently to a second bench, hardwoods intermix with hemlocks. The precipitous slope of Bash Bish Mountain, loden green in hemlock attire, flanks the far side of the gorge. The treadway becomes a little rougher as it leads high above the surging stream. Some large red oaks on the left slope invite notice. In winter, black-capped chickadees and tiny golden-crowned kinglets, hanging from the hemlock boughs in search of insects, may be among the few birds you'll find. After about 15 minutes, you'll reach the Massachusetts border and Bash Bish Falls State Park.

Continue a gentle ascent, skirting denser hemlock growth. Soon you'll reach an intersection with a short gravel service road that leads left up to a metal gate and the highway. Stay straight, guided by the roar of the falls. Reach a kiosk with a donation pipe at a falls viewing area bordered by metal railings. View the falls from above, then walk down native stone steps for a closer look at the spectacle. Be extremely careful when conditions are icy or wet! Massachusetts' most impressive falls (about 60 feet), plunges in twin streams around a jutting granite outcrop into an icy green pool. No swimming signs alert visitors to the potential danger.

Angular slabs of schist surround the pool. In wet seasons, a feeder brook slants down the high-gradient slope from the left, adding its flow. Water tumbling over the falls originates from springs 1,300 feet up, in the Mount Washington State Forest. In winter, wind-blown mist artistically coats tree branches with ice. Climb back up the steps and turn left to walk back the way you came about 150 feet before turning right onto a signed path that angles up the slope. Walk up wooden, then rock steps, and turn right onto a former wood road.

Follow triangular, blue blazes and cross a couple of seasonal flowages under impressive hemlocks, sugar maples, and ashes. You'll ascend fairly steeply toward the head of the ravine past schist boulders—some blazed with blue paint—to a twin log bridge across the upper reaches of the feeder brook. The path ascends under towering hemlocks that impart a primeval forest aspect. Some are nearly 3 feet in diameter. Cross an intermittent drainage on rocks and cover the remaining short distance on railroad tie steps through a small stand of white birch to a kiosk and just before the paved upper parking lot. The kiosk informs hikers about the presence of the endangered eastern timber rattlesnake.

Head right, along the edge of the lot, and turn right at metal fencing to semi-scramble up schist bedrock to a vista point above the gorge. Atop the crag are white pines, shrub-sized oak, and a lone pitch pine. Common polypody ferns fill the crevices of the upturned schist that also contain milky quartz veins. From the vantage points along the metal railing (exercise caution), enjoy splendid views west down the gorge to the Harlem Valley and the distant Catskill Mountains. The falls are audible, but not visible from here; the green mound of Bash Bish Mountain (1,925 feet) looms up to the left, while oak-clothed Cedar Mountain (1,883 feet) forms the opposite wall of the gorge.

From here, you can retrace your steps about 1.0 mile to the lower parking area and your vehicle, or continue on for a more challenging hiking experience.

If continuing on, descend, turn right, and pass around the end of a brown state forest gate. Head easily downhill bearing right, and soon level out on the brook's floodplain, at which point you turn right to follow the stream a mere 125 feet before crossing it on stones. A word of caution—do not attempt this under high flow or icy conditions. Even under moderate flows, you may choose to remove your shoes and wade carefully across. Trekking poles are helpful. Locate the trail on the far side and reach the brook bank at the edge of the restricted area. A wooden sign above the left bank warns of fines associated with continuing down Bash Bish Gorge.

Instead, climb the very steep hemlock-shaded slope following faint blue blazes. A metal fence offers a steadying grip and a large measure of safety. Enjoy a thrilling view down into the gorge where the fence makes a 90-degree turn after you level out. The far side is bounded by Cedar Mountain. Note the name, dating from perhaps 1846, carved deeply into the rock anchoring the corner fencepost. A wooden directional sign indicates that the South Taconic Trail leads up away from the fence. Soon bear right. The treadway soon steepens again and becomes rougher. The roar of the brook is audible. Blazes are few here, but the route is discernible as you bear left, then immediately right in woodland with a number of trees snapped off by high winds.

You'll continue an almost relentless climb through mixed woods dominated by hemlocks until you arrive at a signed intersection with the South Taconic Trail, where the woodland changes to one where broadleaf trees hold sway. The white-blazed South Taconic Trail turns left to climb Bash Bish Mountain, and continues straight toward NY 344 (1.3 miles distant), your return route. Continue straight ahead and walk down under oaks that include chestnut oak; identify it by blocky bark and wavy-edged leaves. White, plastic discs also demarcate the route. White pines join the hemlocks as you reach a border with posted private property on the left. In the fall, pines shed a third of their needles.

Thin soils on these bony slopes don't allow trees to grow very tall. The descent steepens, so watch your footing as you maneuver over rocks that become slippery when wet. When you reach a Y intersection, bear right down a blue-blazed side path about 200 feet to a splendid long-distance view north and west to the alternating farm fields and forested ridges of the Harlem Valley,

A thunderous roar alerts you to the proximity of the falls' impressive 60-foot split drop into a clear pool.

and the Catskills well beyond. Look for turkey vultures soaring past the viewpoint. Return to the main trail and turn right. Blueberries and wintergreen border the path.

Begin a more angular descent over rocks. Note the outcrop on the left covered with rock tripe, lichen that greens up after absorbing moisture, and polypody fern. Here the deciduous trees are again significantly taller than those upslope. Descend into a bowl carpeted in spots by three-leaved hog-peanut, and soon turn right at a twin-trunked tulip tree to continue dropping down. You'll level off near the base of the slope for an easy stroll under hemlocks and hardwoods, including both black and white birches. The route alternates between level and steep pitches and utilizes a switchback to arrive at a tributary stream.

Parallel the brook beneath a dense hemlock canopy and bear left to follow the white blazes to the campground road at the brown shower building. Turn left and walk the camp road to a concrete bridge over Bash Bish Brook and back to the parking area. Just before the bridge, a side trail leads to the old Copake Iron Works site.

DID YOU KNOW?

Legend has it that Bash Bish Falls takes its name from a beautiful Mahican princess named Bash Bish, who was sent over the falls in a canoe to her death as punishment for suspected adultery. Whether true or fanciful, the legend adds romantic appeal to an already evocative scene.

MORE INFORMATION

Taconic State Park (NY) is open daily, year-round, sunrise to sunset, weather and conditions permitting. Free access. Campground is open from the first Friday in May through the first weekend in December. Dogs must be leashed on a 10-foot-maximum leash at all times. Motor and wheeled vehicles are prohibited. Taconic State Park, P.O. Box 100, Copake Falls, NY 12517 (518-329-3993; 800-456-2267 for camping/cabin reservations; parks.ny.gov/parks/default.aspx).

Bash Bish Falls State Park (MA) is open daily, year-round, sunrise to one half-hour after sunset. Access is free. Pets are permitted on a 10-foot-maximum leash; must have proof of current rabies vaccination. Swimming, diving, rock climbing, and alcoholic beverages are prohibited. Bash Bish Falls State Park, Falls Road, c/o RD 3 East Street, Mount Washington, MA 01258 (413-528-0330; mass.gov/eea/agencies/dcr/massparks/region-west/bash-bish-falls-state-park.html).

NEARBY

Kenver Ltd., located at 39 South Main Street (MA 23) in South Egremont, is the Berkshires' largest winter sports store. This full-service shop is open every day, 10 A.M.–5 P.M. (413-528-2330 or 800-342-7547; kenver.com).

TRIP 45
UPPER RACE BROOK FALLS AND MOUNT RACE

Location: Sheffield and Mount Washington, MA
Rating: Strenuous
Distance: 6.2 miles (7.2 miles if you add an out-and-back spur to Lower Race Brook Falls)
Elevation Gain: 1,625 feet
Estimated Time: 4.0 hours
Maps: AMC Massachusetts Trail Map #2 ; USGS Ashley Falls; trail map available online

A hike of superlatives—a spectacular series of waterfalls, a stupendous laurel bloom mid-June to early July, and excellent views from the southern Taconic ridge line on Mount Race make this one of the most picturesque hikes in the Berkshires.

DIRECTIONS

From the junction of US 7 and MA 23 and MA 41 in Great Barrington, take MA 23 and MA 41 southwest for 4.1 miles to where MA 41 splits off from MA 23 in Egremont. Turn left and follow along the Mill Pond shore for 0.1 mile and bear left on MA 41 (Mount Washington Road bears right). Drive for 4.9 additional miles (passing Berkshire School on the right en route at 3.1 miles) and park in a paved pull-off area on the right adjacent to the trailhead. *GPS coordinates: 42° 05.368′ N, 73° 24.667′ W.*

TRAIL DESCRIPTION

Sign in at the kiosk trail register. A large topographic map of the route and other information is posted here. Trail maps may be available. Black bears and occasionally endangered timber rattlesnakes are encountered. A nonnative mulberry tree near the kiosk produces sweet fruit relished by birds and mammals. Turn left and follow blue blazes down an initially eroded path and cross a shallow brook on stepping-stones. The path bears left and is built up in a wet area under white ashes and sugar maples. Cross a rill and skirt the edge of a field on a narrow path through grasses, bedstraw, red clover, and daisies in summer. A few red cedars are scattered about.

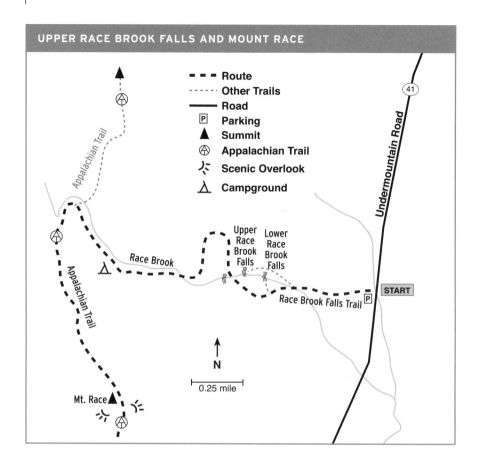

UPPER RACE BROOK FALLS AND MOUNT RACE

- - - Route
······ Other Trails
—— Road
P Parking
▲ Summit
Ⓐ Appalachian Trail
Scenic Overlook
Campground

Appalachian Trail

Appalachian Trail

Race Brook

Upper Race Brook Falls

Lower Race Brook Falls

Race Brook Falls Trail

START

Undermountain Road

41

Mt. Race

N

0.25 mile

Enter a shaded hemlock forest. As the path widens, you'll also note white pines, maples, and oaks—red, white, and chestnut. Chestnut oak sports wavy-edged leaves. Climb gradually and then level out. At a signed intersection, bear left toward the Appalachian Trail (AT) 2.0 miles distant via Upper Race Brook Falls. You have the option on the return of adding a mile to the route by bearing right—to the bottom of Lower Race Brook Falls, 0.5 mile distant.

For now, continue on Race Brook Trail through attractive hardwood-hemlock woods dotted with mountain laurel shrubs. Reach a moss-coated gneiss boulder along cascading Race Brook guarded by sizable hemlocks. The trail bears right, along the stream for a short distance. Descend to the brook, crossing it on stones. On the opposite bank turn left, then right to begin the ascent. Hemlock roots crisscross the pathway. The route climbs higher and higher above the brook on a wide, well-blazed trail. You'll begin a steeper climb. Race Brook rushes along perhaps 60 feet below. American chestnut continues to root-sprout decades after the blight effectively removed this magnificent species from southern New England's woodlands. As you move farther from the stream, a leafy forest of red maple, black birch, and oaks form a canopy over laurel thickets.

You'll reach a signed intersection for Lower Falls Loop Trail on the right, but stay straight on the rocky path up toward the campsite. The grade increases again, highlighted by ledge outcrops. Switchback to climb the slope. In this mixed deciduous-evergreen forest, the songs of scarlet tanager and hermit thrush intermingle. The hemlocks look sickly, perhaps the result of hemlock wooly adelgid infestation. This minute insect has already killed thousands of acres of hemlocks to our south. The path follows the steep hillside contour, but logs and rockwork ensure the path's integrity.

The rough-barked trunks of chestnut oaks are numerous as you catch a glimpse of a falls through the trees on the right. The slope above you is boulder-strewn. An informal path on the right approaches the base of the falls, but footing is potentially hazardous, so use caution. The falls cascade down layered gneiss bedrock into a clear, green pool. Back on the main trail above, pass below a massive hemlock on the left and cross Race Brook— shallow here—on stones. Partway across, take in the view of the high falls from a large, flat rock. This is one of the most impressive falls in the Berkshires. Use caution, as rocks are often slippery when wet.

Pass through a narrow gap between gneiss boulders and continue moderately upward under a leafy canopy. Listen for the loud, effervescent refrain of the tiny winter wren during the nesting season. You'll turn left, ascend rock steps past a 25-foot-high ledge bedecked with leafy rock tripe, a lichen that in time turns green when wet. There is additional steep climbing followed by a few switchbacks. Walk through abundant laurel. Even without the blossoms, this is a very pretty route.

Level out and turn left through more dense laurel. Enjoy peek-a-boo views of the Housatonic Valley through the trees. The sound of fast-moving water presages your return to Race Brook, where cooling breezes prevail. Turn right to closely follow the crystal-clear mountain stream upstream. Turn left and cross the brook on a double-log bridge. Water striders skate across the glassy surface of pools. Emerald green mosses coat the damp stones. Walk along the opposite bank and duck under a pair of wind-thrown trees. Their shallow roots easily separated from the tilted bedrock upon which they grew.

At a sign for Race Brook Falls Campsite, bear left and climb toward a long, low, wall-like outcrop, turning right before reaching it. Shortly bear left and then right past wooden tent platforms to a map board and campsite register.

**Hikers gaze out
over the Housatonic
River Valley from
the thrilling Mount
Race escarpment.**

A privy stands nearby. You have covered 1.8 miles, and the AT is but 0.2 mile farther. Walk up under maple, beech, oak, and hemlock trees. Bear left and ascend schist stone steps. Level out and you will find even more amazing laurel in mid-June to early July. Junction with the AT on the level and turn left (south) toward Mount Race, 1.1 miles distant on a sometimes-steep trail. Cross a wet spot, cushioned by a bit of highly absorbent sphagnum moss, on stones and climb again. A bit of scrambling is required, but nothing major. The wheezy *drink-your-tea* refrain of the robin-sized black, white, and rust-colored eastern towhee indicates you've entered a shrubbier habitat.

The path follows bedrock outcrops—some showing the polished gouges formed by the abrasive force of thick glacial ice. The white flowers of tiny three-toothed cinquefoil bloom in early summer in sunlit spots. This ridge top woodland is much shorter owing to thin soils and a brief growing season. Before too long, the first pitch pines appear, and then patches of huckleberry. The pines soon take on a bonsai appearance. Add the luxuriant laurel blossoms, lowbush blueberry, and shrubby bear oak, and the look is somewhat reminiscent of a Japanese garden. The going is fairly level amid more laurel— the state flower of nearby southern neighbor Connecticut.

You'll reach an outcrop some 20 feet high that you'll have to climb via natural rock steps. The gneiss was melted and recrystallized under tremendous heat and pressure. These rock layers now stand on end. The Taconic Mountains are among the oldest in North America and resulted from the collision of tectonic plates hundreds of millions of years ago. There are panoramic views from atop the rounded rock promontory of Mount Race at 2,365 feet elevation. An official USGS benchmark once marked the summit; only a 0.75-inch diameter hole remains. Looking back in the direction you came, the rounded form of Mount Everett is about 2.0 miles north along the AT. To the right is the saddleback form of Mount Greylock, while New York's 4,000-foot-high Catskills form a blue ridgeline far to the west. Face south and look left to view the Twin Lakes lying across the state line. Short-needled pitch pines no more than 6 feet tall make for a pleasing dwarf forest on this bony spine laced with white quartz swirls.

When ready, retrace your steps to Race Brook Trail on the right to descend. Watch carefully for the blue blazes, as some turns can be missed, especially at the last major brook crossing.

If so inclined, turn hard left when you reach the signed intersection in a flat area under hemlocks for the 0.5-mile spur to the Lower Falls. The path leads gradually uphill through mixed woods to a viewpoint amid huge boulders of the lower falls (not to be confused with the so called Loop Trail to the top of the Lower Falls on the left that you passed earlier on your way down).

DID YOU KNOW?

Some of the head-high pitch pines you brush against as you make your way along the bony Taconic ridge line are well over 100 years old. Scant soil and harsh weather conditions severely limit their growth rate. Similar pitch pines on nearby Mount Everett have been dated at nearly 200 years of age!

MORE INFORMATION

Open sunrise to sunset, daily, year-round. Free access. Pets must be on a 10-foot-maximum leash and attended at all times; owner must have proof of current rabies vaccination. Motorized vehicles, mountain bikes, horses, and alcoholic beverages prohibited. Hunting allowed in season, except along AT corridor and near campsites. Fires allowed in designated areas only. Mount Washington State Forest, RD 3 East Street, Mount Washington, MA 01258 (413-

528-0330; mass.gov/eea/agencies/dcr/massparks/region-west/mt-washington-state-forest-generic.html). The Appalachian Trail Management Committee is responsible for maintenance, management, and protection of the nearly 90 miles of the AT in Massachusetts; volunteers do this work, with assistance from the Massachusetts Department of Conservation and Recreation. Massachusetts AT Committee, Berkshire Chapter AMC, P.O. Box 2281, Pittsfield, MA 01202 (413-528-6333; at@amcberkshire.org; amcberkshire.org/at). Appalachian Mountain Club Regional Trail Coordinator (413-229-9147).

NEARBY

The Shays' Rebellion Monument commemorates the postrevolutionary armed revolt by indebted farmers against the state and wealthy merchants. A final bloody battle with government militia was fought here in February 1787, during which the rebels were routed. Captain Daniel Shays, Revolutionary War veteran, was one of its leaders. The monument is located along the Appalachian Trail at the intersection of Egremont and Rebellion Roads in Sheffield.

TRIP 46
GUILDER POND AND MOUNT EVERETT

Location: Mount Washington, MA
Rating: Moderate
Distance: 4.2 miles
Elevation Gain: 825 feet
Estimated Time: 2.5–3.0 hours
Maps: USGS Ashley Falls

Guilder Pond is locally renowned for its profuse mountain laurel bloom, while ancient pitch pine–topped Mount Everett, the highest point in southern Berkshire County, offers sublime vistas.

DIRECTIONS

From the intersection of US 7 and MA 41/MA 23 in Great Barrington, take MA 23/MA 41 west for 4.1 miles and turn left at Mill Pond in Egremont to follow MA 41 for 0.1 mile to Mount Washington Road on the right. Drive for 7.5 miles (becomes East Street in Mount Washington) and turn left at the sign for Mount Everett State Reservation. Follow the gravel entrance road for 0.1 mile to an iron gate. Park along the right side of the gravel turnout. It is possible to drive all the way to the Guilder Pond Picnic Area in summer (gate open 8 A.M.–8 P.M.), but this hike begins at the lower gate. *GPS coordinates*: 42° 6.220′ N, 73° 27.091′ W.

TRAIL DESCRIPTION

From the metal gate at the bottom of the gravel access road, where a donation pipe is located, stroll steadily uphill on the roadway through a mixed forest of oak, maple, birch, beech, white pine, and hemlock. Mountain laurel is in evidence almost immediately, especially from late June to early July when it flowers. Some bushes are over 12 feet tall. The roadway winds under a canopy of shading eastern hemlocks, as does Guilder Brook on the left a bit farther.

After about 0.9 mile, pass one end of the Guilder Pond Trail on the left and arrive at its namesake water body. At 2,042 feet above sea level, Guilder is either the second- or third-highest natural water body in the Commonwealth. Patches of sweetgale, leatherleaf, and sphagnum moss have colonized the shore. Black whirligig beetles gyrate on the surface in summer. Nearly everything you read labels it second highest, but Tilden Swamp in Pittsfield

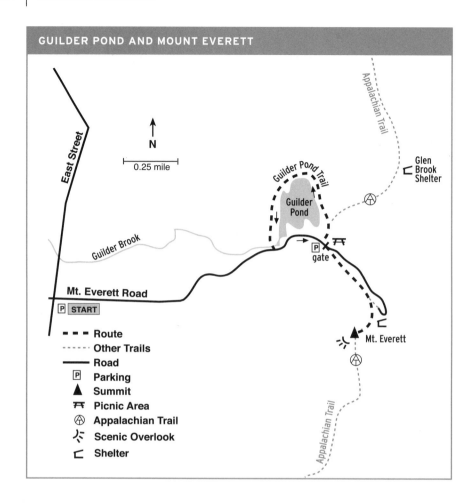

GUILDER POND AND MOUNT EVERETT

East Street

N

0.25 mile

Appalachian Trail

Guilder Pond Trail

Guilder Pond

Glen Brook Shelter

Guilder Brook

P gate

Mt. Everett Road

P START

Mt. Everett

Appalachian Trail

- - - Route
····· Other Trails
——— Road
P Parking
▲ Summit
🏕 Picnic Area
Ⓐ Appalachian Trail
🚶 Scenic Overlook
⊏ Shelter

State Forest, flooded by beavers in the mid-1990s, may be a few feet higher. In any event, it is a beautiful sight, fringed with pink and white laurels as it is in early summer; later you'll walk completely around it. You'll continue on the roadway another 0.2 mile to Guilder Pond Picnic Area, where toilet facilities are located.

In summer it is possible to drive to this lower parking area for the climb up Mount Everett. The gravel summit road on the right is gated. At the far left end of the picnic area is the other access for Guilder Pond Trail, which you'll use upon your return. But first, follow the white-blazed Appalachian Trail (AT) at a large sign (maps may be available at the kiosk on the right) up into beech, maple, yellow birch, and oak woodland on a steady incline. After just 0.1 mile, you'll reach the gravel summit road and turn left. Walk a mere

100 feet and turn right to continue on the AT. It leads up on a rocky path. Striped or goosefoot maple is an abundant small tree here while wood sorrel (with cloverlike leaves and white, pink-veined summer blossoms), *Clintonia* (a.k.a. bluebead lily), and Canada mayflower grow in the rich soil.

Soon notice that the summit road parallels the footpath on the left. The AT bears right, climbs a short distance, and turns left and ascends a stone "stairway" adjacent to rocky outcrops. Blue-green spinulose wood ferns soften the sharp angles below yellow birch and mountain ash.

At a short rocky side path, bear left to a bench and shelter in a grassy clearing offering an expansive view all the way to Mount Greylock, 37 miles north. It's easy to imagine how its other name—Saddleback Mountain—came to be.

Return to the trail and resume your uphill climb and then level out briefly. Mountain azaleas put on quite a show in May. In late June and early July, laurel bushes festooned with clusters of flowers crowd the path. The modest leaves of trailing arbutus beneath the laurel are easy to overlook. Hiking so close to the Connecticut border here, it's fitting that the two state flowers are in such close proximity as well. Adding much to the overall ambience are shrubby red maple, mountain ash, wild raisin, huckleberry, and lowbush blueberry. The latter two offer tasty treats as well.

After the wooden sign indicating 0.1 mile to the summit, tread over schist bedrock that stands on end due to the collision of continental plates hundreds of millions of years ago when these mountains were formed. The thin soil atop the bedrock provides nourishment to bear or scrub oak, also found on Cape Cod. Its tough, leathery leaves limit water loss in this harsh environment; note its tiny acorns. At a blue blaze on the right, step up onto a ledge outcrop and vista point to gaze eastward over the Housatonic Valley, Berkshire Plateau beyond, and the Twin Lakes just over the Connecticut line. You might even be able to pick out the sloping meadow on Hurlburt's Hill (Trip 49).

Soon you'll reach the site of the former summit fire tower, erected in 1915, and surrounded by little stiff-needled pitch pines at 2,624 feet (signage erroneously indicates its height as 2,602 feet). Only the concrete footings remain. The tower, which had fallen into disrepair, was removed by helicopter in 2003. The summit is an unusual and fragile environment, so remain on the trail and bedrock to not trample the vegetation. Studies of the summit vegetation have revealed that some of the gnarled dwarf pitch pines are between 100 and 200 years old—an old growth forest in miniature! Views of the bluish ridgeline of New York's Catskill Mountain—50 miles to the west-southwest—are yours to enjoy.

Guilder Pond, one of the state's highest water bodies, presents a lovely sight at any time of year.

After taking in the panoramic vistas, retrace your steps down to the Guilder Pond Picnic Area, but turn right to follow the joint AT/Guilder Pond Trail. Ignore the almost immediate unmarked side path on the left, and continue straight through northern hardwoods blended with hemlock, oaks, and laurel. At the Y intersection, where bog bridges lead through a seasonally damp area, turn left instead to follow the blue-blazed Guilder Pond (Loop) Trail. Some hemlocks have attained a seemingly advanced age based on their girth. The cushioned path undulates through and around old laurel bushes that tower over your head. This woodland in summer is filled with the birdsong of vireo, warbler, and thrush.

After passing through a fern glade dominated by New York fern (the fronds taper to a point at the bottom as well as the top), ascend the rocky ledge on stone steps that bring you to a viewpoint across the pond of the rounded "Dome of the Taconics," as Everett is known. You may be surprised to see stumps cut by industrious beavers quite high up the slope. However, hemlocks and oaks are not among their preferred foods. Their lodge is visible on an island in the pond. A ledge runs parallel with the trail. Walk across bedrock again close to the shore. The schist is laced with the white veins of milky quartz.

To your left are a concrete water control structure, wooden decking, and a black plastic culvert that transports water under an old vegetated beaver dam to the pond's outlet stream—Guilder Brook. Water from this side of the mountain eventually finds its way into the Hudson River. Enter a narrow path ahead to cross a single log span over Guilder Brook. A few feet more and you are back on the gravel entry road. Turn right and walk about 1.0 mile back to your vehicle.

DID YOU KNOW?

Mount Everett is named for Edward Everett, the fifteenth governor of Massachusetts, who served in that capacity from 1825 to 1835. The name was suggested by geologist Edward Hitchcock in 1841. Up until that time, the mountain had been known as "Bald Mountain" or "The Dome."

MORE INFORMATION

Open sunrise to sunset, daily, year-round. Access is free. Toilet facilities located at Guilder Pond Picnic Area. Pets permitted, but must be on a 10-foot-maximum leash; proof of rabies vaccination required. Motorized off-road vehicles and alcoholic beverages are prohibited. Mount Everett State Reservation; East Street, Mount Washington; c/o RD 3 East Street; Mount Washington, MA 01258 (413-528-0330; mass.gov/eea/agencies/dcr/massparks/region-west/mt-everett-state-reservation-generic.html). The Appalachian Trail Management Committee is responsible for maintenance, management, and protection of the nearly 90 miles of the AT in Massachusetts. Massachusetts AT Committee, Berkshire Chapter AMC, P.O. Box 2281, Pittsfield, MA 01202 (413-528-6333). Appalachian Mountain Club Regional Trail Coordinator (413-229-9147; amcberkshire.org/at).

NEARBY

Pick your own organically grown blueberries on weekends, 9 A.M.–5 P.M., in season, at Blueberry Hill Farm, 100 East Street, Mount Washington. The farm's 10 acres contain three varieties of highbush blueberries. Call ahead for more information. You'll need to bring your own containers. The farm does not accept credit cards (413-528-1479; austinfarm.com).

TRIP 47
ALANDER MOUNTAIN TRAIL

Location: Mount Washington, MA
Rating: Moderate
Distance: 5.0 miles
Elevation Gain: 790 feet
Estimated Time: 3.0–4.0 hours
Maps: USGS Ashley Falls; trail map available online

Alander is one of the most scenic summits in the Berkshires. Throw in a roaring mountain brook and attractive mixed woodland alive with birds, and you have a real winner.

DIRECTIONS

From the intersection of US 7, MA 23, and MA 41 in Great Barrington, turn onto MA 23/MA 41 and drive southwest for 4.1 miles. Turn left onto MA 41 south (at Mill Pond) and in 0.1 mile, turn right onto Mount Washington Road. Follow it for 9.1 miles (the road becomes East Street in Mount Washington) and go past the entrance to Mount Everett State Reservation until you come to the Mount Washington State Forest headquarters on the right. Follow the drive around to the right and the large gravel parking area. A chemical toilet is located at the lot's far end. *GPS coordinates*: 42° 5.185′ N, 73° 27.725′ W.

TRAIL DESCRIPTION

Trail maps are available at the trailhead kiosk and hikers are asked to sign in and out. A money pipe for donations is located to the left. Stride across the mowed field where lowbush blueberries and tiny four-petaled bluets attract pollinators in spring. Hunts Pond, with its resident Canada geese, lies serenely in a bowl to the left. Soon you'll enter woods of eastern hemlock, beneath which Canada lilies bloom in May. The route is blazed in blue. Listen for the whistled *weeta-weeta-weeteo* song of the black, yellow, and white magnolia warbler, and the buzzy notes of the black-throated green warbler in spring and early summer. After strolling through mixed woods, amble gently down through a second field where fiery wood lilies brighten the brushy meadow in July. Your destination is visible 2.0 miles to the west.

At the far end of the meadow, cross Lee Pond Brook on a wooden bridge and turn right onto an old roadway. A stone foundation lies across the stream.

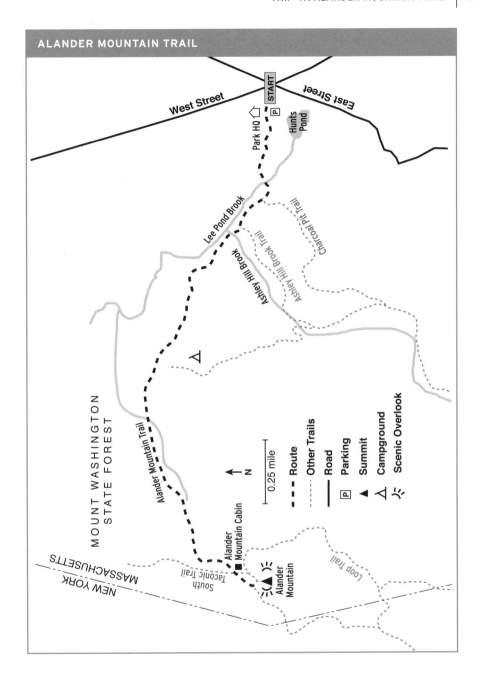

Charcoal Pit Trail soon leads uphill to the left, but stay straight. This forest was clear-cut between the late 1700s and mid-1800s to make charcoal—fuel for the many area iron furnaces. Note the significant yellow birch on the left, perhaps one of the first to grow back after the last clear-cut. The bark of young trees is

A group of hikers enjoy a snack and expansive three-state views from Alander's open summit.

much brassier. At a sign post, reach the Ashley Hill Brook Trail junction on the left; that trail leads south to Connecticut.

A short descent through hemlocks brings you to cascading Ashley Hill Brook (first audible from some distance) just above its confluence with another high-gradient stream. Cross the roaring flow via a well-built wooden bridge. The water has polished the schist bedrock to a silvery patina.

Soon you'll arrive at the stone remnants of a millrace. Across the stream, water cascades down small falls to join the main flow. Climb moderately on the old wood road under the dense shade of deep green hemlocks as the slope drops off sharply to the right. Shade-tolerant American beech, readily identified by its smooth gray bark; yellow birch; and red oak join the conifers. A sign on the right proclaims the distance to the primitive campground as 0.5 mile. Striped maple, black birch, and black cherry all grow here. Striped maple has green bark, cherry has scaly bark, while that of young black birch is tight.

The roadway continues on level ground through mixed woodland. Little spring beauty blooms in early May with five delicate white petals veined with pink. Former heavy use and flowing water has eroded the rocky road that levels out and then steepens as you bear left. The rocks are schist, the tough material that makes up the Taconics. A side trail soon runs left uphill toward the primitive campground. Continue straight and soon you'll find yourself among mountain laurel shrubs. Laurel boughs support the nests of black-throated blue warblers in spring and summer. Listen for their *beer-beer-bee* songs during the breeding season. After crossing a generally dry stony streambed, the path follows along a short stretch of brook through a shallow hemlock gorge.

More evergreen laurel and a small stream crossing on rocks takes you into a maple and oak forest. The small stream will be on your left. Reach a landing that may be a former charcoal-making site. A clue is that the earth is black from years of use. This is a good spot to pause for a moment, as the trail turns right and climbs sharply from here. Head uphill and bear left under hemlocks. This is especially attractive woodland. A tiny metal sign handmade with a sharp pointed instrument and affixed to a hemlock warns that this is the last source of water during the dry season. Should you use it, be sure to purify it first!

Walk up through lush laurel and along a ledge outcrop that parallels the trail on the right. Ahead sits a cabin where hikers may spend the night. Wood smoke aroma permeates the structure and a rock tied to a rope serves as a clever counterweight that closes the door behind you. A few feet beyond the cabin, Alander Mountain Trail joins South Taconic Trail. Turn right to follow both up over steplike schist outcrops. Shortly you'll reach an intersection with a small rock cairn and sign. Turn left through brushy scrub (a.k.a. bear) oak and bend right toward the splendid open rock summit of Alander Mountain at an elevation of 2,239 feet. The footings of a former fire tower are still obvious on the banded schist.

Lowbush blueberries and glossy-leaved bearberry both produce delicate whitish bell-like blossoms in May. Be attuned to the hoarse chewink call and the sweet whistled *drink-your-tea* song of the eastern towhee, a large black, rusty, and white member of the sparrow family. Gaze skyward for migrant hawks in spring and fall and vultures all year except winter.

This is the most open and arguably the most spectacular summit in the region, and it offers wonderful views of the Catskill Mountains, some 45 miles to the west (right). Nearby, but behind you, is the rounded form of Mount Everett (Trip 46). To your left is an undulating wooded ridge with three bumps. Mount Ashley is the leftmost, Mount Frissell sits in the middle, and Mount Brace (in Connecticut) stands farthest right. Note the rock cairn on its open summit. Ahead and below you lies the Hudson River Valley. New York's Route 22 is the ribbon of blacktop that runs south and north along the western side of the Taconics, one of this country's oldest mountain ranges, at approximately 400 million years. When ready to return, retrace your steps, but be sure to turn right at the small cairn in the trail.

DID YOU KNOW?

Although Bear Mountain is the highest summit entirely in the state of Connecticut, and was once thought to be its highest point, the true high point is on the southern slope of Mount Frissell at 2,380 feet, 64 feet higher than nearby Bear Mountain.

MORE INFORMATION

Open sunrise to sunset, year-round. Free access. Pets must be on a 10-foot-maximum leash and attended at all times; must have proof of current rabies vaccination. Motorized vehicles and alcoholic beverages prohibited. Mount Washington State Forest, RD 3 East Street, Mount Washington, MA 01258 (413-528-0330; mass.gov/eea/agencies/dcr/massparks/region-west/mt-washington-state-forest-generic.html).

NEARBY

The highest point in Connecticut—on the south slope of Mount Frissell—can be reached via Mount Frissell Trail. The trailhead is located off East Street in Mount Washington, on the right, just north of the Connecticut state line. After walking 1.2 miles, cross the summit (which is actually in Massachusetts), and continue south 0.1 mile to reach the Connecticut high point. A rock cairn and USGS marker pinpoint the site.

FEEDING THE FIRES OF INDUSTRY

In the mid-nineteenth century, Massachusetts was only 25 percent shaded by a forest canopy. Fully 75 percent was devoid of tree cover. Beginning in earnest during the previous century, the ancient forests that greeted the first white settlers were systematically cut. Colonists used timber for house construction and firewood, and they cleared the land for agricultural use to be sure, but not until the Industrial Revolution did the wholesale clear-cutting of Massachusetts woodlands move into high gear.

Early in the life of our young nation, this area was the center of a booming iron industry. In his book *Exploring the Berkshire Hills: A Guide to Geology and Early Industry in the Upper Housatonic Watershed*, historian and geologist Ed Kirby chronicles this little-known period in the area's past when the nation's industrial epicenter was right here. Iron was discovered in 1731, and eventually there would be 43 blast furnaces processing locally mined ore. The iron was used to manufacture cannons and cannon balls for the American Revolution and, later on, wheels for railroad trains. Not until large quantities of a higher-quality grade ore was discovered in the upper Midwest did the prominence of the Berkshire industry diminish.

The fires of the mammoth Richmond Furnace, which had operated 24 hours a day, went out for good in 1923. The fuel that fired the blast furnaces was not coal, but more abundant and therefore cheaper locally produced charcoal. Thousands upon thousands of forested acres were cleared to make charcoal to feed the insatiable blast furnaces. Charcoal making was a laborious proposition. Early on, men called colliers cut up to 30 cords of wood that required seasoning for a year in order to dry it. Later, the collier constructed a mound from the 30 cords of wood in the shape of a wigwam, which was covered with ferns and sod to slow the combustion process, while airflow was controlled by vents at the base of the mound. The smoldering mound was tended for four weeks as the wood was slowly transformed into charcoal.

Of course at first, the furnaces burned charcoal from the abundant woodlands so close at hand, but as those were exhausted, sources radiating farther out from the furnace were required. Eventually, with local forests decimated, charcoal had to be imported from elsewhere, making it too expensive as a fuel when compared with coal. But by then the landscape had virtually been laid bare. Today's woodlands are only now recovering from the far-reaching effects of the iron industry.

TRIP 48
LIME KILN FARM WILDLIFE SANCTUARY

Location: Sheffield, MA
Rating: Easy
Distance: 1.75 miles
Elevation Gain: 135 feet
Estimated Time: 1.5 hours
Maps: USGS Ashley Falls; trail map available on-site and online

This biologically diverse property in the Housatonic valley boasts rolling hayfields with magnificent vistas and hardwood forest alive with songbirds, almost in the shadow of Mount Everett and the Taconic Range; a fine walk for families with small children.

DIRECTIONS
From the north: From the center of Sheffield, at the U.S. Post Office, travel south on US 7 for 1.1 miles to Silver Street on the right (note tourist-oriented directional sign) and follow it for 1.1 miles to the sanctuary entrance and crushed stone parking lot (suitable for twelve vehicles) on the right.

From the south: From US 7 at the Connecticut border, drive north on US 7 for 3.6 miles to Silver Street on the left (note sign) and follow directions above. *GPS coordinates*: 42° 04.963′ N, 73° 21.766′ W.

TRAIL DESCRIPTION
From the parking lot, there is a wonderful view of Mount Everett (2,624 feet elevation and 3 miles distant). You'll approach a large, colorful map with trail information, and an adjacent donation box among apple trees. Trail maps are available here. Blue plastic discs indicating outbound travel mark the route, with yellow ones indicating return travel.

Amble under a canopy of apple trees down the former dairy farm lane—hayfield to the right and marsh to the left—where sweetflag, with greenish-yellow flower spikes the size and shape of your pinkie and cattail-like leaves, thrives; it's actually a relative of jack-in-the-pulpit. Pink-flowering hairy willow herb fills the wetland in summer. Reach a former small farm pond on the left, just before a trail junction.

Here Lime Kiln Loop splits. Continue straight up into another hayfield, passing weathering marble outcrops on the right. Marked by a signpost, the

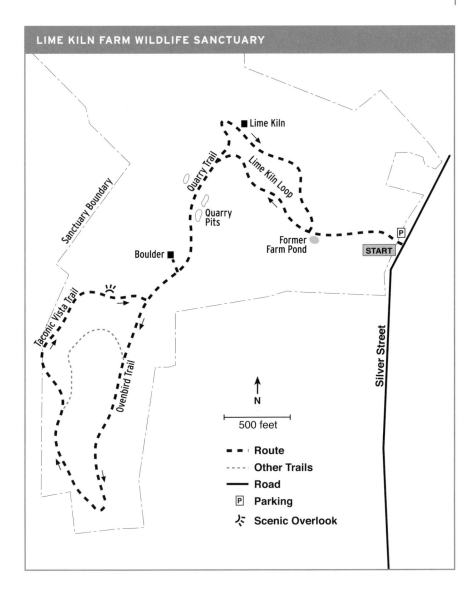

path soon bears right and briefly enters regenerating woody vegetation that includes columnar eastern red cedars (junipers) and invasive exotic autumn olive trees that sport silvery-red fruits. Emerge into the field again briefly, turn right, and then bear left at another post. Follow the broad path over soggy ground and pass a small quarry area on the left largely hidden by woody growth.

The trail leads gently uphill and passes several corky-barked hackberry trees unusual in these parts. Two species of butterfly caterpillar—hackberry

The rounded mass of Mount Everett, the highest point in the southern Berkshires, presents a picturesque image from the sanctuary's parking lot.

emperor and tawny emperor—feed exclusively on their leaves. After bearing left, you'll notice the cement footings of a former trestle on the right, over which marble rock was conveyed to the top of the limekiln (not visible from here). A few feet farther, a wooden bench is a fine spot for a snack as you survey a larger sloping hayfield and its Taconic Mountains backdrop. Sanctuary hayfields are cut annually by a neighboring dairy farmer—but not until late summer— giving grassland-nesting birds time to bring forth their broods.

At this point, Lime Kiln Loop turns right and follows the field edge down past the limekiln, and back to the parking lot, but turn left instead to follow Quarry Trail. You pass a monument to the three women who formerly lived on the property and are responsible for its donation as conservation land in 1990. Reenter woodland edge and shortly bear left. Soon you'll reach several former marble quarry pits. The largest is often filled with water and may serve as a vernal pool. Red and yellow blossoms of columbine grace the path's borders in June.

Continue over the wide, grassy treadway where oriental bittersweet vines drape the trees. This invasive exotic is a real curse as it strangles native trees and robs them of sunlight. In fall, the yellow fruit husks split open, revealing bright red-orange fruits consumed and spread by birds such as cedar waxwings and robins. Before long, enter deciduous woodland and arrive at Boulder Spur on the right. Walk a short distance down this side path for a close look at an imposing angular glacial erratic, and a bench facing the Taconics.

Back at Quarry Trail, turn right to continue. You'll soon pass a junction with Taconic Vista Trail on the right, but continue straight. The old farm road—now designated as Ovenbird Trail—passes through mixed woodland that includes hemlock and white pine. Another junction with Ovenbird Trail comes up on the right, but continue straight. Interestingly, yellow-rumped warblers nest among the pines on the left, although they are much more apt to choose high-elevation nest sites in the Berkshires.

Ovenbird Trail eventually turns right and makes its way along the property line. This path through woodland of oak, black birch, bigtooth aspen, hemlock, and witch hazel parallels a linear ledge outcrop rising on the right. At a junction on the right, Ovenbird Trail climbs up a modest slope and returns to Quarry Trail, but continue straight on Taconic Vista Trail. Later it bears right, then left, to pass over and around the end of the ledge softened by moss. Even after heavy snowfall, the ground is relatively bare below the hemlocks as their dense foliage intercepts and holds much of the fluffy white stuff. So far at least, these hemlocks appear to be unaffected by the hemlock wooly adelgid, which is advancing northward from Connecticut.

After passing a large fallen hemlock trunk cut to make way for the trail, you'll walk through a patch of Christmas fern before turning right to follow an old barbed-wire fence line up into mixed woodland that includes yellow birch. At a signpost marked "Vista," turn left and walk a few feet to the upper edge of a hayfield that affords a stunning view north and west. These fields are loaded with butterflies and dragonflies in summer.

Continue on the main path gently uphill. The path soon rejoins the wide former roadway known as Quarry Trail. Turn left and follow the yellow blazes back to the monument to the property donors and the junction with Lime Kiln Loop on the right.

Instead of turning right, however, to retrace your steps past the bench, stay straight and walk along the large field edge down to a signpost. After leaf fall, the 40-foot-high limekiln is visible to your right. At the post, turn right and approach the cement cylinder that is the former kiln. Built in 1909, this enterprise lasted only three years before it was abandoned. The marble rock was dumped in the top and cooked at temperatures of 1,400 degrees until the moisture was driven off and the rock reduced to powdery lime used in agriculture and many industrial applications. Be sure to stay clear of the kiln and adjacent structures.

Past the kiln on the left stand two enormous hemlocks that must be several hundred years old. Continue down the wide former roadway lined by prickly, ash shrubs. While not an ash at all, the branches are certainly prickly and you'll want to avoid contact with them. Walk along the left margin of another field and turn right where a couple of deciduous conifers—American larches (a.k.a. tamarack)—stand. Their needle tufts turn yellow in fall before dropping off. As you continue, note the vegetated wetland on your left. Here alder flycatchers nest in summer. Their diagnostic breeding "song" is a rapid, hiccupping *fee-bee-o*.

In summer and fall, American woodcocks sometimes flush from beneath the shrubby growth right of the path just before you close the Lime Kiln Loop near the farm pond. Turn left to stroll back to your vehicle.

DID YOU KNOW?

The 248-acre Lime Kiln Farm is part of the much larger 13,750-acre state-designated Schenob Brook Area of Critical Environmental Concern (ACEC), established in 1990. The ACEC, with its associated wetlands, comprises one of the most significant natural communities in Massachusetts, featuring the largest continuous calcareous seepage swamp, the finest examples of calcareous fens in southern New England, and more than 40 state-listed rare species.

MORE INFORMATION

Open daily, year-round, dawn to dusk. Admission free. Donations appreciated. No toilet facilities. Dogs, vehicles, hunting, fishing, trapping, and collecting prohibited. Owned and managed by Mass Audubon, 472 W. Mountain Road, Lenox, MA 01240 (413-637-0320; massaudubon.org).

NEARBY

Sheffield Covered Bridge, rebuilt in 1998, is a 93-foot-long lattice truss bridge across the Housatonic River. Only six such bridges remain in Massachusetts. The original, constructed in 1854, was the oldest covered bridge in the state until it was destroyed by fire in 1994. The bridge, open only to pedestrian traffic, is located 0.8 mile north of the center of town, and east of US 7.

TRIP 49
BARTHOLOMEW'S COBBLE RESERVATION

Location: Sheffield, MA
Rating: Moderate
Distance: 3.2 miles
Elevation Gain: 310 feet
Estimated Time: 2.0–2.5 hours
Maps: USGS Ashley Falls; trail map available online

Long beloved by botanists and fern enthusiasts, The Cobble offers terrific birding and wildflower-viewing opportunities, interesting geology, and fabulous panoramic views from the crest of Hurlburt's Hill.

DIRECTIONS

From the center of Sheffield (at the U.S. Post Office), follow US 7 south 1.7 miles to the US 7 and US 7A intersection. Turn right onto US 7A and follow it 0.4 mile to Rannapo Road on the right. Cross the railroad tracks and drive 1.5 miles to Weatogue Road on the right. Follow Weatogue Road 0.1 mile and turn left into the Reservation's gravel parking area with space for more than twenty vehicles. *GPS coordinates*: 42° 03.452′ N, 73° 21.042′ W.

TRAIL DESCRIPTION

Check in at the visitor center or, if visiting when the center is closed, examine the kiosk with map at the trailhead to the left. Trail maps are available at the visitor center (both inside and out). Trail intersections are signed. Much of the route is blazed in yellow.

From the kiosk, walk left and follow Eaton Trail up the rocky slope under junipers (a.k.a. eastern red cedars). You are ascending the smaller of two cobbles, composed primarily of erosion-resistant quartzite rock and softer marble. The amalgamation of these two rock types and the soils they produce gives rise to great botanical biodiversity here. Note the large rock outcrops, capped by polypody ferns, on both sides of the trail. Delicate maidenhair spleenwort, just one of 43 ferns and allied species to be found in this botanist's wonderland, thrive at the base of the rocks. You'll soon reach the top, and a screened view of the Housatonic River valley from a well-placed wooden bench.

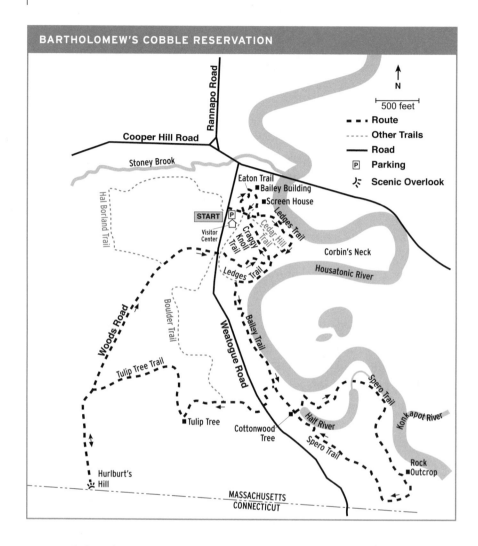

BARTHOLOMEW'S COBBLE RESERVATION

Rannapo Road

Cooper Hill Road

Stoney Brook

N

500 feet

- - - Route

- - - - Other Trails

——— Road

P Parking

Scenic Overlook

Hal Borland Trail

Eaton Trail
Bailey Building
Screen House

START P

Visitor Center

Cedar Hill Trail

Ledges Trail

Craggy Knoll Trail

Corbin's Neck

Housatonic River

Ledges Trail

Woods Road

Boulder Trail

Weatogue Road

Bailey Trail

Spero Trail

Tulip Tree Trail

Konkapot River

Tulip Tree

Cottonwood Tree

Half River

Spero Trail

Rock Outcrop

Hurlburt's Hill

MASSACHUSETTS
CONNECTICUT

Bear left and proceed downhill under junipers to the old Bailey Building, the former museum. Bear right under white pines on a wide path, and soon arrive at a three-way split. Continue straight ahead (the middle branch), where invasive garlic mustard dominates here in spring. Eastern hemlocks and white pines soon shade the intersection with Ledges Trail that leads left toward the river. Turn left. The larger of two moss-and-fern-covered quartzite cobbles hems in the path on the right. Steps lead down to the edge of Housatonic floodplain, where spring's rising waters deposit silt. This flat pasture, nearly encircled by the river, is known as Corbin's Neck. One day it may be cut off by the flow and become an oxbow pond. Watch for fish-hunting ospreys here during their spring and fall migrations, and for wintering bald eagles.

The larger of two moss and fern-capped quartzite cobbles is skirted by the Ledges Trail.

In early spring, watch for pleated leaves of false hellebore rise from the silt and the dainty pantaloons of Dutchman's breeches closer to the cliff face. The latter are among "spring ephemerals" that flower before unfurling tree leaves shade the ground. White ashes predominate, but maples are present too. Bear right and climb a bit to the Cedar Hill Trail intersection under large oaks; continue left on Ledges Trail, which skirts the cobble. After a few steps up, note the massive white ash, more than 3 feet in diameter, on the right. The path continues past Corbin's Neck, above and adjacent to the Housatonic and along a marble and quartzite cliff face topped by junipers. Sinewy ironwood and hophornbeam (both have hard wood), and birch clothe the slope down to the water's edge.

At a small clearing, turn left onto Bailey Trail and cross a small brook. Skunk cabbage and red osier dogwood thrive in the moist soil. A "hairy" poison ivy vine snakes up the black cherry on the right. A bit farther, large wild grape vines hang from the trees. Follow the river downstream, cross a few small feeder streams and walk beneath some sizable white pines, until you reach the Spero Trail/Tulip Tree Trail junction. Continue straight to Spero Trail under more towering pines. Listen for the sweet trill of pine warblers during spring and early summer. Shallow pools dot the floodplain in spring.

You'll arrive at Half River, an oxbow pond that was once part of the river's main stem. Here Spero Loop turns left. A cottonwood of truly monumental proportions dominates the intersection. This giant, hollow at its base, is more than 6 feet in diameter. Turn left and tread through a floodplain dominated by silver maples tolerant of periodic inundation, and then along the edge of a wet meadow that may not always be passable. This is the site of recent floodplain forest restoration work. If flooded, return to the giant cottonwood tree and turn left, then return along that stretch of Spero Trail.

Climb out of the floodplain and bear left at the signed fork to remain on Spero Loop. An angular schist outcrop juts from the oak woodland on the left. Schist is also considerably harder than the eroded marble bedrock that underlies the river valley. Enjoy a wonderful view south into Connecticut upon reaching another meadow before beginning another gradual climb on Spero Trail into a forest of hemlock, pine, and black birch. The cooling effect of deep evergreen shade is readily apparent under hemlocks as you close the loop and arrive back at Half River. Check the protruding logs for basking painted turtles.

After crossing a boardwalk spanning a trickle, you'll find yourself once more among quartzite boulders. Strikingly emerald green mosses pad the face of one low vertical rock face on the left. Maidenhair fern and round-lobed hepatica do well in the nutrient rich soil at the bottom of the slope a bit farther along. When you reach the giant cottonwood, continue straight for a short distance to Tulip Tree Trail on the left.

Climb moderately through pines and hemlocks; soon you'll reach gravel Weatogue Road. Cross it and follow the trail up into mixed and rocky woodland of oak, ash, hemlock, and pine. Turn left at the intersection with Boulder Trail to remain on Tulip Tree Trail. After traversing a series of bog bridges, marvel at a massive tulip tree more than 3 feet in diameter and with a spreading crown. This imposing species, near its northern range limits in the southern Berkshires, is the largest species of our eastern forests. The treadway may be a bit muddy here during wet weather, but yellow blazes mark the trail. Bits of rusted barbed wire and a luxuriant growth of invasive Japanese barberry and multiflora rose bushes indicate former disturbance by humans and livestock.

As you enter a small field, be on the lookout for wild turkey and ruffed grouse, two game species that thrive in a mosaic of habitats. Bear left and walk up to meet Woods Road. Turn left to follow it steadily uphill on a mowed path toward the summit of Hurlburt's Hill. Bluebird nest boxes on wooden posts flank the trail. A splendid view awaits as you continue up the hillside hayfield. From two wooden benches facing north near the crest, a magnificent 180-degree vista offers unobstructed views of Mount Everett (Trip 46) and the southern Taconics to the northwest and East Mountain (Trip 40) to the northeast. This is also a fine spot from which to spot southward-migrating hawks in the fall. An interpretive panel identifies both distant landscape features and the hawks that one might see. A stone monument just to the right delineates the state line.

Retrace your steps down the hill, past the intersection with Tulip Tree Trail, and enter pine, hickory, ash, and cherry woods with barberry and another invasive, exotic: winged euonymus. Both escaped from cultivation long ago. A few old apple trees along the field edge produce fruit for deer and other wildlife. Continue steadily downslope and cross Weatogue Road to Craggy Knoll Trail (crossing Ledges Trail); walk under junipers—some dead—up to the top of the larger cobble.

Ledges heavily padded with mosses and ferns rise on the left. The rock has been intriguingly eroded over the eons. In late spring, the delicate pink blossoms of herb Robert are ubiquitous. Finally, descend rather steeply from the promontory around a quartzite boulder, reaching the Cedar Hill Trail/Ledges Trail intersection. Bear left to the visitors center.

DID YOU KNOW?

Today's twin Cobbles had their origin some 500 million years ago. During those ancient times, layers of sediment (quartzite is metamorphosed beach sand, and marble is metamorphosed limestone composed of the shells of sea creatures) were pushed upward. The property is named for farmer George Bartholomew who purchased the land in the late nineteenth century.

MORE INFORMATION

Trails open daily, year-round, sunrise to sunset. Museum and visitor center open year-round, daily, 9 A.M.–4:30 P.M. (closed Sundays and Mondays, December to March). Nonmember adult entrance fee $5, child (6–12) $1. Trustees members free. Pets and mountain biking are not permitted. Public programs presented on a regular basis. Bartholomew's Cobble, P.O. Box 128, Ashley Falls, MA 01222 (413-229-8600; westregion@ttor.org; thetrustees.org).

NEARBY

Visit historic Ashley House, built in 1735 and located on nearby Cooper Hill Road. Also owned by The Trustees of Reservations, it is on the National Register of Historic Places. It was the residence of Colonel John Ashley, who amassed a 3,000-acre estate in the eighteenth century. The house was also the residence of Mum Bett, an enslaved African American who sued Ashley for her freedom in 1781 and won, effectively ending slavery in Massachusetts. Guided tours of the house are offered seasonally on weekends. For more information, call 413-298-3239 x3013.

TRIP 50
SAGES RAVINE AND BEAR MOUNTAIN

Location: Mount Washington, MA; Salisbury, CT
Rating: Strenuous
Distance: 3.9 miles
Elevation Gain: 915 feet
Estimated Time: 2.5–3.0 hours
Maps: USGS Ashley Falls, AMC Massachusetts Trail Map #2: E3

**A journey into a charming chasm—a veritable mile of delights.
Contrasting with that is a short but tough climb to Connecticut's
loftiest perch, offering sublime views.**

DIRECTIONS

From the intersection of US 7 and MA 41/MA 23 in Great Barrington, turn
onto MA 23/MA 41 and drive southwest for 3.9 miles. Turn left onto MA 41
South (at Mill Pond) in Egremont. Follow MA 41 for only 0.1 mile (bearing
right) to Mount Washington Road. Follow Mount Washington Road (its name
later changes to East Road) for 11.4 miles, past the entrances to Mount Everett
State Reservation at 7.3 miles and Mount Washington State Forest at 8.8 miles.
The last 2.3 miles are on gravel. A small parking area, with space for about
five vehicles, is on the left, approximately 100 feet beyond the 1906 granite
marker signifying the Massachusetts/Connecticut border. Be sure not to block
the metal gate. The road may be closed in winter. Additional parking space is
located 150 feet back the way you came. *GPS coordinates*: 42° 02.959′ N, 73°
28.011′ W.

TRAIL DESCRIPTION

From the parking area, walk around the metal gate on wide, grassy Undermountain Trail. Showy mountain laurel (the Connecticut state flower) is profligate to the right, while dense ferns—tall interrupted fern and shorter New
York and hay-scented ferns—populate a glade on the left. At the trail fork,
stay left to cross a feeder stream on stones. The right fork leads to the AMC's
Northwest Camp, wonderfully situated on a rise under hemlocks. Soon Sages
Ravine Brook comes into view to your left and the forest diversifies into multiple shades—hemlock and beech—and then virtually pure deciduous growth.

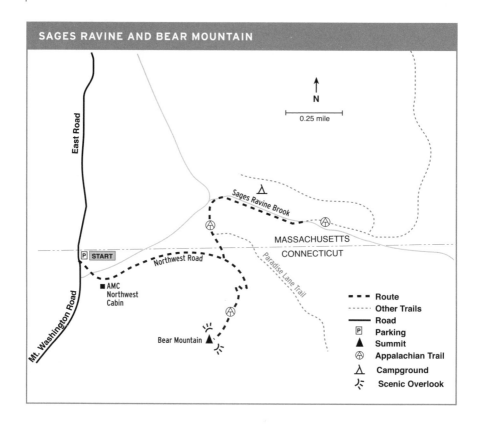

SAGES RAVINE AND BEAR MOUNTAIN

East Road

N

0.25 mile

Sages Ravine Brook

MASSACHUSETTS
CONNECTICUT

Northwest Road

Paradise Lane Trail

Mt. Washington Road

■ AMC
Northwest
Cabin

Bear Mountain ▲

Route
Other Trails
Road
P **Parking**
▲ **Summit**
Ⓐ **Appalachian Trail**
⚶ **Campground**
⋇ **Scenic Overlook**

You are walking on an old built-up roadway, and it doesn't take long to come upon the first cascade, but this is only a teaser. Cross a plank bridge over another feeder brook just before the narrowing path turns rocky and the grade increases through laurels. American beech sprouts, striped maple, and laurel fill the space between yellow and black birches, then maples, ashes, and oaks. Soon you're treading on level ground through open woodland along the base of Bear Mountain, which you'll climb later. The oaks—sporting more than one trunk—hint at past logging.

A sign on the left announces that you've entered the 500-foot-wide Appalachian Trail (AT) corridor, and within moments you reach the fabled footpath. Here you have a choice. Turn right to scale Bear Mountain first, or turn left to visit Sages Ravine. If weather is not an issue, turn left and stride downhill under a mixed evergreen-deciduous canopy to arrive at a wooden sign that reads, "You are entering a very fragile environment. Please camp at designated sites only. Help this area to recover from overuse and abuse. Thank you." Here the blue-blazed Paradise Trail takes off to the right, but turn left to continue on the white-blazed AT as it proceeds moderately downhill through

Gazing up Sage's Ravine Brook from an elevated perch reveals a series of falls and cascades in a sublime setting.

a thick stand of striped maple saplings and over stone steps toward Sages Ravine Brook.

The grade eases along Sages Ravine Brook, where the path bears right and runs along steep ledge faces. The next mile or so is without doubt one of the loveliest stream strolls in the region. Spinulose woodfern blankets the lower reaches of the mountain as you arrive at a long double-split-log bridge leading across the stream to Sages Ravine Campsite on a hemlock-shaded bench. But continue straight ahead on the AT, now a rocky, narrow path edging the brook. Pools that harbor native brook trout are interspersed with little cascades. Some "brookies" here attain all of 6 inches in length.

At one point, a large pool is hemmed in by sheer ledge. As you proceed downstream, the scene becomes progressively more enchanting. Take your time moving through the ravine. American yew caps boulders and wood sorrel, with clover like leaves, thrives in patches on the forest floor under hemlocks.

A high-gradient tributary empties into Sages Ravine Brook and a laurel shrub marks the confluence. The AT climbs jauntily above the rock-lined chasm. From above, note that the flow has scoured the sides of the vertical walls.

Soon you cross a flow that bounces precipitously down the right slope from one rock ledge to the next in multiple cascades. It's only a sideshow to the main act, but a delight nonetheless. These rocky tributaries cause the main stream to flow with even more gusto. Work your way down through angular schist boulders. The battlements of a formidable ledge rise above on the right slope. The path leads down to the brook's bank again at a 3-foot-high falls. The volume of water charging down the ravine is impressive. Where the stream makes a serpentine bend under hemlocks, you'll delight to another plunge. This second, actually split into two, is more than 12 feet high. Gazing upstream from an elevated location, the falls align themselves into a truly sublime scene. Note the trough the torrent gouged into tilted bedrock to the right during flood events.

After reaching a lofty height of about 45 feet above the churning flow, you'll descend again over expertly constructed stone steps into a cool microclimate streamside. Here grows long beech fern, a small fern identified by its bottom two leaflets, which point downward. Soon you'll notice a sign affixed to a tree on the right that welcomes hikers to Connecticut. You are actually in Massachusetts here, but only about 1,000 feet north of the state line. The AT crosses the brook on large stones, but this is the turnaround point for this portion of the hike. The good news is that you'll have a second opportunity to revel in the many delights of Sages Ravine. Retrace your steps to where the initial access trail enters from the right.

Now it's time for a very different hiking experience. If your energy level is low by this point, pass up the ascent of Bear Mountain's steep north face for another day, as it gains over 500 vertical feet in 0.3 mile. Otherwise, forge on, following the AT as it bears left along the slope contour under a deciduous canopy. But make sure you still have enough drinking water. Descend, and then climb a series of stone staircases over slanting bedrock. The path zigzags up the steep gradient. You'll negotiate rock ledges where some easy handholds will aid your progress. White blazes are few heading up, and the going can be tricky, so watch your footing; this hike is certainly not recommended during icy or wet conditions.

A few herbaceous dogwoods—bunchberries—have gained a foothold in the scant soil, while mountain azalea, common polypody fern (the little one clinging to rocks), and lowbush blueberries eke out a living in sun-dappled spots. The first pitch pines appear on the right and more laurel—loaded with blossoms in late June and early July. Ascend more bedrock, but not as steeply.

Glaciers scoured this stone some 14,000 years ago. If you have a compass—and you should—note that the grooves line up north/south, the direction of flow of the mile-thick ice sheet.

An evocative pine-resin aroma wafts in the air of sunny gaps as you near the summit. Blueberries and related huckleberry shrubs (note huckleberry's shiny resin dots on the undersides of its leaves) populate the top, as do gray birch, oaks, and cherry. A stone tower appearing as a giant rock cairn sits atop the highest peak (at 2,316 feet) entirely within Connecticut's boundaries. The tower has been rebuilt three times.

Climb the mound of schist flagstones from the backside for sublime views—some stones are loose, so step gingerly. To the near north are Mount Race (Trip 45) and Mount Everett (Trip 46) along the AT, while the Housatonic River valley and Twin Lakes in Connecticut lie seemingly at arm's length to the east. On a completely clear day, five states may be visible. When ready to start back, retrace your steps to Under Mountain Trail on the left and follow it back to your vehicle.

DID YOU KNOW?

A plaque placed on the summit rock "tower" in 1885 refers to Bear Mountain as being the highest point in Connecticut. It has since been discovered that the high point is actually on the south slope of Mount Frissel at 2,380 feet, a peak whose summit is across the border in Massachusetts.

MORE INFORMATION

Camping permitted in designated areas only. Carry in, carry out all trash. Motorized vehicles, horses, hunting, and fires prohibited. Appalachian Mountain Club, Connecticut Chapter, Northwest Camp Committee (nwcamp@ct-amc.org; ct-amc.org/nwcamp). Appalachian Trail Conference, P.O. Box 807, Harpers Ferry, WV 25425.

NEARBY

The boyhood home site of African American intellectual and civil rights leader W.E.B. DuBois (1868–1963) is located just south of the MA 71 intersection along MA 41/MA 23 in Great Barrington. Designated as a National Historic Landmark, the site contains foundation remnants of his grandfather's home, where DuBois spent his first five years, an informational kiosk, and a commemorative boulder. The 5-acre property was donated to the state in 1987 and is administered by the University of Massachusetts, Amherst.

INDEX

ABOUT THE AUTHOR

RENÉ LAUBACH, who holds a bachelor's degree in Wildlife Biology and a master's degree in Museum Science, retired in 2014 from Mass Audubon's Berkshire Wildlife Sanctuaries, which he directed for nearly 30 years. While at Mass Audubon, he developed and conducted numerous and varied public programs and outdoor excursions. He has organized and led 75 natural history tours around the US and overseas, and continues to do so. René has been an avid birder for many years and has authored seven books on natural history subjects as well as written for *AMC Outdoors*, *Audubon*, *Sanctuary*, and other publications. For 35 years, René and his wife Christyna conducted bird banding programs. Currently René conducts an annual Breeding Bird Survey for the U.S. Fish & Wildlife Service, compiles the Southern Berkshire Christmas Bird Count and the Southern Berkshire Fourth of July Butterfly Count. René's other natural history interests include bats, butterflies, and dragonflies. René and his wife Christyna are both enthusiastic Highpointers and in 2014 summited Africa's Mount Kilimanjaro. René resides in the Berkshires Hills community of Becket.

APPALACHIAN MOUNTAIN CLUB

At AMC, connecting you to the freedom and exhilaration of the outdoors is our calling. We help people of all ages and abilities to explore and develop a deep appreciation of the natural world.

AMC helps you get outdoors on your own, with family and friends, and through activities close to home and beyond. With chapters from Maine to Washington, D.C., including groups in Boston, New York City, and Philadelphia, you can enjoy activities like hiking, paddling, cycling, and skiing, and learn new outdoor skills. We offer advice, guidebooks, maps, and unique lodges and huts to inspire your next outing. You will also have the opportunity to support conservation advocacy and research, youth programming, and caring for 1,800 miles of trails.

We invite you to join us in the outdoors.

YOUR CONNECTION TO THE OUTDOORS

ABOUT AMC IN WESTERN MASSACHUSETTS

AMC HAS A LONG STANDING COMMITMENT TO THE FORESTS land, and rivers of Western Massachusetts. AMC works closely with the Connecticut Forest and Parks Association and the National Park Service to administer and maintain the New England National Scenic Trail which runs along the historic route of the Metabesset–Metacomet Trail (M–M Trail) and stretches 215 miles from the Massachusetts–New Hampshire border south to the Long Island Sound. AMC has also worked to build support to restore and increase funding for Massachusetts State Parks across the state. With funding from the Fields Pond Foundation and in cooperation with the Massachusetts Department of Fish and Game, we have also developed a video and brochure promoting ways property owners, paddlers, and others can balance paddling safety, aesthetics, and ecological values along our state rivers.

AMC also manages properties in Western Massachusetts. The Upper Goose Pond Cabin, located on the Appalachian Trail and run exclusively for thru-hikers and section hikers, is owned by the National Park Service and managed by volunteers from AMC's Berkshire Chapter. AMC's Noble View Outdoor Center in the Pioneer Valley accommodates groups of many sizes in cottages and campsites. The 360-acre property features 50-mile views over the Connecticut River Valley and trails suitable for hiking, snowshoeing, and cross-country skiing.

AMC's Berkshire Chapter is integral in conservation and trail maintenance efforts in the region. The chapter offers hundreds of activities like hiking, mountaineering, paddling, snowshoeing, and family outings.

Members maintain local trails—including the Appalachian Trail, M–M Trail and New England Trail—lead outdoor skills workshops, and promote stewardship of the region's natural resources. AMC also offers a Teen Volunteer Trail Crew program in the Berkshires. To view a list of AMC activities across the Northeast, visit activities.outdoors.org.

AMC BOOK UPDATES

AMC BOOKS STRIVES TO KEEP OUR GUIDEBOOKS AS UP-TO-DATE as possible to help you plan safe and enjoyable adventures. If after publishing a book we learn that trails have been relocated or that route or contact information has changed, we will post the updated information online. Before you hit the trail, check for updates at www.outdoors.org/publications/books/updates.

While hiking or paddling, if you notice discrepancies with the trail description or map, or if you find any other errors in a book, please let us know by submitting them to amcbookupdates@outdoors.org or in writing to Books Editor, c/o AMC, 5 Joy Street, Boston, MA 02108. We will verify all submissions and post key updates each month. AMC Books is dedicated to being a recognized leader in outdoor publishing. Thank you for your participation.

New England Trail Map & Guide

AMC Books and Connecticut Forest & Park Association

This two-map set is the indispensable day-hiker's companion to the entire 215-mile New England National Scenic Trail, extending from Long Island Sound to the New Hampshire border. The map and guide pairs two topographical trail maps—one for each state—with relevant information such as safety tips, Leave No Trace, natural history and more.

$14.95 • 978-1-628420-15-4

Quiet Water Massachusetts, Connecticut, and Rhode Island, 3rd Edition

John Hayes and Alex Wilson

Fully updated with an all-new layout and design, this easy-to-use guide will help paddlers of al skill levels discover 100 of the best flatwater lake and river trips in Southern New England. Featuring an "At-a-Glance" quick trip planner, GPS coordinates to parking locations, improved maps, and new trip planning/safety information, this guide will appeal to locals and visitors alike.

$19.95 • 978-1-628420-00-5

Southern New Hampshire Trail Guide, 4th Edition

Compiled and Edited by Steven D. Smith

Fully revised and updated, this trusty guide from the editor of the best-selling *AMC White Mountain Guide* describes more than 200 trails and nature areas. With included full-color, GPS-rendered, pull-out paper map, this guide is a must-have for every avid hiker who sets out to explore the central and southern regions of the Granite State.

$23.95 • 978-1-934028-96-4

AMC's Best Day Hikes near Boston, 3rd Edition

Michael Tougias and John S. Burk

From the barrier beach on Plum Island, the Middlesex Fells and the Blue Hills, to the South Shore and Cape Cod, this guide offers a variety of trails for all ability levels and interests. This fully revised new edition adds ten more hikes for beginner and intermediate hikers.

$18.95 • 978-1-934028-47-6